W9-BPR-730

THE COMPLETE BOOK OF

HOME DESIGN

REVISED EDITION

THE COMPLETE BOOK OF
HOME DESIGN
REVISED EDITION

MARY GILLIATT

LITTLE, BROWN AND COMPANY
BOSTON TORONTO LONDON

COPYRIGHT © 1983, 1984, 1989 BY LITTLE, BROWN AND COMPANY (UK) LTD.
TEXT COPYRIGHT © 1983, 1989 BY MARY GILLIATT

ALL RIGHTS RESERVED, NO PART OF THIS BOOK MAY BE
REPRODUCED IN ANY FORM OR BY ANY ELECTRONIC OR
MECHANICAL MEANS, INCLUDING INFORMATION STORAGE AND
RETRIEVAL SYSTEMS, WITHOUT PERMISSION IN WRITING
FROM THE PUBLISHER, EXCEPT BY A REVIEWER WHO
MAY QUOTE BRIEF PASSAGES IN A REVIEW.

This is a revised edition of
The Complete Book of Home Design,
published in 1984 by Little, Brown and Company.

Library of Congress Catalog Card Number 88–83396
10 9 8 7 6 5 4 3

Published simultaneously in Canada
by Little, Brown & Company (Canada) Limited

Printed and bound in Italy by New Interlitho S.p.a. Milan

FOREWORD

I hope you will find, as I do, that this new *Complete Book of Home Design* lives up to its title of being as complete a guide to every room in your house or apartment as you can get. To the original volume, which dealt with living rooms and halls, kitchens and dining rooms, and bedrooms and bathrooms, I have added further chapters on children's rooms, studies and work spaces, as well as general more up-to-date information where required. There's also a special section on decorative paint finishes for floors, walls and furniture, which, as many of you will no doubt already be aware, can make an overwhelming difference to a previously characterless room.

Each component of the rooms is covered as exhaustively as possible. So, whether you are interested in decorating just one room, or several, planning on doing up a whole house, flat or apartment, or simply adapting part of a room for another use, you should find information in this book to help you. In addition, the rooms illustrated have been chosen from affordable and easily manageable examples in a huge variety of styles from all over the world, so the book is as full of inspiration for schemes as it is for practical information, and should work as a valuable resource and help for years to come.

LIVING ROOMS AND HALLS

INTRODUCTION

Every other room in the house—kitchen, bathroom, bedroom, dining room, study—has its own fixed function that to a certain extent dictates the arrangements within it. The living room is the only one that does not at least partly arrange itself, which makes it, of course, the most taxing on the imagination. It's the one room that has in some way to accommodate the changing interests of all members of the family; it's also the room that is most on show, the room where your guests stay the longest.

Since a living room is literally the room for general living it often has to serve as a study, playroom and dining room as well and still manage to reflect your tastes and be a comfortable extension of your personality—or personalities. Everybody, including the family pets, should be able to stake a claim in the living room and feel thoroughly at home there. So how do you set about decorating it for all its possible different uses? How do you make it a room that is as pleasant to live in as it is to look at? Should comfort come first, or practical considerations, or style? Or can all three be happily reconciled?

Any decorator asked to help design a room for a client would start by asking certain obvious questions. You must do the same. Ask yourself: What sort of life do you lead? Do you entertain much? What are you going to use the room for—sitting, talking, reading, listening to music, tv, parties, cards, hobbies? Will there be people of different ages all doing separate things or do you go in for family activities or both? Do you possess any furniture, furnishings or equipment already that will need taking into consideration? If so, do they need altering, adapting or re-vamping? Re-covering perhaps, or re-painting to fit in with their new circumstances? Are you starting from scratch or just hoping to re-style an existing room?

The answers should help you to keep a realistic grip on your decorating ideas and these should be as flexible as possible. An idea isn't wonderful if it doesn't work. If you've set your heart on some specific feature—say, white carpet—and find it's not feasible or practical or that it's too expensive, then look sensibly at the alternatives and find a less impossible compromise. Furniture should be versatile enough to suit different needs and situations which might well change over the years. Surfaces—floors, walls, upholstery, table tops—should be practical so that you're not constantly worried about spoiling them. The arrangement of the room should be as efficient and convenient for several people moving about as for one person sitting reading. Above all, it should be as physically comfortable and relaxing as it is easy on the eye. So try not to be too rigid or too carried away; a happy balance will help the general feel and atmosphere of the room in the end.

Any room is easier to plan, decorate and arrange if you imagine it divided into three basic parts: *the background*—walls, ceiling, floor, windows and lighting; *the furniture and furnishings*; and *the accessories*—the personal possessions that will give it personality and character. The background provides the framework; get this right and the rest will follow. And take comfort from these two decorating truths, confirmed by much experience: that too perfect rooms are as boring as too perfect people, and that most successful decoration is the result of successful elimination.

A comfortable, relaxed and stylish room in which the emphasis is on softness, harmony and homeliness. The matching floral pattern in the curtains and soft furnishings combine to give a fresh, country feel which is enhanced by the plants and foliage in the background, while personal possessions add character.

LIVING ROOMS

Faced with an empty room what do you do first? You have a long, hard think about it, because it's a great mistake to simply accept or adapt to whatever space you have, however cramped or awkward it is, without questioning whether it's right for you. So, long before you rush into the basic decoration and furnishings you must first of all make a proper plan of the room and its needs and then work out how best to spend what money you have.

Think, plan, budget

Obviously there are certain key factors to any sort of reasonable living space: walls and ceiling will have to be decorated along with all the woodwork; windows and floors have to be treated in some way; there must be light both to see by and to enhance the space; there should be something to sit on and probably to eat from and almost certainly somewhere to work at times. Finally there are the decorative accessories like pictures and ornaments and the entertainment equipment—books, stereo, tv, video, records, tapes—for which there must be storage space.

So the next step is to write down everything that you consider absolutely essential to an individual furnishing/decorating or renovating scheme. Not the frills; they can come later. Then cost it all out and work backwards from there seeing

what you really can afford—and can afford to be without. The total sum might give you a shock but will also help you to be more ruthless at the start and put changes into effect.

Work out a budget

A realistic budget will do three things for you: it will sort out the urgent essentials from the details which can wait; make you feel good if you manage any or all of it at a lower price than your original estimate; and inspire you to improvise, to consider if you could achieve an equally good effect and still fit in with what you can comfortably afford. This way you'll not only get more personality into the room but you'll also go more slowly, giving yourself more time to think around problems.

The process of budgeting will send you out on more research. If you cannot afford the furniture or floorcovering you want, further trips to shops or markets, or looking at suppliers' catalogues, should give you more inspiration.

Problems of size and shape determined the look of these rooms. Right, mirror, wicker and old pine give a casual feel to a smallish space, while left, low shelves and cool colours smooth out an awkward angle.

LIVING ROOMS

Learn to make lists

Once you are sure of your priorities start to make lists. Write down any repairs that are needed and/or any alterations you think desirable. Transfer to paper any thoughts or suggestions on how to treat the walls, the floor, the windows. Think about what sort of lighting you're going to need and how you can achieve it. If the space is very small and you want to enlarge it, put down all the possibilities. Can your furniture be made to serve several purposes? How is the room going to be heated? How much or how little storage do you need?

Start off with a basic check list

along these lines; then you won't leave out anything important.

Fill in details about the present state of the room in the first column; then what you would like or propose to do about it in the second, and finally, in the last column, what it's going to cost you. Date the list and keep it in a file. If you have to compromise, change your mind or adapt an idea, make a new list, date it and file it so that you end up with a master check list that is a complete record of the whole procedure. With everything committed to paper you're less likely to forget details and it will help you tackle the situation in a very or-

ganised way. You'll also see how ideas progressed and developed as well as how much they cost.

When to spend, where to save

Once you have a clear idea of the essentials you can decide where to compromise and where you must make an investment. Again, take time to come to your decision because you won't get everything right first go off. Some things are going to have to last you a very long time and withstand a great deal of wear so these must be the best of their kind that you can possibly afford.

Comfortable seating is essential. You can do without carpet but

you've got to have somewhere to sit and the least you can make do with is one sofa or two good chairs. If you're young you might think that cushions or even a thick rug will be fine for sitting on but not everybody would be happy—or able—to put up with this and certainly older people would prefer something more comfortable.

You don't have to have curtains; blinds are a good alternative or if the room has a marvellous view you might want to do without any form of window dressing. Lighting, however, you can't do without for obvious reasons and also because it adds a great deal of extra interest to a room (see *Lighting is important*, page 35).

You can easily make your own coffee table and improvise on dining and side tables (see *Improvise with flair*, page 70) until you can afford better, but generous storage and some large healthy plants will make all the difference between a comfortable, relaxing room and a stiff, conventional one. Better to eat off an orange box and get pleasure from a plant than to spend the money on a cheap and nasty table which is going to be an unsatisfactory stopgap. Save money and effort right at the start by sorting out priorities—which should include enjoying the room you live in—and try not to stray too far from your original objectives.

DATE:	PRESENT STATE	REPAIRS/ALTERATIONS	DECORATIVE TREATMENT	£
LIGHTING	Central light only	Replace with recessed down-lights on dimmer switch	Add uplights and table lamps	
ELECTRICITY	One wall socket	Put new sockets in each corner. Add TV socket	Check out hardware – brass, brushed steel or white?	
HEATING	Gas heater in fireplace	Restore fireplace, add two radiators under windows	Add coal-flame effect fire	
WALLS	Shabby paper	Strip and line	Stipple and add border below ceiling	
CEILING	Cracked	Line with paper	Paint white emulsion	
FLOOR	Floor boards - fair condition	Strip, sand and polish	Buy rugs	
WINDOWS	Peeling paint	Strip and repaint	Roman blinds initially later add curtains	
DOORS	Undistinguished	Strip to original pine	Replace hardware	
ACCESSORIES	No storage facilities or pictures	Fit glass shelves in recesses	Remount old prints	

uplight makes
interesting tracery

wall-mounted reading lamp
takes no floor space

skirted table
for working/dining

aquamarine
rag-rubbed
walls

blinds are
economical
with space
and fabric

a mass of
cushions in
the colours
of the blind

old sleep-sofa
recovered

perspex
fold-up
chairs

*This room was planned on a tiny
budget but looks fresh, comfortable
and interesting. Candy-striped
Roman blinds, wall lamps, glass-
topped table and pale coir matting all
help to visually enlarge the rather
small space. The wicker sofa, palm
and blue/green rag-rubbed walls help
the freshness, while cushions piled on
the sofa-bed spell comfort. The table
(above) is both pretty and practical;
folding chairs save space but can
accommodate four diners.*

affordable coir
matting provides
attractive texture

glass-topped table takes up
less visual space and
provides storage

inexpensive wicker
sofa blends with
coir matting

LIVING ROOMS

Be creative with colour

Colour can transform a room – or wreck it. Just by changing the colour of the walls and soft furnishings you can provide a completely new background that may have a profound effect on the existing furniture, making it look entirely different.

Some people have very firm ideas on colour schemes. They decide they want a mainly blue or green or apricot room and know just how to set about achieving it. This sort of assurance is very rare and really only

Different shades of one colour

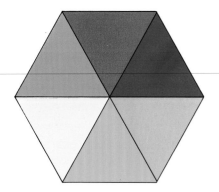

Colour wheel

comes with experience. But because mistakes are expensive and we have to live with them for a long time we tend to play safe and go for rather bland schemes. This is a mistake in itself because the result is often uninspired and therefore uninviting. How can we overcome this?

Be confident with colour

Should I put green or purple against that dark blue? Can I live with all those reds? Would I find a brown background restful or depressing? If you are not sure what goes with what or even which colours you feel comfortable with there are several things you can do to improve your confidence.

Start by noticing colour all around you. Then try to look at it as an artist would look at it, really *analysing* it. Look out of the window; which colours look particularly good next to each other? Those red-tiled roofs against the blue-grey sky; do they please you more than the slatey-purple ones? Which shades of green blend best with each other, with pale colours, with vivid colours? Look no further than your own garden to see the most interesting and often surprising colour combinations.

Train yourself to be conscious of colour wherever you go: in hotels, shops, restaurants, theatres, stately homes. Which schemes make you feel excited, relaxed, on edge? Go

and look at paintings in art galleries just to see what effect the artist is trying to achieve. Look at the marvellous build-up of colours in oriental rugs or tapestries and embroidery. It all helps to get your eye in and is far better than trying to rely on memory. You'll soon find yourself developing a pretty sure grasp of what colour is all about.

It's a good idea to buy as many magazines and books on interior decoration and home-making as you can afford and study their colour pages carefully. Pull out the magazine schemes that appeal most to you and stick them in a file; mark the pages you like in books. Then take time to look at them all together and see what they tell you. Is there a definite theme running through them all? Do the illustrations you have chosen have certain colours and styles in common? Be guided by them because they're obviously the ones you feel most comfortable with and they'll provide a reliable starting point.

The colour wheel

The primary colours are red, yellow and blue. Equal amounts of these mixed together produce secondary colours eg red + yellow = orange. All other colours are formed by mixing together various amounts of these colours and by adding black or white to make lighter or darker versions.

The secrets of colour schemes

When you have decided on the main background colour for floor or walls or both, you can set about building up the scheme throughout the room. A very simple but effective way is to stick to one major colour livened up with accent colours in cushions, rugs, the odd chair, blinds, borders, prints, paintings, books and plants. A fairly neutral background will make any small splash of colour sing out with particular vibrance and significance.

One very exciting and yet subtle way to treat the subject is to keep to one main colour but to introduce it in all its different shades and tones. Learn how to do this by taking one colour, say yellow, and thinking of all the objects that come within that category.

This should remind of you of the infinite varieties in any one colour and also set you thinking about texture. It will help you when it comes to choosing upholstery, blinds, curtains, rugs, carpets and general accessories. Varying the textures within this sort of monochromatic colour scheme can be just as interesting and lively as a scheme full of more obvious contrasts. At the same time it's worth remembering that at least one contrast colour, even if only a large plant or a mass of flowers or cushions, will help to emphasize the clever harmony of the background colour scheme.

Above: Flecks of orange in the sofa have been skilfully picked up in the curtain linings and cushions to give an air of co-ordination and elegance.

Far right: Here, paint colours and techniques have been used to maximum effect. The blue of the fireplace matches that on the window frame and chest. Stencilling on the chest and around the floor adds the finishing touches.

Right: The harmonious range of creams and yellows, toned with white and green, was inspired by the colours in the large painting.

LIVING ROOMS

Make a floor plan

Taking time to plan your space to its best advantage is essential when you are starting from scratch. This way you'll make quite sure that anything you buy in the way of furniture, equipment and accessories will be the right shape, scale and style to suit the room and your lifestyle. It's perhaps the one time you'll bless starting with a completely clean slate; at least there are no existing possessions that might perhaps prove difficult to accommodate.

So the most helpful thing to do before you start shopping is to draw up a scale plan of the room. It's quite easy. All you have to do is measure the length and width of the room and draw it lightly out in pencil on a sheet of graph paper allowing say, 1 cm ($\frac{1}{4}$ in) to represent 25 cm (1 ft) in reality.

Long narrow rooms are a difficult shape to furnish if you want to avoid a corridor feeling. This room gets over the problem with see-through occasional tables and pale colours for walls and seating. The squared dhurrie rug (washed to pale the colours) effectively makes the room seem wider, as does the fact that its colouring is picked out by the cushions or pillows. Huge plants soften the angles of the walls. Note the simplicity of the single stem glass specimen vases.

THE FLOOR PLAN

Now measure and mark in door openings with their clearance, windows, radiators, electrical points, fireplace, alcoves and any fixtures, again making sure that everything is completely accurate; the slightest inaccuracy can ruin the brightest idea. Correct measurement of doors and windows is particularly important as far as the moving of furniture is concerned. Many a large sofa, armchair or piano has had to be sent back at unnecessary cost because it wouldn't go through the door. Make sure to measure the ceiling height as well because if you multiply this by the wall measurements (see *Calculating quantities* on page 53) it will give you an idea of the amount of paint or wallpaper you will need.

Take your plan and a tape measure with you whenever you shop and always make sure you measure whatever you are thinking of buying. Try to avoid making instant decisions; instead, go home and draw the proposed piece to scale on some card. Cut it out, mark it with 'armchair' or whatever and juggle it around on your plan together with any other pieces you're planning to buy until you're sure it fits in. If quick decisions are needed, say during the sales, then at least work out the approximate size of the spaces you have in mind and look out for pieces of furniture that will best fit into them.

How to take measurements

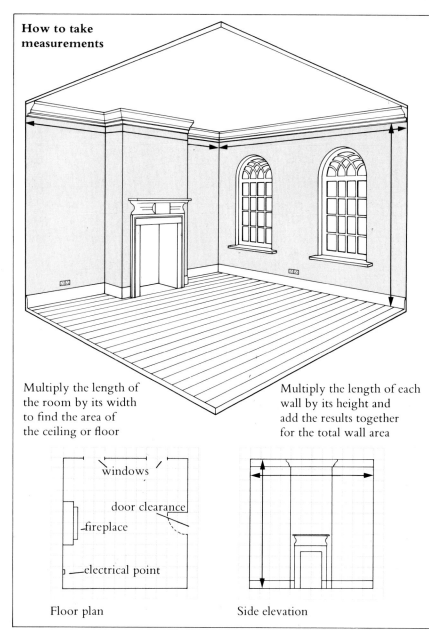

Multiply the length of the room by its width to find the area of the ceiling or floor

Multiply the length of each wall by its height and add the results together for the total wall area

windows

door clearance

fireplace

electrical point

Floor plan

Side elevation

How to draw up a plan
First make a sketch of the room or rooms. Then measure the length of walls, the width of doors and openings, the thickness of partitions, as well as the position of electrical outlets, radiators, telephone attachments and any other permanent fixtures like pipes and ducts. Mark them all out clearly on your rough sketch. This is the preliminary step.

Now decide on a scale. A quarter of an inch to a foot or 1 in 50 cm is fairly general, but half an inch to a foot or 1 in 25 cm is usually better for kitchens, bathrooms and utility or laundry rooms which have to take a lot of equipment and where every fraction of space counts. If working in inches, use graph paper with the inch square divided into eights and then take two (a quarter of an inch) for a foot.

Take a sharp pencil and an eraser and draw the perimeter of the space to the chosen scale. Erase door openings to the exact widths, and mark in windows, radiators, outlets, fixtures and the thickness of current partition walls, *making sure that everything is completely accurate* (many a bulky piece of furniture has proved impossible to get in because it wouldn't go through a door or window).

LIVING ROOMS

MAKING DO WITH WHAT YOU HAVE

Very few people have the luxury of starting completely from scratch although those who do seldom see it as an advantage. Most of us have possessions we want, or have to go on using, so the best thing to do is to take a very positive attitude and use them as jumping-off points. Let a rug or painting suggest or inspire the colour scheme; if you can't re-vamp old curtains (though beware! re-making can sometimes be just as expensive as starting afresh) turn them into cushions; cut down carpets which no longer fit but are too good to be thrown out, and make them into small rugs.

Existing rooms which need a face-lift or which you would like to have a completely new image are much more of a problem. Here we have to work around not only a collection of possessions which have become part of our lives, but also carpets or curtains or wall coverings we feel we can't afford to replace. How can we achieve a new look when some things are going to stay exactly the same?

'Use it up, wear it out; make it do or do without!' the old New England maxim goes. But if we have a conscience about our familiar old things what can we do?

Make the best of it

The best solution is to analyse each item in the room. If the existing carpet is in reasonable condition but you're sick to death of it you could add rugs to cheer it up. If it is in very bad condition but you really can't afford to buy new carpet then see what the floor is like underneath. If there are boards that seem in good shape they could be stripped, sanded and polished. If they are rather worse for wear you could always just paint and perhaps stencil them. Replacing an old, dark-coloured carpet with bright, painted boards can transform the character of a room, giving it the visual 'up-lift' it needs.

New-look curtains

If there's nothing wrong with your curtains except that you've grown rather bored with them there's quite a lot you can do to give them a new lease of life. Consider adding a border to the leading edges and making tie-backs to match; or having tie-backs where none existed before. If your curtains are plain you could stencil them (see page 378). Another solution would be to keep the curtain tied back and to add

Different cushions, massed plants, and new curtains all help refresh the room to the left, injecting colour and pattern, while the room on the right owes its crispness to vertically striped cotton blinds over a horizontally striped sofa bed.

LIVING ROOMS

Tailored tie-backs

Even if you feel you are not up to making curtains you can improve the looks of existing adequate but dull ones by looping them back with tie-backs. You can use cord or special metal fitments, but it is really quite easy to make your own tailored variety.

You will need per pair:
Some fabric to match or contrast with the existing curtains
Iron-on or fusible interfacing
11.5 cm ($4\frac{1}{2}$ in) diameter plastic rings
2 largish cup hooks
Plenty of pins
Sharp shears or scissors

Find out the best size by experimenting with a spare piece of material to make a rough model. Do this by cutting a strip 5–10 cm (2–4 in) wide, and about half as long as the width of the curtain. Loop it around the curtain and move it up and down, tucking in the edges and folding it until you see what looks like the best position and the best width. When you have decided these, mark the right size on the fabric with pins, and pencil a mark on the wall where the cup hooks should go. Repeat the mark in the same position on the opposite side. Screw in the cup hooks.

Fold the fabric in two and lay the rough pattern on it. Double the width, leave a 1.25 cm ($\frac{1}{2}$ in) seam allowance and cut out the two tie-backs. Cut out two interfacings the same size but without the seam allowance.

Centre each interfacing on the wrong side of each of the strips and iron in place according to the manufacturer's instructions.

Next, fold the tie-backs in half lengthwise with the right sides together. Stitch along the strips 1.25 cm ($\frac{1}{2}$ in) in from the cut edges and leave the ends open.

Fold them right side out and press with the seam running down the centre (this will be the back). Turn the cut edges inside, press again and stitch up neatly.

At this stage you can sew on the plastic rings to the back of the tie-backs (the seamed side), centring them about 0.6 cm ($\frac{1}{4}$ in) from each end, avoiding sewing through the front of the fabric. All you have to do now is loop them round the curtains again and attach each ring to the cup hook, gently pulling out the curtain fabric to its best advantage.

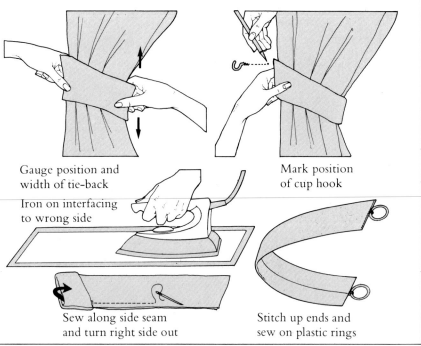

Gauge position and width of tie-back

Mark position of cup hook

Iron on interfacing to wrong side

Sew along side seam and turn right side out

Stitch up ends and sew on plastic rings

Roman or roller or Austrian blinds underneath. Or you could make under-curtains in a lighter, toning or contrasting fabric to pull backwards and forwards while the original curtains remain stationary.

Upholstery

If the upholstery is still in too good a condition to change, add plain coloured cushions in one of the colours taken from a patterned fabric or patterned ones if the upholstery is plain. Either of these could match the new borders or blinds or under-curtains, perhaps bringing out a colour that had not been emphasized before. Pale *plain* loose covers could be dyed a different, darker colour and occasional chairs changed round with old ones relegated to another room in the house. Old close or tight-covered sofas and chairs can be utterly transformed by giving them new loose covers.

Don't make the mistake of thinking that any changes must be major ones, on a smaller scale it's amazing what a few new accessories will achieve—paintings and prints, plants, perhaps a new round table with a floor-length cloth on it, a small but eye-catching rug, some concealed uplights in the corner (see pages 37 and 39). You'll find that quite often this sort of selective improvement will give a room the new look it needs for far less money than a drastic change-around.

Top left: A rather uninteresting room has been enlivened by 'panels' cut from contrasting wallpapers, which serve to balance the proportions of the room. Shelves and cupboard doors are two-tone painted to match the predominant colours of pale lilac and primrose.

Above: Dual-purpose library-dining table widens a narrow room.

Left: Matching sofas, side tables and vases give an air of graceful symmetry to this room, freshened by contrasting loose covers and a profusion of plants and dried and fresh flowers. Overmantel mirror and long, low glass coffee table placed unconventionally in front of the fireplace add extra sparkle and a sense of added space.

LIVING ROOMS

Left: A deep paper border gives an interesting distinction to these plain walls. Note also the painted stripe between ceiling moulding and cornice which further helps to delineate the space, as does the mirror, carefully chosen to repeat almost exactly the width of the fireplace surround.

Above: Added moulding around the architrave of this doorway turns what was a very plain opening into a most distinguished feature.

DECORATIVE DETAILS

Details that make a difference

You have only to look through one or two stately homes to see what a great difference the architectural details–the cornices, mouldings, hardware on doors and windows, doors themselves–make to a room. If your house doesn't possess them already, there's nothing to stop you adding your own.

You can buy one of the many reproduction plaster or fibre-glass cornices by the foot and have it added to your room just under the ceiling or, if you cannot afford this luxury, go for a stylish compromise with a paper border. There are some good-looking ones on the market. Choose one that contrasts with the current wall colour or wallpaper and see how it totally changes its character. If you can't find a pleasing paper border, there are other alternatives: look amongst the fabric borders in soft furnishing departments. You could even run a contrast border of webbing around the walls just under the ceiling, and around doors, windows and skirting board as well if you like.

Another way to transform walls is to form false panels on them. Do this by making squares or rectangles (or both, one above the other, depending on ceiling height and proportion) either with the same sort of webbing or with lengths of picture frame edging, or plain wood moulding from DIY stores.

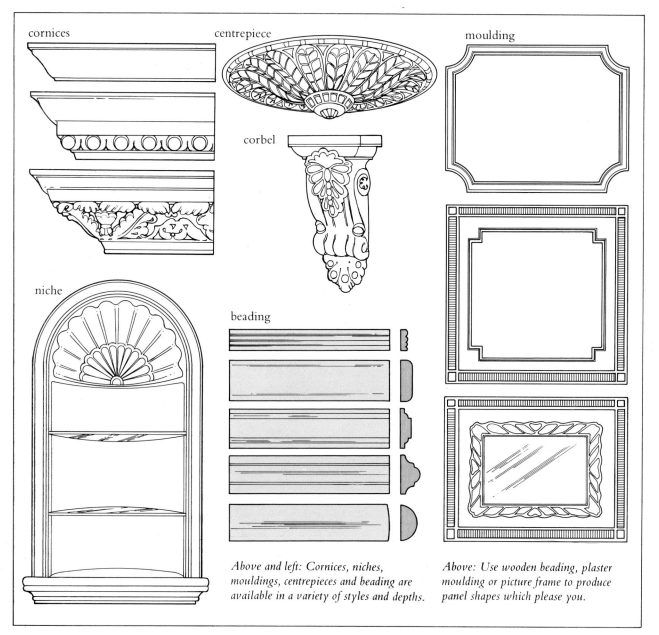

cornices centrepiece moulding

corbel

niche

beading

Above and left: Cornices, niches, mouldings, centrepieces and beading are available in a variety of styles and depths.

Above: Use wooden beading, plaster moulding or picture frame to produce panel shapes which please you.

LIVING ROOMS

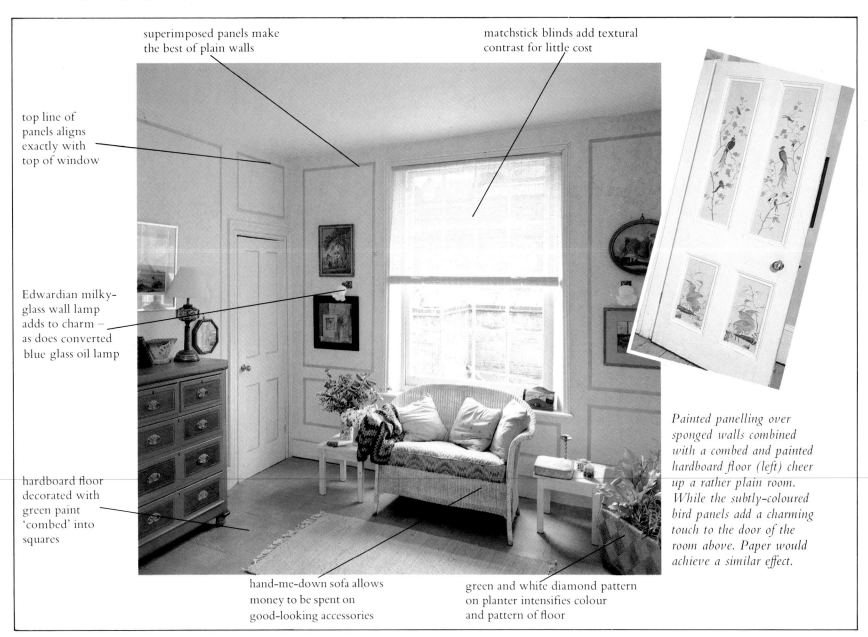

superimposed panels make
the best of plain walls

matchstick blinds add textural
contrast for little cost

top line of
panels aligns
exactly with
top of window

Edwardian milky-
glass wall lamp
adds to charm –
as does converted
blue glass oil lamp

hardboard floor
decorated with
green paint
'combed' into
squares

hand-me-down sofa allows
money to be spent on
good-looking accessories

green and white diamond pattern
on planter intensifies colour
and pattern of floor

*Painted panelling over
sponged walls combined
with a combed and painted
hardboard floor (left) cheer
up a rather plain room.
While the subtly-coloured
bird panels add a charming
touch to the door of the
room above. Paper would
achieve a similar effect.*

If your doors have rather ugly or undistinguished knobs and finger plates change them. Handsome new brass, china, enamelled metal or anodized steel all look very impressive, and if you can afford it you could have matching light and dimmer switches. Again, for remarkably small outlay, you will have added new interest and improved the quality of the room.

Changing the style and/or structure of the doors will have an immediate effect on the feel of a room. Unattractive old doors might look better stripped; they are very often a handsome pine underneath. Really ugly doors can be replaced or left off altogether and the space widened to form an archway, although this will inevitably increase draughts and the demands on your heating system.

Rather ordinary plain hardboard doors can look quite special if they are 'panelled out' — that is, given false panels with picture framing or beading. Purpose-made door panelling kits are now produced, ready-cut to size, to make this job even easier than before.

The main thing is to try to reassess all those long familiar features in a room that are taken completely for granted because you are so used to them. Look at them long and hard with a fresh eye, question their presence and their use; there are very few that don't lend themselves to ingenious transformations.

Right: The architectural presence of these magnificent double doors has been emphasized by wood graining, heavy brass door furniture and gold-painted moulding.

Bottom right: Motifs on the hallway wallpaper, stained glass door panels and the carpet bring an immediate sense of thoughtful harmony.

Below: Even a plain door can be enlivened by the addition of heavy beading to form panelled features.

The treatment of space is what good design is all about but far too many people think that if they cannot afford to change a room *structurally* nothing else is going to alter the look and feel. Yet it is quite possible to change the feeling of space *cosmetically*, that is by the clever use of colour, pattern, texture and arrangement, all of which can make space *seem* much larger as well as unifying and simplifying it. It might sound dull to advise using the same pale colour for walls, floors and larger pieces of furniture but this treatment will make the most confined area seem lighter and airier and will make bulky objects like sofas, armchairs and beds recede into the background. And you can avoid monotony to a quiet remarkable degree by using the same colours in different textures against which any extra added colours like plants, scatter cushions, pictures or books will stand out with dramatic intensity.

Diagonal designs, whether painted on bare floor boards or woven into carpets, will always seem to push space out. Any wall-covering design that produces a sense of perspective like some geometrics, trellis patterns or inexpensive garden trellis itself fixed on top of walls, will seem to give extra depth. Shiny and reflective walls, ceilings and floors will also make space seem much bigger because they throw out extra light. And light itself has a blurring, softening effect on the hard edges of a room, making them seem further away and less constricting.

Make space with mirror

Mirror can work magic on a room. Cleverly used it will double, treble, even quadruple the size. Mirror panels are expensive of course and you must ensure that large slabs of it can be got through doors, up stair-wells, and onto lifts or elevators. There is no way it will bend and it can break en route only too easily. But once safely in position it will be worth its weight in gold for the extra light and space it will create. You can always save on something else. If you use mirror in this way, be careful where you position it. Putting it at one end of a long, narrow room will make it seem even longer and narrower. So work out just how you want to affect the look of your room.

This brilliant platformed solution to a small space (left) was made entirely from hollow core doors. The angular table has a twin panel which hangs on the wall like sculpture.

This light and airy modern living room is decorated in a monochrome scheme. The hard black metal furniture is softened by the gentle cream carpet and walls.

LIVING ROOMS

If you use mirror from floor to ceiling and at right angles to a window or opposite a window it will give you twice the light and twice the view. If you use it from floor to ceiling in a recess—say the recesses either side of a chimney breast—it will look as if you can walk into a whole extra room next door. Mirror tiles on a ceiling will gain height for the room and a miraculous sense of spaciousness.

Mirror tiles are also a good substitute for panels and are very much cheaper if you don't mind the obvious break in reflection caused by the lines. Plastic mirror is another possible substitute and has the advantage that it won't steam over; on the other hand it can crack very easily when it is being fixed into place and it does seem to give a more distorted reflection.

Pre-cut panels of mirrors sold for hanging on wardrobe or cupboard doors are often surprisingly cheap compared to custom-cut pieces and they can be hung side by side or used in certain places to look like slit windows in a wall. Strips stuck on skirting boards or used instead of a cornice between ceiling and walls can greatly expand the sense of space for very little cost.

More space by arrangement

Built-in furniture—window seats, wall units all down one wall—will always take up less space than free 'floating' pieces and if you can manage good storage space under a window seat or built-in seating around a wall so much the better. All you need do is have a lift-up lid instead of a solid base or shelves added under the actual seat part and you have immediately doubled the usefulness of the piece as well as gained some footage.

If you have a small room use as much transparent and fold-up-and-put-away furniture as possible. See-through desks and small tables of glass and metal, or plexiglass, or perspex will appear to take up much less space. Fold-up furniture can either be stacked neatly in one place, hung from a large hook on a wall or stashed away out of sight when it isn't in use. Cane and wicker will look lighter than wood; white-painted pieces will look less conspicuous and therefore less space-consuming than dark. The most common advice is to place large pieces of furniture around the sides of a room but there are exceptions. Two sofas placed back to back in the centre of a space can often define the divisions of space very well. And in a one-roomed flat or apartment a large bed placed in the middle of the room can be used as an island lounging unit. By positioning a bolster in the middle of the bed instead of at the end the mattress will look as if it is divided into two separate areas.

Above: Arched mirrored corners make this room appear spacious.

Right: More mirror at right angles to the window seems to double the space and increase the light.

Left: With space at a premium in a city studio, a sofa bed placed in a window recess offers the perfect answer. At night, the sofa becomes a bed, transforming a stylish living area into an equally elegant bedroom – finely detailed with matching cushions and co-ordinating bedspread.

Above: Ceiling, walls and floors have all been decorated in the same pale colour to create an illusion of light and space.

Left: Here are several excellent space-cheating ideas combined in what is, but does not look, a very small room. Various shades of the same colour, mushroom, add to the effect of space. A desk top suspended across a corner between recessed window and mantelpiece effectively disguises an awkward space as well as taking advantage of every square inch, and a slim platform built on the diagonal gives relaxation and tv space while at the same time providing an area behind for plants and lighting.

Clever ways to win space

Useful tips for stretching a room without changing the structure.

Use very light colours and limit the colours of accessories. Or stick to one basic colour but vary the textures.

Give ceilings, walls, floors and furniture the same light colour to increase the illusion of space. Use light or natural coloured wall-to-wall flooring. No rugs.

Achieve a three-dimensional effect with pattern by using a colour against white.

Create perspectives as much as possible so that the eye is always drawn along. Go for geometric, directional or diagonal lines on a floor or wall, especially dark colours on a light ground which will give depth as well; stand objects in front of a mirror; set a table and lamp or plant in front of the hinges of a screen; use blinds in conjunction with curtains; have vertical louvres half open.

Expand space by mounting mirrors on wall, doors or storage cupboards; on ceilings; in the reveals of deep-set windows; across corners; in recesses. Economise with mirror tiles, pre-cut mirror or mirrored laminate.

Use a minimum of furniture at the lowest level; have it custom-built along the walls as much as possible. Keep all the surfaces as uncluttered as possible.

Gain extra storage space over and around doorways, under banquettes and window seats, under and around beds.

Make short walls look longer with strong horizontal lines like bookshelves or countertops.

Divide space without constricting it with a pair of screens, or trellis or even large plants.

Use fold-up, stack-away furniture.

Have occasional furniture in glass, perspex or plexiglass or surfaced in mirror; it will look lighter than wood, marble, chrome or plastic.

Cane, wicker and open-work furniture is better than anything with more solid lines.

Use spotlights to highlight details, objects and plants for a three-dimensional effect. Soften hard lines and make them recede by washing walls with light using wall-washers or uplights (see *Lighting*, pages 36-9).

Use reflective surfaces to make space seem larger.

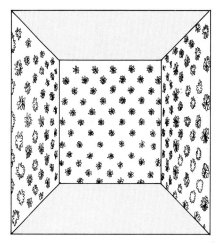

Any patterned paper with a white or pale ground will give the illusion of more depth to a smallish room.

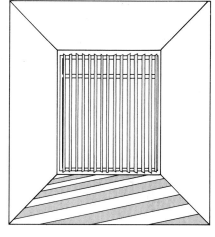

A diagonally-striped floor and vertical louvered blinds will both lengthen and widen any room.

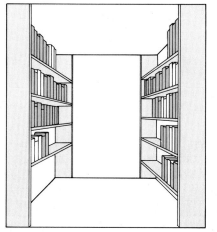

Short walls can be made to look longer by the strong horizontal lines of shelving.

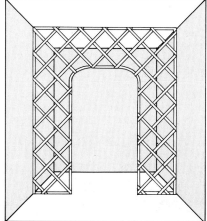

An archway formed from garden trellis divides this space without in any way constricting it.

LIVING ROOMS

room enlarged by taking down corridor wall
leaving book-lined passage (detail left)

philodendron
trained to make
a charming
natural border

large mirror,
airy side table
visually enlarge
space

black shades
on lamps match
paintwork

floor and ceiling
are slightly darker
tones of the walls
to enlarge space

*A corridor wall was
taken down in this classic
thirties flat to increase
living space. Black has
been used to define the
skirting and door frames
and is repeated in the
lampshades. A
foreshortened corridor
leads to the bedroom
(detail, above).*

portrait colours
are repeated
in cushions

rugs repeat colours
of walls, upholstery
and portrait

Some structural solutions

If cosmetic changes are not enough there are some fairly obvious and simple ways of altering the structure of a room to gain extra space. If you own your house or flat you can take down partition walls, improvise new ones, block up old doors and make new openings in more convenient places to improve on the space. Compared to the visual and practical differences these sort of changes make, the cost is small.

It pays, first of all, to get hold of a plan of the place (managing agents of blocks of flats should be able to provide one) or draw a rough one up yourself, as described on page 17, and see on paper where more space looks possible. For example, if you have a large hall or corridor you might be able to slice off bits to add to your living room.

Walls can be cut half-way down or at either side to form dividing slabs rather than solid masses. Or once the partition walls are down, you can create your own flexible dividers, with bookcases, shelving units, screens or screen-like structures like trellis, or even Murphy beds that let down at night from what looks like a panelled screen.

You could consider making internal windows or openings in a dividing wall to get more light and airiness. They could be conventionally square or round or in the shape of long slits so that the adjoining room shows through and gives extra perspective.

In a very small studio or one-roomed flat where space is at an absolute premium it would pay to build in multi-purpose furniture that would solve the problems of sleeping/working/eating and sitting all in one area.

Above left: Partition walls cut half-way down add space and light to this studio flat, and make a useful and attractive divider between sleeping and living areas.

Above: A cut-away stair wall makes an effective backing for a sofa covered with multicoloured pillows backed by plants and a painting. What could have been an area of blackness has become an interesting useful corner.

Lighting is important

Lighting is one of the most important elements to get right in any room, but particularly in the living room with its many different functions, all of which need to be appropriately lit. It is also the quickest way to change atmosphere and mood, to exaggerate space or diminish faults, to bring out texture, pattern and colour, and to highlight special possessions and achieve particular effects.

Yet when people think of lighting they mostly think of lights or lamps—the actual fittings—rather than of a flexible medium, just like heat, which can be manipulated by the flick of a switch or a turn of a dimmer. When they buy fittings they buy them mainly for their shape or colour or looks, but neglect to find out what sort of light they will give.

Ideally lighting should be planned and installed before the walls and ceiling are decorated in case any re-wiring is necessary. All too often, lighting is an afterthought superimposed on the final decoration instead of being planned from the start. In most housing a centre light fitting, for example, goes unquestioned, although people would find even daylight very harsh and glaring if it poured from the centre of the sky all day. Plugs or outlets too, are often fitted in a haphazard way around the room, with the result that when a lamp is placed where it seems most needed, it frequently has to trail a dnagerous mess of flex or wire with it. If spots or downlights are bought, they're often used without benefit of a dimmer switch.

Light where you need it

So how do you plan an efficient lighting system? Before you start it helps to understand the differing functions of the various types of fixtures available. Remember you are aiming for not one lighting effect but several. All living rooms need a mixture of light: background lighting; local light for working by; and decorative accent lighting.

From firelight to fluorescent

There are basically four main groups of domestic lighting—five if you count candlelight and firelight. These are:

● Conventional pendant and ceiling lights, wall lights, table lamps, floor

Top right: A floor-standing halogen lamp can provide enough background lighting for a whole room. Placed as here, it offers a good reading light as well as blending in with the rather geometric feel of the room.

Lighting should be both atmospheric and practical. Left, concealed light illuminates both the ceiling and floor and a spotlight provides light for working by. Table lamps, bottom right, and a wall-washer give dramatic illumination.

LIVING ROOMS

lamps and strip lights.
- Fluorescent lighting.
- Downlights, wall-washers and uplights, spotlights, track lights.
- The more ambitious kinds of 'effect' lighting, like neon and rotating lenses.

Conventional lights

These come in a huge choice of shapes, colours, materials and prices. The pendant or hanging variety give good overall light but tend to flatten shadows and do not provide enough light by which to read or work comfortably. The amount of actual light they throw out depends on the type of shade used and the height at which they are hung. Ceiling mounted lights also give good general light, but the effect is flat unless used in conjunction with other types of light.

Wall lights are best if they are directional and used to bounce light off a ceiling or floor, or to light a picture or piece of wall. Table lamps should provide concentrated areas of light. They will bounce light up or down or spread it horizontally, depending on the type of shade. Directional desk or table lamps for working by should be adjusted to let light shine down on the work in question. Floor lamps can give general or directional light depending on the type. Some are fitted with halogen bulbs for overall punch, or spots to light specific ob-

jects or to highlight. Hooded brass or chrome floor lamps make especially good reading lamps since they can be moved around to various chairs or sofas, and set to shine on books, or they can be directed onto a wall or ceiling. If you prefer shades, the translucent silk variety are the best light diffusers followed by linen, card or paper.

Incandescent strip lights (as opposed to fluorescent tubes) are good for concealed lighting behind pelmets or baffles, or down the sides of cupboards.

Fluorescent lights

Fluorescent tubes give about three times as much light as a tungsten or incandescent (normal everyday) bulb. They come in straight or circular shapes and are best concealed behind a baffle of some sort. They have an average life of 5,000 hours and are, therefore, much more economical to use in places where high levels of light are needed for long hours at a time.

Fluorescent lighting, however, can look cold; the best colour to go for is 'de luxe warm white' (not just 'warm white' — which is neither warm nor white) as this is nearest to warmer incandescent light.

The Halogen light

One of the newest and most interesting additions to domestic lighting has been the tungsten-

halogen, or quartz-halogen light bulb. The halogen bulb's unique regenerative cycle means that the filament does not wear out, the glass does not blacken, and the bulb lasts much longer than ordinary bulbs – in fact, for between 2000 and 400 hours – all of which makes the halogen bulb an extremely efficient form of lighting. Its great efficiency means that bulbs can be very small – a 500-watt halogen bulb is only about 7.5 cm (3 in) long, and about the same thickness as a slim pencil or pen. The light is much stronger and whiter than normal tungsten, but, like normal bulbs, they can be

Above: A thoughtful combination of table lamps, wall lights, free-standing floor lights and uplighters gives flexibility and a sense of intimacy in this large, formal room.

used with a dimmer switch.

Halogen bulbs usually require special sockets and lighting fixtures. The standard variety is tubular with electrical contacts at either end, though there are now single-ended bulbs on the market which have conventional bayonet or screw ends to fit normal lamp-holders. Another variety – the low-voltage miniature halogen lamp – is designed for use in

Top centre: A period table lamp. Top right: A spotlight used to highlight specific features in the home gives added sparkle to glass ornaments. Left: Hiding the source of the illumination, here behind a large ornamental fan, gives a soft, diffused effect.

a special fitting complete with a transformer and is excellent used on its own or with a miniature track for lighting objects and paintings, as is the new low-voltage halogen reflector lamp.

Halogen lamps' small size makes them ideal for integrating into sculptural uplights or slim wall fittings. One 250-watt bulb is capable of giving enough background light for a whole room.

Downlights

These are round or square, natural or painted metal canisters that can be recessed or semi-recessed into a ceiling, or ceiling mounted to cast pools of light on the ground or any other surface below them. The kind of pool of light depends on whether the bulb fitted inside is a spot, flood or an ordinary bulb. There are many types, but make sure you observe the unit's wattage rating.

A spot will throw a concentrated circle of light and is therefore best directed down on to, say, a bowl of flowers or a plant. A floodlight will give a wider, less intense, cone-shaped light. An ordinary bulb will provide soft, all-over light. Downlights can also be used for wall-washing. This means literally washing a wall with light. Several downlights angled close to a wall of paintings (say 60 cm [2 ft] out from the wall and 60–90 cm [2–3 ft] apart) will give a dramatic effect by

splashing light on to various surfaces with contrasting shadows in between. They won't light individual paintings unless they can be manoeuvred to direct light to a specific place. Downlights should be, if possible, fitted with some sort of anti-glare device or any unfortunate standing underneath could feel that he or she is in an interrogation chamber.

Uplights

Uplights are simply downlights in reverse and meant to stand on the floor. Of all lights in the room these make the biggest difference and are a blessing since you can plug them in and put them behind plants, or in corners, or behind large pieces of furniture to give a beautiful, dramatic accent light, creating mood and interest that could never be imagined by day. A good mixture of uplights and downlights supplemented by spot and reading lights will give a particularly warm and interesting atmosphere to a room.

Spotlights

These are used for accent lighting, to pin-point objects and give a strong punch of light whenever and wherever needed. They come in a great many varieties and can be mounted straight on to a ceiling, on to walls or on to tracks, and then pointed towards whatever needs special lighting. Miniature free-

LIVING ROOMS

standing spots can be stood amongst objects and collections on a table, or amongst books and ornaments on a shelf.

Some spotlights have a magnetic backplate so that they can be attached to any surface and pointed in any direction or can be set to swivel around inside a container.

Track lights

Track systems make it possible for one electric source to supply a number of separate fittings without extra expensive electrical work and all the making good, or restoration work, afterwards that this entails. Mount them on or recess them into a ceiling or down the side of a wall. Arrange them in lines or rectangles and fit them with spots or floods or downlights or a mixture, depending on your needs.

Dimmers

These are absolutely essential for any sort of lighting scheme that involves spot or floorlights. They save energy, prolong the life of the bulbs and mean that you can control the intensity of your light at will.

Good lighting needs planning

When you are still in the planning stage of a room but with the furnishings decided upon, work out what type of light you want where; should it be direct, indirect, concealed, background, very bright?

Decide too, what style of lighting fixture would be best for each area and whether you're going to need any more electrical outlets, switches or dimmers, and where they should go. If spots or downlights are to be inset into a very high ceiling, make sure you have the longest-lasting bulbs possible and that they are very easy to change; otherwise you'll be for ever climbing ladders to deal with them.

Are they safe?

Many electrical accidents are caused by ignoring common safety rules; for example, failing to replace old and faulty wiring; by loading too few outlets or points with too many appliances; and with the thoughtless placing of wires or cords leading from outlets to table or floor lamps. Always check the recommended wattage on any light shade purchased and do not fit bulbs which exceed it. And never try to do any sort of re-wiring yourself unless you are absolutely sure you know what you're doing; have it done and tested professionally.

Improving what you have

How do you improve the lighting in existing houses, flats or apartments when the electrical lay-out is far from ideal and far from flexible? You can either add new points or outlets to existing circuits, if they can take the increased load (which is

good but expensive) or install lengths of track to the odd ceiling outlets that are there already. If there are no ceiling outlets, make do with the kind of floor lamps that have adjustable spots or, if there are wall points, get wall-mounted spots. Buy uplights and put them anywhere you think would make a difference—in corners, behind sofas, on mantelpieces, behind plants, in deep bowls or vases.

The colour of bulbs will change the feeling of room colours. White

Track lighting and adjustable downlights light window, plants and seating area. Adjustable floor lamps in foreground are right for reading.

bulbs cast a yellowish light; pink ones give a mellow effect. Plain white walls can be radically changed at night by using coloured filters over downlight, uplight, spot or wall-washer fixtures. Most reds will be emphasized by artificial light; blues and greens tend to be diminished by it.

How to create special effects

Light and shade should be balanced. An evenly lit room can be boring and often curiously depressing, whereas areas of strong light where it's needed, with dark shadows between, can be dramatic and interesting and still comfortable to live with.

Washing walls with light using wall-washers will make a space seem much larger.

Uplights set into corners will draw attention to the limits of a room. Uplights set under glass shelves or glass side tables will add sparkle. Uplights behind big plants will cast intricate shadows on the ceiling and upper part of walls as well as highlighting the leaves.

Low lamps and lamps placed at a low level with the light coming from underneath an opaque shade will make a room seem more intimate and a high ceiling much lower.

Spotlights and downlights carefully positioned will flatter the textures in a room. A downlight mounted close to the wall will show off a textured wall covering by just grazing it with light, while a spotlight fully trained on to it would cancel it out completely.

The lighter and whiter the surfaces in a room, the more they will reflect light, but a dark-walled room with a light carpet and ceiling will still look surprisingly light.

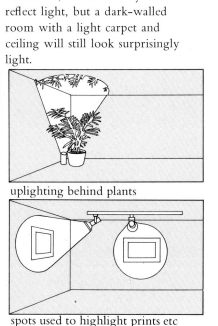

wall washing

uplighting behind plants

low lighting for atmosphere

spots used to highlight prints etc

uplight

angled uplight

sandbag uplight

recessed downlight

semi-recessed downlight

exposed downlight

shuttered wallwasher

angled wallwasher

spotlight on track

moveable eyeball spot on track

clip-on spotlight

parabolic spot

high framing projector

low voltage spot

box spotlight

LIVING ROOMS

Radiators

single convector radiator

convector radiator panel

compact steel column radiator

steel column radiator

electric
low level radiator

electrically-heated
skirting panel

flat-fronted
convector radiator

*A variety of radiator shapes is
available to fit in with most heating
systems.*

Heating

Central heating is actually fairly easy to sort out right at the beginning provided you are clear about certain facts. To get some idea of the best system for your particular way of life you should ask yourself the sort of questions a heating contractor would ask:

Who goes out during the day and who stays in?

If you are out all day what time do you get back in the evening?

What sort of temperatures do you prefer?

Do you want different temperatures in the living room and the bedroom?

Does your living room face north or south?

How old is your home?

How big are the rooms and how high?

How compact is your home and how well insulated?

Do you have room to store oil or solid fuel or wood?

Would you prefer a wood-burning stove, conventional radiators, skirting or baseboard heaters, warm air ducts, underfloor or ceiling heating (given a choice in a new house) or, if you can't have a central heating system, storage heaters?

With the uncertainty about oil prices and the expense of both gas and electricity, many people are opting for wood-burning stoves

These have long been a favourite in Northern Europe and America, and they can be amazingly efficient in heating most of the house, quite apart from being decorative.

Living room heat

The living room needs to be a warm room. Generally speaking, people in this room are sitting around relaxing; they aren't bustling about generating their own heat so the atmosphere around them needs to be kept at a comfortable temperature. The average would seem to be about 70 degrees Fahrenheit/21 degrees Centigrade. On the other hand, a lot of bodies could make it too hot for comfort, so you need to be able to control the temperature with a room thermostat. You must also consider where to put heaters and radiators, and whether you still need a fireplace as a focal point in the room. Many people who took out their fireplaces several years ago now find they want to restore them to have a real open fire or some acceptable substitute like gas logs or a gas coal effect. You may like to have 'top-up' portable heating for very cold weather. There's quite a lot to choose from: electric fan-assisted or convector heaters, free-standing stoves, oil heaters, calor gas fires.

Bear in mind that different types of heat source produce different levels of humidity.

Far left: The comforting, almost hypnotic glow of a real fire, apart from making a fine contrast with the black-painted fire surround, becomes an immediate focal point in any room.

Left: A small, wood-burning stove is both utilitarian and attractive.

Above: Even in centrally-heated homes, people are now realizing the decorative value of a fireplace – here framed picture-fashion.

LIVING ROOMS

Fireplaces can be retained as decorative features even when their use is somewhat altered.

Top left: Once completely tiled, the inside of this fireplace provides an ideal setting for dried flowers and grasses.

Top right: A shirred fireguard adds a homely touch.

Right: Lined and fitted out with a series of racks, a fireplace is perfect for wine storage.

Electricity, for example, is a drying heat which produces a slight condensation. Do check before installation as too dry an atmosphere may affect furniture adversely.

You need insulation

However efficient the method of heating, it will be of no use if the room (and of course, the house) is not well insulated. It has been calculated that in an average semi-detached house only twenty-five per cent of the heat generated actually warms the house: twenty per cent may be lost through unlagged upstairs ceilings and the roof; twenty per cent through windows, doors and flues; twenty-five per cent through external walls and ten per cent through the ground floor. An atrocious waste. On the other hand, don't attempt to stop up every opening. The room will get muggy, the fire won't draw properly, the boiler, if you have one, won't work to its full capacity and the doors may warp. You need a healthy amount of ventilation.

Walls are generally the greatest source of heat loss and correspondingly expensive to tackle. If the home has cavity walls, they can be filled with an injected cellular compound. Dry walls can be covered with polystyrene sheeting and lined, then painted or papered. Or walls can be battened and covered with another layer of plasterboard with more insulating material. Damp walls can be given a damp-excluding lining as well as being insulated. If the plaster is in bad shape, get it ripped off, line the walls with corrugated bitumastic building paper and then re-plaster with plaster containing insulating vermiculite. If the plaster is still in reasonable condition, have the walls lined with bitumin paper or brush them with a waterproofing liquid, adding battens treated with a preservative, and hang with plasterboard to make a new surface in front of the old one.

Doors with gaps underneath could have a draught-proofing strip fixed. The best kind is the flexible bronze variety.

Windows can have their heat loss cut down by double glazing and, in the US by storm windows, but it is expensive. If you have large draughty windows on the east- and north-facing walls, it might be worth the expense for the resulting extra comfort. A cheaper alternative to glass is to double glaze them yourself with plastic sheeting, but this will obviously affect their appearance. Otherwise you can only tuck insulating tape in the cracks or fit draught-proofing strips as for doors.

Heat loss through any window can be substantially reduced by using curtains which are lined. The quality of the lining is irrelevant.

Sheets of simple pegboard can be joined and trimmed to any size to make attractive screens for wall-mounted radiators. A wide frame completes the job.

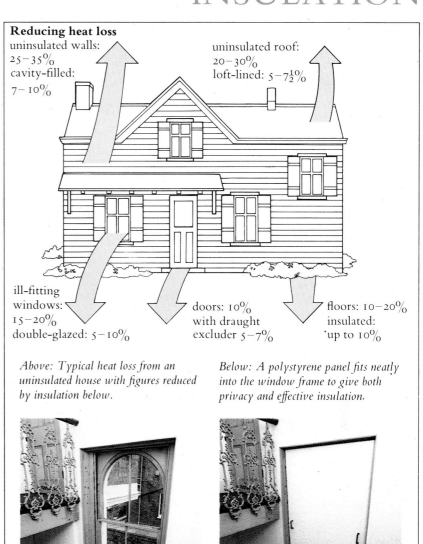

Reducing heat loss

uninsulated walls: $25-35\%$
cavity-filled: $7-10\%$

uninsulated roof: $20-30\%$
loft-lined: $5-7\frac{1}{2}\%$

ill-fitting windows: $15-20\%$
double-glazed: $5-10\%$

doors: 10%
with draught excluder $5-7\%$

floors: $10-20\%$
insulated: up to 10%

Above: Typical heat loss from an uninsulated house with figures reduced by insulation below.

Below: A polystyrene panel fits neatly into the window frame to give both privacy and effective insulation.

Clearly, the largest surfaces to be covered in any room are the walls and the floor, and there are invariably two schools of thought about which should have preference in the budget. I usually start at the walls because I find it easier to think up the general colour scheme first, but many people prefer to start with the floor because they automatically think of carpet and presume that this will be the most expensive item. But flooring need not cost the earth; nor is carpeting the only solution. In fact, floors are not necessarily improved by having a cover at all.

Old floors

Wood floors in reasonable condition – that is to say, without gaps, splits and frayed or splintered ends – can be made to look like new with some sanding and polishing. Sanding can be done yourself as long as you wear a medical mask (from chemists or drug stores) and are prepared for a lot of noise. Look in your area trade directory to see where you can hire a machine with a dustbag attachment, or ask at your local hardware or DIY store. You will probably find that the sander will not work up to the very edge of the floor, so you will have to hire a smaller unit to finish off the job. Even so, the end result will be well worth the effort.

When the surface is completely free from all dust you can seal it with clear polyurethane in an egg-shell finish if you want a good gleam, or matt if you prefer. Apply it with a roller in a thin, even coat and let it dry without disturbing it for a good 24 hours. After this time, apply a second coat and repeat the drying procedure. Finally, you should hire an electric floor polisher, rub on two coats of floor wax and buff it all up. (You may need to sand down and revarnish once every three or four years.)

Another quick improvement can be achieved by dyeing or staining the boards or parquet. If the floor does not need sanding, at least give it a good scrub and a final wash of white spirits, or a mixture of two parts water to one of ordinary vinegar. If it does need sanding, get this done and then give the scrub and wash treatment. This will leave the wood immaculately clean, dry, smooth and receptive to the stain or dye. You can either use a water-based or an oil-based stain. The water-based ones are quite easy to apply and dry quickly but they often look patchy afterwards unless

Right: A highly polished parquet floor acts as a perfect mirror, returning light from the fireplace and the elegant windows.

A bordered carpet of 'body and border' looks well in a large living room (left). Borders can be chosen from a range or can be specially designed.

LIVING ROOMS

you finish off with a water-based varnish instead of the usual oil-based polyurethane. A range of oil-based stains in a reasonable choice of shades have recently appeared on the market; these give a more even colour, but they do dry more slowly. Again, let the surface dry and finish off with two coats of polyurethane and wax as for the straight sanding process.

Try bleaching Bleached boards can look quite spectacular provided the surface has been well prepared. Sometimes it is enough to scrub with ordinary bleach and rinse off, sealing with polyurethane after-wards as usual. Or, you could try a stronger chemical bleach, taking good care to follow the instructions on the packet. More professionally, you can lighten them to that bleached-bone look by staining them with a white stain, thinned down with fifty per cent white spirit. Apply it over the boards with a roller, wait a few seconds, then wipe it up with a clean cloth. Let the surface dry, then apply another coat of white stain mixed with matt polyurethane on a five per cent stain/ninety-five per cent polyurethane ratio. Let this dry for 24 hours, then apply a second coat of unadulterated polyurethane. When dry, rub on two coats of white floor wax and finish off by polishing it well.

Paint to the rescue If boards are in too bad a condition to be revived by any of the preceding methods they can almost certainly be retrieved by paint topped up with several coats of polyurethane. Boards can be painted all over in one colour, or individually to form a formal or striped or variegated pattern; they can be stencilled, given a border, or topped with all sorts of imaginative decorative effects (see *Paint Finishes*, pages 368–79). You do not need to use expensive gloss or enamel paints, because you have to finish off the surface with polyurethane anyway. Eggshell paint will be fine – or deck paint, although this often looks rather dense. The important thing to remember when painting is that boards should first be given a couple of coats of undercoat and left to dry properly. Tint the undercoat with whatever you are using for the final colour and you will get a good, even finish.

Stencils can be bought from art and craft shops and come complete with instructions for use. There are also a number of excellent books on specialist painting and decorating techniques which will provide you with inspiration as well as practical help.

New hard floors

If your existing floor is beyond improving and needs a fresh start in life, there are several solutions. If it's

Above: Black and white floor tiles set on the diagonal make this room look very cool and large – a feeling helped by the white wicker furniture. Distressed pink walls, leafy plants and period knick-knacks lend the room an air of a Victorian conservatory.

a concrete floor you could either put down a new wood floor or tile it with some sort of composition tile or sheeting like vinyl or linoleum which is showing quite a revival. You can cheer up an expanse of plain flooring by setting in borders and designs which can look very handsome, or make two-tone squares: black and white; brown and white; brown and cream; or two shades of the same colour, like two blues or two greens.

Above: A terrazzo floor such as this needs the minimum of room decoration. By its very presence it immediately becomes the major feature in any setting.

Top left: Floorboards painted in a tile design of muted cream, grey and white harmonize with the grey and white colour scheme of the walls, fireplace surround and tiles, and introduce a welcome area of patterning into an otherwise plain room.

Top centre: The stencilled border on this stripped, sanded and polished floor matches the wall frieze and painted motifs on the alcove cabinets.

Top right: A sense of unity has been created through the use of a co-ordinated frieze design on the white-painted floor and walls.

Left: A subdued colour scheme provides a neutral backdrop for furnishings and floor.

LIVING ROOMS

Soft floors

If you still decide on carpet for comfort, warmth and quiet, it should be as expensive as you can afford. It is one item you should never skimp or compromise on, and you should make sure you buy the right quality and the right grade. Since a much-used living room has to stand up to a lot of traffic, it needs a superior quality, heavy duty carpet of either 100 per cent wool or 80 per cent wool/20 per cent nylon. They don't come cheap but they do offer the sort of value, wear, sound and heat insulation and dirt-resistance that you're going to expect. They'll also look very good and have great durability giving you years and years of good wear for your money. Then too some of the new man-made fibres are improving; they are losing their old harshness of touch and are being produced in a better range of colours. They're worth considering because they are less expensive and have strong wearing qualities.

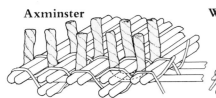

Axminster

Cut pile tufts are put in position as the backing is woven and are not visible underneath. Any number of colours may be used and any pile effect produced.

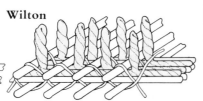

Wilton

Surface pile is woven in a continuous thread with the backing for added strength, and taken to the base when a new colour is introduced.

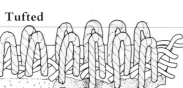

Tufted

Made by needling tufts into a woven backing and securing on the reverse side with a latex coating.

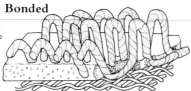

Bonded

Made by bonding a sheet of surface yarn directly onto backing and cutting pile afterwards.

Taking care of carpets Good carpet needs a good underlay. Sometimes this is built-in to the carpet in the form of a heavy foam backing which only needs layers of newspaper underneath it. Otherwise you'll have to buy it separately. There are many kinds of underlay –felt, foam rubber, pvc, latex. Some have a secondary woven-type backing to give added strength. Felts come in various thicknesses, the thicker they are the more they cost and the better protection they'll give your carpet. Felts are best for 'bedding-down' seams and joins. Rubber or foam backings provide resilience and firmness underfoot but tend to push carpet joins up making them prone to wear. When choosing either foam or felt remember that the more resilient the underlay the more it will improve and therefore prolong the life of your carpet. Underlay forms a necessary cushion between carpet and floor which helps to even the wear, absorb sound and cut down on heat loss. It should be laid with care, preferably by an expert, so that there are no gaps, creases or folds which will cause the carpet to wear quickly in those places as well as making it look unsightly. Before you make your final purchase, do shop around and check whether or not fitting is included in the price. Having bought the best you can afford and laid it properly, you should keep it clean. Vacuum at least once a week and shampoo whenever it starts to look grubby– probably once or twice a year. If you can afford to have it shampooed professionally it'll need doing less often. Old dirt is obstinate and also begins to destroy the fibres if left.

Good alternatives

Other cheaper and very hard-wearing forms of floor covering well worth considering are sisal, coir or coconut matting or hair and woolcord. Although rougher and hairier in texture than wool and man-made carpet and not so soft or luxurious, they come in good colours–the natural shades are particularly attractive–and are tough enough to withstand the most active family on its feet. You won't sink into this sort of flooring but it has a neat appearance and will pull together a disparate collection of furniture and styles and make a roomful of old things look firmly set in the twentieth century. Again, it is especially important to keep matting regularly cleaned to avoid a build-up of dirt and stains. Carpet tiles are marvellously practical because they can be moved around stress areas–under chairs, in front of sofas–and worn ones replaced as necessary. They are particularly useful for temporary and rented accommodation because they can be so easily taken up and put down.

Top left: Coir matting looks neat, and works perfectly with a mixture of styles as well as being an excellent contrast to rugs.

Above: Wall to wall Berber carpet, can also be a good link between the traditional and the modern; its neutral shades and chunky texture makes it an interesting contrast for different colours.

Far left and left: Geometric carpets and rugs look fresh and modern.

LIVING ROOMS

What to put on the wall

There must be countless ways to cover a wall but let's narrow it down to the three basic choices: paint, paper or fabric. Of these, painting is generally the easiest and least expensive. Clever painting can disguise faults in a room, lose unsightly features like too many doors, ugly pipes or angles, emphasize good proportions and minimize bad ones. And these days, it can do more than this: it can introduce all sorts of excitements in design, colour and texture. Up till recently, ceilings, walls and woodwork were either done in gloss, eggshell or flat paint, with perhaps the odd contrast border or super graphic thrown in as an added bonus. Now the increasing sophistication in most paint ranges, plus a new interest in the purely decorative aspect, has resulted in the revival of old traditional crafts and techniques such as stippling, rag-rolling, colour-washing, dragging and lacquering which can all be learnt and practised without too much difficulty. If you've never tackled these techniques before you should experiment off the wall first, using lining paper.

Simple tricks with paint

You can make a ceiling seem much higher by painting it a lighter colour than the walls and keeping the floor a light tone as well. Lower a too-high ceiling by painting it darker.

Liven up dull-looking spaces with bands or outlines of colour. Keep a simple, light background and paint skirting or baseboards and mouldings in a contrasting shade. You could paint two or three bands of different colours in different widths, starting from the baseboard or skirting. If there isn't a false cornice or cove, form one by painting a stripe or two immediately under the ceiling. This could be continued down corners to the skirting and around doors. Draw the stripes lightly in pencil first and take great care to get them precise.

Create impressive graphic designs on your walls; all it takes is courage and a little sleight of hand. If not graphics, then try free-flowing bands of colour in varying shapes. Sometimes the shape of a bedhead or a mirror or storage unit can be echoed over the object proper in 1920's or 1930's style and then exaggerated with a contrasting edge of another colour. Have a little fun with it and let shapes drawn down a wall spill over a dresser or chest of drawers.

Get the feeling of panelling by sticking rectangles of contrasting tape on a plain painted wall; or by drawing rectangular stripes in panel

shapes and carefully painting them in contrasting colours.

Disguise eyesores—a confusion of unboxed pipes, off-centre doors or windows, breaks in ceiling levels, awkward angles and unsightly radiators—by painting the area in a dark colour. This makes everything melt away into the background. Alternatively, a messy jumble of pipes could actually be picked out to look like an interesting feature in its own right.

Create interesting striped effects with paint and invent your own striped patterns as an inexpensive alternative to striped wallpaper. First paint a background colour and let it dry. Next stick strips of low-tack masking tape over the areas of background colour that you want to remain. You can then paint between the strips of tape with a second colour and remove the tape when the paint is dry. The result will be neat, accurate stripes, which can be vertical, horizontal, or even diagonal – and in any width or colour you like.

Pick out any interesting mouldings, dado rails or picture rails in different colours to emphasize these features.

For more ideas, see the section on *Paint Finishes*, pages 368–379.

Paint is obviously very versatile and adaptable but wall coverings of paper or fabric can cheer up a dull room, obliterate uneven, cracked walls, help to even up proportions and generally soften the look of a room, and needn't cost the earth.

Left: Lengths of picture framing are used here to create false panelling on what otherwise might have been a bland-looking wall. Panels like this make an excellent background for prints. Similarly, a dado can be added to a wall to give additional interest, as here, painted in the same shade as the panelling border; the wall beneath it is given a different treatment.

Below: A dado painted in a contrasting colour can add interest to an otherwise bland wall. Here, an unusual effect had been achieved by using different finishes on either side – marbling above and stippling below.

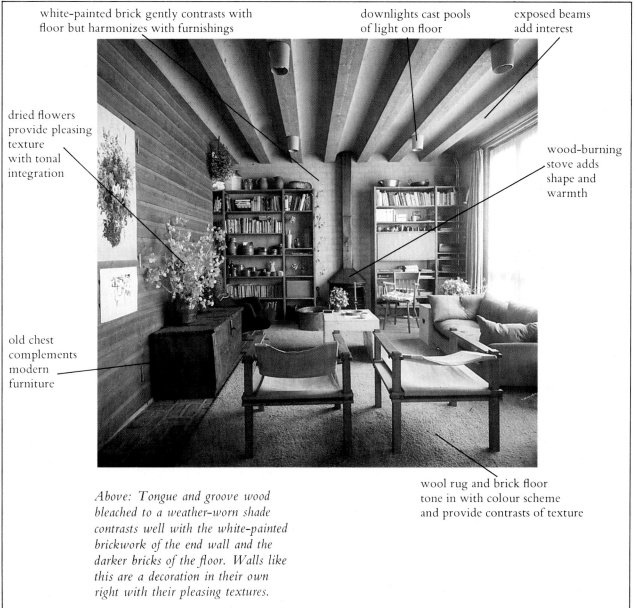

white-painted brick gently contrasts with floor but harmonizes with furnishings

downlights cast pools of light on floor

exposed beams add interest

dried flowers provide pleasing texture with tonal integration

wood-burning stove adds shape and warmth

old chest complements modern furniture

wool rug and brick floor tone in with colour scheme and provide contrasts of texture

Above: Tongue and groove wood bleached to a weather-worn shade contrasts well with the white-painted brickwork of the end wall and the darker bricks of the floor. Walls like this are a decoration in their own right with their pleasing textures.

LIVING ROOMS

Achieving expensive effects

The choice of wallpapers is enormous, with prices to match at every stage up and down the scale, but you don't have to pay the earth to achieve a very luxurious look. Fairly inexpensive papers can be made to seem—and last—like very expensive versions if you know some of the tricks:

● Use a heavy lining paper to hide any defects in the wall. Hang it horizontally and be careful to stick it precisely edge to edge so that no bulge will show through the paper proper.

● Paint over inexpensive non-vinyl paper when it is hung, with a coat or two of either matt or eggshell polyurethane. Test the varnish out on a small piece of leftover paper first to make sure that the colours don't run. The varnish will deepen or 'yellow' the paper slightly but this generally makes it look richer and more interesting. It will last longer and you'll also be able to sponge it gently to clean it.

With a little careful planning, an expensive-looking room need not cost a lot of money to decorate. Stunning and luxurious-looking effects such as this can be achieved by combining wallpaper and fabrics in co-ordinating colours.

How to afford the best

It's easy to make one very expensive roll of wallpaper stretch all round a room which, if you could ever afford it, would normally take 10 or 12 rolls. The trick is to paint the walls the colour of the background of the paper, using a matt emulsion paint, then cut the paper into equal rectangles or squares and stick them on the walls in regularly spaced 'panels'. If the paper has a border, use it as a finishing edging. Again, you can make it more durable and cleanable by giving a coat or two of polyurethane. Test the paper first for colour fastness.

You are better able to afford good wallpaper if you hang it yourself. The pre-pasted range is a boon to the DIY expert. Being self-adhesive it only needs wetting and sticking on. It takes about 20 minutes to adhere – time enough to correct mistakes.

Fabrics look fabulous

Wall fabrics are generally more expensive than papers but can often make the walls look so luxurious that you can get away with minimal furnishings. They will also completely cover up imperfections, have good sound and heat insulation properties and, if they've been treated with protective spray, will last for years and years – long after paint has become chipped and discoloured, and paper faded.

Calculating quantities

Paint To work out the area, multiply the perimeter of the room by the height from skirting board to ceiling.

Quantity	Gloss		Emulsion	
	sq yds	(sq m)	sq yds	(sq m)
1 pt (0.568 l)	10	(8½)	12	(10)
1 qt (1.135 l)	20	(17)	24	(20)
1 gal (4.54 l)	80	(67)	96	(80)

Wallcoverings Check the size and origin of rolls of wallpaper before ordering. English papers generally have different measurements from American varieties. For example: English papers are more or less 10.98 m (12 yd) long and 0.64 m (21 in) wide when trimmed or 7.03 sq m (7 sq yd) in area; most European papers are 8.25 m (9 yd) long and 0.46 m (18 in) wide when trimmed or 12.35 sq m (40.5 sq ft) in area; most American papers are 7.32 m (8 yd) long and 0.46 m (18 in) wide when trimmed or 3.34 sq m (4 sq yd) in area. Check if paper is trimmed before buying; allow extra to match pattern drops. Order more paint and wallpaper than you think you'll need.

English wallpapers Table for calculating number of rolls required

Height of wall — Measurement around the walls in feet (metres)

Feet	Metres	28 (8.53)	32 (9.76)	40 (12.19)	44 (13.41)	52 (15.08)	56 (17.01)
7–7½	2.13–2.29	4	4	5	6	7	7
7½–8	2.29–2.44	4	4	5	6	7	8
8–8½	2.44–2.59	4	5	6	7	8	8
8½–9	2.59–2.74	4	5	6	7	8	9
9½–10	2.94–3.05	5	6	7	7	9	9
10–10½	3.05–3.24	5	6	7	8	9	10
10½–11½	3.24–3.39	5	6	7	8	9	10

Feet	Metres	60 (18.29)	64 (19.50)	68 (20.73)	72 (21.95)	80 (24.38)	84 (25.60)
7–7½	2.13–2.29	8	8	9	9	10	10
7½–8	2.29–2.44	8	9	9	10	11	11
8–8½	2.44–2.59	9	9	10	11	12	12
8½–9	2.59–2.74	9	10	10	11	12	13
9½–10	2.94–3.05	10	10	11	12	13	14
10–10½	3.05–3.24	10	11	12	12	14	14
10½–11½	3.24–3.39	11	11	12	13	14	15

American wallpapers Table for calculating rolls required

Feet (metres) around room	Height of wall 8 ft (2.44 m)	9 ft (2.74 m)	10 ft (3.05 m)	11 ft (3.35 m)	12 ft (3.65 m)	14 ft (4.27 m)
28 (8.53)	7	8	9	10	11	12
36 (10.98)	9	10	11	12	13	16
44 (13.41)	11	12	14	15	16	19
52 (16.08)	13	15	16	18	19	22
60 (18.29)	15	17	19	20	22	26
68 (20.96)	17	19	21	23	25	29
72 (22.18)	18	20	22	24	27	31
80 (23.38)	20	22	25	27	30	34
88 (25.84)	22	24	27	30	32	38
92 (27.06)	23	26	28	31	34	39
96 (28.28)	24	27	30	32	35	41

LIVING ROOMS

Making it stick Some fabric wall coverings—ranging from hessians or burlaps, felts and flannels to suedes, wool, silk and moiré—come with a paper backing which makes it easy to stick them to the walls. However, if you use the correct adhesive and somebody with the right sort of skill, almost any fabric of reasonable weight and texture can be stuck to walls. You can then choose from a very wide range indeed, from lengths of artists' or sail canvas (available quite cheaply from art supply stores or marine goods suppliers) to upholstery fabrics and velvets. It is best to go for fabrics which are stretch- and fade-resistant as well as stain- and mildew-resistant.

When sticking fabric up apply the paste to the walls and not to the fabric. Cover any frayed edges with braid, or a thin painted beading, or lengths of narrow picture-framing wood, polished, silvered, gilded or lacquered. (This can often be bought by the foot from the picture framers.) As well as being practical, the end result will look as if it cost many times as much.

Fixing fabric There are special wall-track systems for attaching materials of all weights to the wall. The fabric stays neat and taut without the need for adhesive. These track systems are comprised of long plastic strips with 'jaws' to hide ragged edges and an adhesive strip to hold the fabric tight. You simply screw the strips to the walls just under the ceiling and just above the skirting or baseboards to make a kind of frame, and use the special tool provided to push the fabric into the frame and secure it in position. Although it is obviously more expensive than sticking with applied adhesive, this method means that you can change fabrics if you like to achieve a fresh effect, and also clean the fabric as necessary. Do check therefore that you use fabric that will not shrink. This makes it a good bet for rented accommodation as you can take both the material and the wall-track with you when you leave.

Upholster the wall Pre-cut fabric can actually be stapled to the wall and any raw edges covered with braid or trim, but you can get a much softer, more professionally upholstered look if you batten the fabric. This means nailing or stapling (with a proper staple gun) lathes or thin strips of wood (about 5 cm [2 in wide]) horizontally, just below the ceiling or moulding and just above the skirting. Similar strips of wood are then fixed vertically at 1.8 m (6 ft) intervals. If paintings or prints are to be hung on the walls it is important to work out beforehand where they are going to go, and to make sure that battens are

Above: In this more tailored room, fabric is attached to the wall just below the cornice and caught up at intervals in graceful folds like elaborate curtains, and, like curtains, left to sweep the floor. The effect is both graceful and original.

Left: Tropical in feel, the tent-like effect of this fabric-draped ceiling, supported by bamboo poles fixed above the picture rail, is accentuated by the centrally located ceiling fan and cane furniture.

fixed in these particular areas. This applies equally to light switches and electric sockets. When the fabric is up, these battens can be felt through the fabric, making it easy to fix nails and picture hooks to them.

When all the strips of wood are fixed, staple lengths of synthetic fibre padding between them. You are now ready to attach the fabric which should have been cut in panels to fit the wall measurements and seamed where necessary to join the lengths.

Attach the first fabric panel by centring it between the outside edge of the first vertical batten and the middle of the second one. When the top of the fabric is level with the top horizontal batten, lightly tack it—with thumb tacks—in the middle. Stretch it to either side, tack it, then staple into position.

You can keep the whole thing very neat by using 5 cm (2 in) wide cardboard strips cut to the height of the walls. Place the second panel, right side down, on to the edge of the first panel so that their two cut edges line up. Lay one of the long strips of cardboard over this join and staple through card and fabric on to the batten. Continue all round the room, remembering that any staple marks and rough edges can be covered with lengths of matching or contrasting braid. Braid should also be used around the top and bottom of the fabric and around doors and windows.

Wall fabrics that hang If you have rented accommodation and can't or don't want to put fabric up permanently—or are not allowed to paint, for that matter—then you can hang fabric instead.

Inexpensive cottons can be hung from rods or poles and left to hang free at the bottom, although they should be caught back over doors and windows with tie-backs.

Lightweight inexpensive fabrics like cheesecloth and muslin can be shirred and hung between rods, wires or traverse poles attached below the ceiling and above the skirting or baseboards, and either caught back at doors and windows or fixed around them (with rods or wires attached to the top of the frames). If you use this method you will need a generous amount of fabric, about three times the width of the wall. You can then either hem and gather it with shirring tape before it is fixed to the walls; or let it gather itself naturally as you push the rods through the turned-over hems at top and bottom. Make the casing only just large enough for the rods, so that they fit tightly.

Fabric you can afford
Wall fabric always sounds like the last word in luxury but in fact need not cost much. For instance:
Cheesecloth muslin
Painters' dust sheets or drop cloths in clear colours and simple patterns such as checks and stripes
Indian cotton quilts
Removers' quilts in plain or printed cotton or satin
Artists' canvas
Sail canvas
Book-binding cloth
Khaki and navy suiting cloth from Army and Navy surplus stores
Reject fabric of any sort
Rolls of embroidery canvas.

Safety factor
To avoid any fire risk, you can treat fabric with a flame retardant spray.

LIVING ROOMS

Windows are like eyes: they are looked *at* as much as they are looked *out of*. They also provide light, ventilation, protection and, very often, a focus. But they usually have to be covered, which means yet another thing to budget for in a room. For even when the proportions are beautiful and unusual, the view stupendous, the privacy assured, a window covering is still the most practical way of shutting out the depressing sight of rain, avoiding too much heat loss, preventing draughts in winter and the discomforts of too much sun in summer. The sort of windows that need little or nothing in the way of treatment are usually narrow slits of glass, small ovals, round, arched, stained and etched glass windows that only show a glimpse of the outside and are often unopenable anyway. In cases like this, a decorative object on the sill, like a plant, a single flower in a vase, a piece of old glass or china, a sculpture, a small lamp or candle, even a beautiful book, is often far better than attempting any sort of curtain. However, most of us have very ordinary windows and want to know how to treat them well and interestingly for the least possible expense.

Curtains

The variety of curtains is enormous. They can be as simple or as elaborate as you like, depending on the fabric, the heading, the pelmet, whether they hang free or are tied back and, of course, on your taste and what suits the room. Headings range from simple gathers to complicated arrangements of pleats and include the popular French heads – groups of three pleats – single goblet pleats, pinch pleats, pencil pleats, double pleats, gathers and smocks. If you're making them yourself use the appropriate heading tape. Swags and tails, done by draping and folding, are another fairly elaborate form of heading and can look enormously impressive. Pelmets can be hard or soft. Hard ones are usually of wood in straight or fancy shapes, painted or fabric covered. Soft pelmets, in the same material as the curtains are lined, gathered or ruched. If you do not want to use a pelmet, curtain rails and poles can also provide great visual variety. They come in a wide range of shapes, from simple flat rails that disappear behind the heading, to elaborate wooden and metal poles with ornate finials and decorative brackets. Many types take pull cords.

If windows are a handsome shape and not overlooked just leave them be. The triple set to the left is complemented by an array of healthy plants. The graceful curtains on the right are gathered high to show off arched panes.

LIVING ROOMS

How long is a curtain?

Short windows don't necessarily have to have short curtains which only really look good in small cottagey or attic windows. Short, neat café curtains that cover half the window can sometimes be the answer to shut out an ugly view. If you have short windows and don't want long curtains, use blinds.

Generous, full-length curtains look rich, graceful and generally room-enhancing. They should either just touch the floor—no gap between hem and floor—or be allowed to fall down to it in folds, Thirties style. Give long curtains good hems to allow for shrinkage.

Fabric

Whatever you buy, don't skimp on the amount. Curtains should look full so it's better to have yards and yards of a cheaper material than meagre amounts of an expensive one. It won't even look expensive if you've been mean about it. Bound, edged, or bordered curtains, or all three, look sophisticated and beautifully finished off. Lining is a must—except for sheers—and interlining recommended for insulating—both keeping in the heat and keeping out any cold air—cutting down noise and dirt absorption. Properly lined curtains hang nicely; unlined ones just droop.

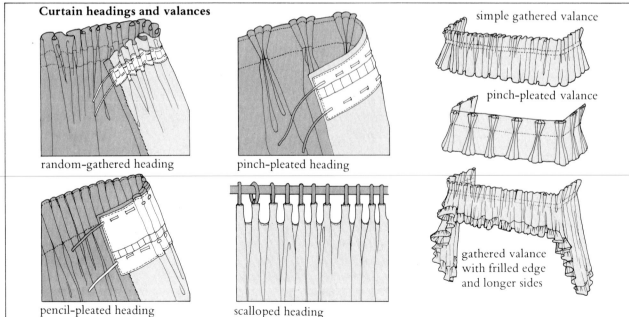

Curtain headings and valances

random-gathered heading

pinch-pleated heading

simple gathered valance

pinch-pleated valance

pencil-pleated heading

scalloped heading

gathered valance with frilled edge and longer sides

Above left: Double café curtains are made specially interesting with their frame of stencilled flowers. The smaller pattern seems to be repeated by the leaves trailing from the hanging basket, and the larger pattern by the tulips on the table.

Above: In this room elaborately painted shutters, which are more like decorated panels, give a better effect than curtains. The table, with its patchwork overcloth in front of the window adds to the picturesqueness.

Right: Loose cream linen weave curtains on this bay fall gracefully to the floor over Holland blinds. False panels of wood beading give distinction to the wood below.

Blinds

These have now become as popular as curtains and range from the plain and simple roller fabric blinds or shades to elaborately frilled and ruched varieties. As well as those you can make yourself, there are the wood and metal blinds, including Venetian and louvred. See the Blind identikit (page 317) for description of available types.

Good alternatives

If your insulation is reasonable, and heat loss and energy conservation not therefore serious considerations, or if the window is more useful for its light than its view, or the view needs disguising, then see what you can do with the frames. These can often be very imaginatively treated. Short windows can be given extra height by fixing wood trim to the frame from floor to ceiling and perpendicular to the wall. It will also give the window more depth. Add a blind or shade to drop from the ceiling level as well and you will suddenly have long graceful windows, or what will pass for them very well. The frames can be painted, papered or covered in with the walls or painted a contrasting colour or white.

Another possibility is to have double-hinged solid wooden shutters or panels made for each side of the window, again from ceiling to floor. Were you to feel particularly

LIVING ROOMS

extravagant you could have the room-facing side mirrored – worth it for the wonderful effect of light and space. Alternatively, you could make the screens or shutters easily detachable and have one surface painted or covered in fabric so that you could ring the changes when you felt like it or have different ones for summer and winter. Other good ideas are to fill the window with plants hung from the ceiling; to fit glass shelves for a collection of coloured china or masses of pretty pot plants. (Always check first that the plants are suited to a position where they will be subjected to extremes of light and heat, like some hardy ivies.) Or surround the window with shelves for books and interesting collections of objects.

Cheerful improvements

It is quite possible to cheer up existing curtains, blinds or shades that are perfectly adequate but tired and boring. And what's more, it needn't cost very much.

● Long curtains or draperies hanging loose will look better – and different – immediately if you loop them back with tie-backs made from lengths of cord and attached to hooks fixed to the window frame. Or make your own fabric tie-backs (see instructions on page 20).

● Add a border or binding down

the leading and bottom edges of curtains for a real interior designer touch. Choose a colour from the existing design or a contrast colour if the fabric is plain. Make fabric tie-backs to match.

● If you are handy with a needle you could sew in another lining or backing in a contrasting or toning fabric to the existing one. Add a print lining to a plain material; a small scale design in the same colours to a large scale design; a geometric in the same colours to a mini-flower pattern; an abstract pattern to a more clear-cut one. If you then loop the curtains back you will get glimpses of the new lining, which will give it fresh interest.

Top right: Permanently tied-back drapes allow plain under-curtains to be drawn. Note the matching colours of the tie-backs – a useful designer customizing touch. This budget-minded design allows you to create a luxury look relatively inexpensively. The yardage for the costly patterned fabric is small compared to that of the low-priced plain cotton sateen.

Right: Elaborate festoon blinds behind rather tailored curtains add an air of depth and perspective to this room. This is reinforced by the use of mirror on the wall, and glass to support the unicorn head and act as a coffee table.

Above: The colour scheme of pale yellow with turquoise blue trim used to decorate this charming Regency period room, was based on that used in the drawing room of the Sir John Soane Museum in London. In keeping with that period, the window treatment has been confined to shutters with Holland blinds for privacy. The small table, which like the rest of the furniture is contemporary with the house, was originally backed with mirror. New distressed mirror has been cleverly used between the long windows to continue the effect of enhanced space. The faux bois treatment used on the skirting board and the Greek key pattern of the border are also period features which have been added.

Know your window terms

Here is a brief guide, in alphabetical order, to the names you're most likely to come across once you start thinking about window treatments.

Austrian blind Arched blind or shade more commonly known as a festoon blind or pull-up curtain. It has rows of vertical shirring and can be raised and lowered by cords threaded through rings concealed at the back of the blind.

Backing This is the special material laminated to roller shade fabric to act as a lining, a stiffener and a blocker-out of unwelcome light.

Balloon blind A shade or blind with deep inverted pleats which create a billowing balloon-like effect.

Blind A vertical window covering which can be rolled up on a spring-roller attachment, or drawn up by cords threaded through rings.

Café curtain A short half-curtain hung from a rod going across a window, as in French cafés. This sort of curtaining is sometimes hung in a double tier, and is a useful treatment for windows that open inwards, or face the street. The tier system gives both light and privacy.

Casement window A window that opens on vertical hinges.

Cornice A wooden frame or pelmet mounted over a window treatment to hide the hardware.

Festoon blind See Austrian blind.

Finials The decorative ends of a curtain rod, either wood or brass.

Heading The top of curtains or drapes. Different varieties include gathered headings, pencil pleats, pinch pleats, box pleats, scalloped headings and smocked or shirred headings.

Leading edge The inner edge of a curtain or blind which is often bound or bordered.

Mullions The vertical, narrow wood members that separate panes of glass.

Muntins US term for mullion.

Pattern repeat A design term for one or more motifs repeated either vertically or horizontally on a fabric. It is useful to quote the size of the repeat when ordering fabric for curtains or blinds so that you do not cut off in the middle of a formalized pattern. Large repeats in fabric make curtains very expensive

Pelmet: See cornice and valance.

Pull-up curtain See Austrian blind.

Ring-shirr tape Fabric strip with regular rings and two enclosed cords used for shirring blinds like the Austrian or Festoon variety.

Ring tape Fabric strip with rings used for Roman and Balloon blinds.

Rod pocket The open-ended casing at the bottom hem of a Roman or Roller blind through which a rod, batten or wooden slat is passed to add extra weight.

Roller blind A flat blind that is controlled by a spring-mechanism.

Roman blind A shade or blind that draws up into neat horizontal folds by means of cords threaded through rings attached at regular intervals to the back of the fabric. You can either use rings alone or, on heavier fabrics, you can attach light battens to keep the folds crisp.

Sash curtains A flat piece of fabric or curtain panel with rod pockets sewn at top and bottom. Ordinary brass or tension rods are then threaded through and mounted at top and bottom of the window to stretch the curtain between them.

Shirring A permanent gathering of fabric achieved by drawing up material along two or more parallel lines of stitching, or over cords or thin rods threaded through casings or rod pockets.

Tie-back A piece of fabric, cord or chain attached to the window frame and used to loop back curtains.

Valance Or pelmet. A decorative, horizontal panel of fabric usually attached to the top of the window frame, or just above, to hide rods and provide added interest.

LIVING ROOMS

Measuring curtains

Accurate measurement is essential. Don't guess–looks are deceptive. Measure every window with a steel tape (fabric ones stretch). Double check each measurement and write it down immediately, identifying each window if you are measuring several at once.

Once you have measured the window, decide where the hardware–the tracks and screws and so on–is going to go (above the frame; overlapping the sides; tucked neatly inside a recess); buy what you have decided upon and install it before you start calculating the fabric. If you are going to replace existing hardware, make pencil marks to show the new position. This is important because hardware measurements will affect your calculations as you will see from the more detailed instructions for measuring curtains which are given on page 63 opposite.

Above left: Venetian blinds are used both for window and room divider in this large Hi-Tech living space.

Above: Clear blue shades are fitted to draw up from the bottom on these overlooked windows. Fixed like this they ensure maximum privacy with the benefit of maximum light as well.

Right: A light, fresh, modern look with blinds reminiscent of the orient.

How to measure curtains

Before you can estimate how much material you are going to need, you must first decide what style of curtain you want, whether a heading is required, what sort of fabric you want to use and what length they should be. The appropriate curtain track or rod should also either be in position or its precise location and dimensions marked with a pencil.

The first thing you need to establish is the final length and width of the area the finished curtains are to cover when drawn.

The width

To find the width of the curtain area (**AA**), you only need measure the length of the supporting track or rod, or the combined length of both tracks where two overlap.

The total width of the curtains is this measurement multiplied by the fullness required by the type of heading you have chosen, plus 7.5 cm (3 in) for each side hem. Curtains look mean when they don't have sufficient fabric to hang in luxurious folds, so don't skimp. Multiply the width by two for a standard gathered heading, by two and a quarter for a pencil pleat heading, two and a half for pinch pleats and three for sheer and lightweight fabrics.

The length

To find the finished length of curtains you must know where they are to start and finish. Measure from the top of the curtain track or rod (or pencilled position) for headed curtains, and from the bottom of the rings where the curtains are to be suspended below a rod.

Measure from there to the point where you want the curtain to finish. This is usually the sill (**AB**) or floor (**AC**).

Add 15–25 cm (6–10 ins) to this length for hems and heading (15 cm [6 in] for lightweight and sheer fabrics and 25 cm [10 in] for heavy ones).

How much fabric to buy

To find out how many fabric widths you will need, divide the total width of the curtain by the width of the fabric you want to use, always rounding up the total (i.e. $6\frac{1}{2}$ widths should be seven widths).

If you are using a plain fabric, multiply the number of fabric widths by the length in centimetres and divide by 100 to get the number of metres. Do the same for yards but divide the inches by 36.

Matching patterns

If you are using a patterned fabric you will have to allow for repeats of design

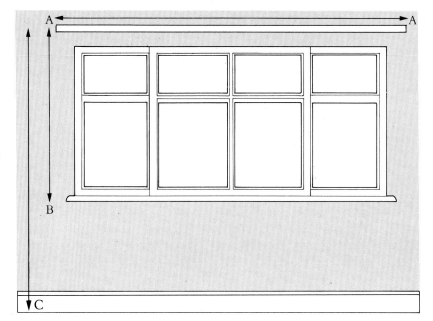

in the length. With floor length curtains or drapes you usually start off with a full repeat just below the heading; short curtains and blinds have the repeat at the bottom. Repeats on each width must match exactly; so should every window in the room.

This applies not just to large designs; even tiny all-over patterns jar if they are out of true. To test this in a store, simply unroll enough fabric for you to see two pattern sections side by side. If, when you shift one section slightly, you can't see any

difference in the pattern, you won't need to bother about measuring the repeat. If it looks odd, you must measure.

You do this by measuring the length of a complete pattern before it repeats again. Make a note of it along with all the other measurements. Then measure lengthwise from the dominant motif within a repeat to the next identical one. Since you want to keep the repeats even and not cut off in mid-air as it were, you usually have to buy more patterned fabric than plain.

CHOOSING THE RIGHT FURNITURE

People often get very guilty about choosing furniture. They feel that they should know what they want in a room from the very beginning, and feel incompetent if they cannot make up their minds right away. But any truly individual room has to evolve slowly; this is half the fun and certainly half the charm.

If you have existing furniture and are merely re-doing a room, you will almost certainly know what you want to keep and what to re-place – or re-upholster, re-cover, re-finish or re-paint. If you are start-ing from scratch, make a list of all the pieces you think absolutely essential, with a note of what they are likely to cost. If you get into the habit of always checking the prices of furniture you like in shops, sales or auction rooms, you will soon have a pretty clear idea of most values whether antique, second hand, reproduction or modern. Make a second list of other pieces you think you would like when you can afford them, say over the next five years or so. This will be a more flexible list because prices tend to creep upwards (except when you want to sell anything) and your tastes and finances might well change a little or a lot along the way.

Choosing a style
The style of a room is what gives it its own particular character. Style often becomes as big a bugbear as colour schemes and for the same reason; it means laying what passes for your taste on the table for all to judge. But I cannot emphasize too strongly that you should only choose furniture and furnishings that make you feel comfortable. If they don't, they won't make other people feel comfortable either. Once again it boils down to confidence, and the small test I recommend on page 14 for finding out the colours that make you feel secure, can apply just as well to style.

The most unusual styles to see around today could include what pass for country, city-sophisticated, improvised junk, garden room, Ita-lian modern, French (Louis Le-whatever) uncompromisingly anti-que or whatever period is chosen (Georgian, Jacobean) industrial (high-tech or creative salvage), art deco and art nouveau. In addition there are the individual, mixed styles of decoration that contain ele-ments from several sources and are often called 'eclectic mix'.

Left: This room features a carefully selected range of furniture and rug in almost an identical shade of beige. It is the objects in the room that provide contrast and variety.

Different styles for different tastes. Thirties furnishings contribute comfort to the room on the right.

LIVING ROOMS

SEATING

Far left: Antique furniture, fake wall panelling and subtle colours serve to create the atmosphere of a period room – enhanced even further by the tapestries on the wall.

Top left: A Country or Cottage style is achieved here by the presence of comfortable upholstered furniture, soft furnishings and wallcovering, all in complementary floral prints. This is reinforced by the use of cane, wicker and an abundance of fresh flowers.

Bottom left: Contrasting colours, streamlined storage space and an overall Minimalist feel create a look that epitomizes the modern room.

Above: Garden style is brought into this living room through the massed display of plants in front of the lattice-effect windows and in other parts of the room. Rattan cane chairs and floral and leaf chintz fabrics set against a light background are equally appropriate.

They all have a sort of recognisable shorthand: *Country*, for example, would include delicate flower prints or stencils, comfortable sofas, and stripped pine furniture. Slate or quarry tiles and faded rugs complete the look. *Junk* would pride itself on a collection of re-vamped, painted-up old pieces and found objects. *City* would conjure up sophisticated leather and chrome, glass, marble and wall-to-wall carpet. *Modern Italian* would be bright, primary coloured, or 'dolly-mixture' lacquered furniture, white floor and walls, with perhaps a strong dash of Memphis daring. 'Memphis' is the name of the design partnership set up by the Italian designer Ettore Sottsass in 1981 when he exhibited the furniture which has now become pseudonymous with this name at the Italian Furniture Fair. *Antique* relates to any room which is consistently furnished in the style of one period, such as Victorian, Georgian, Art Deco. Art Nouveau would relate to furnishings of the 1890's, typified by the use of images inspired by plants and the sea reflected in sinuous curves in pale and subtle colours. Art Deco has come to mean brilliant colours, curved upholstery and angular, geometric designs. *Industrial* style uses hard-edged black and grey, and furniture originally designed for hospitals or factories. *Garden* would be lattice-patterned wallpaper, cane furniture, plants and flowery chintzes. And the *Eclectic mix* is what most of us are probably happiest with; a little bit of everything, old and new, treasures, heirlooms and favourite things collected from all over.

Sitting comfortably

If you are starting from scratch, or just about, decide what has to be bought and what improvised in the way of seating. Whatever you buy, make it the best you can afford. If comfort is important to you – and if it isn't now, it almost certainly will be at a later date – anchor pieces like sofas and large armchairs should be the best looking and most comfortable you can pay for and find. Second best is not good enough. In upholstery you really do get what you pay for and you usually have to take the quality on trust since you cannot see all the underpinnings of frames, filling and springs unless you are shown a sample cross section and have it all explained to you in the shop.

Most good stores display a whole section of upholstered pieces from traditional to modern in a range of different shapes and sizes, but most pieces come in a far greater variety of sizes, covers and colourings than those on show. So, if you like the shape of something but not the size and colour, do not give up on it. For instance, you may like the look of a sofa but think it too small; it may

LIVING ROOMS

well come in other lengths from 137 cm to 229 cm (54 to 90 in). Arm and back heights too, can be varied since they have to be built separately in the first place, and there is almost always a large range of covers available for the choosing within the price range. If you are willing to pay the difference in price there is usually even more choice. It pays to inquire. Living-room seating should be as adaptable as your lifestyle demands and able to cope with crowded parties as well as quiet evenings if need be. Try to plan to seat at least six comfortably, and also have some really occasional chairs that can be stashed away in a cupboard somewhere or brought in from the hall or a bedroom. If they can fit in with the room's general style, so much the better.

Other furniture

Most other furniture – tables, desks, storage and occasional pieces – will either be made of wood, glass and some sort of metal or perspex or plexiglass or even marble. Whether you choose antique, modern, reproduction or a mixture of all three is purely a question of personal taste, combined with the sort of style you're aiming at. Some people are ardent collectors of 20s, 30s and 50s furniture, or even the 40s utility pieces which are now enjoying a new vogue. If you are far from rich but hanker after earlier furniture,

Far left: Comfortable and flexible modular seating units in toning coloured upholstery, which is removable for easy cleaning.

Above: Regency drawing room with real candle candelabra, and genuine period furniture. Original window surrounds have been painted then combed to look like grained oak.

Left: Stylish simplicity is produced by the framing of a classic black Corbusier chaise longue against the unexpected combination of vivid green stippled walls and pink carpet. Note the empty frame.

scour the second-hand shops, junk yards, charity shops and sales.

Most good modern furniture is expensive and if you have set your heart on a piece you can't afford it is better to improvise for the moment.

Flexi-furniture

If you plan to eat in the living room, try to buy as generous a table as possible but one which will look quite in keeping with the room when it is not laid for a meal. Round tables are best for this because when they aren't being used for dining they can be piled with books, magazines and plants, and have the look and feel of a library table. You can make up round tables from cheap wood and cover them with long cloths and changeable overcloths. Alternatively, try to find the sort of rectangular table that can also double as a long desk or work table when required. Chairs should look just as good for occasional seating as for dining. If you feel more comfortable having at least a visual dividing line between sitting and dining areas you could make a dividing 'wall' with a low storage unit. This could act as a bar and serving area as well. Even a large sofa with its back to the table can make an effective divider.

Small space seating

If a room is tiny, don't despair. Try to work out the best solution to your background problem (see pages 27–33), then forget altogether about conventional seating (one or two sofas, armchairs, occasional chairs). Instead, plan on using a set of very comfortable chairs spaced round a low round table. This will create a seating island which is probably all you need in a confined space. It will work for most occasions, especially if it is properly lit.

Get the scale right

The size of a piece of furniture can look amazingly different when placed in different surroundings – lost in a vast, tall room, overpowering in a small one. You can prepare for this by having a scale plan of your room as described on page 17, and drawing your furniture on it to scale too. There is also the question of height: getting some height into a room can make all the difference between a monotonous and an interesting space. Most furniture today is fairly low which means that a good deal of the furniture in your room is going to be exactly the same height. So, if you can get the occasional high point in to vary the scale, the difference will be as important as an interesting flash of colour or pattern. Even if you can't find or afford tall elegant pieces of furniture much the same effect can be produced with a tall plant or lamp, wall-fixed shelving, mirrors and, of course, pictures.

LIVING ROOMS

Improvise with flair

Since most of us have very limited budgets for furnishing it is essential to know when to spend, when to save and how to improvise. For example, comfortable anchor pieces like large upholstery and capacious storage should, and will, certainly have first call on your money. This leaves the smaller pieces like coffee tables, ordinary tables, work tables, side tables and occasional chairs and low storage to make demands on your ingenuity and imagination. Most of them can be put together quite cheaply but without ruining the style or atmosphere of the room; on the contrary it's often these that add most of the character to a room and reflect your personality better than the bought pieces which can look like everyone else's.

Style on a shoe-string

● Find black tin trunks to act as coffee tables or side tables. Or use oriental packing cases—or occidental ones come to that, if they are waxed or painted—topped with a rectangle of glass cut to size.

● Ready-cut slabs of thick glass on top of painted, lacquered or carpeted wooden cubes make stunning tables and provide storage space.

● The same cubes, padded and covered are fine for occasional seating. Add semi-concealed castors for easy manoeuvrability.

● Old flush doors (or new flush doors) set on painted or natural wooden trestles; or on 60 cm × 60 cm (2 ft × 2 ft) steel supports, make good-looking desks.

● Shabby [not valuable] old oriental rugs can be used to cover large floor cushions.

● Forget about conventional sofas and seating. Build a plywood platform at one end of the room, cover it with a carpet and pile it with floor cushions. If storage space and seating are both at a premium, try building in boxes around the perimeter of the room. Give them hinged lids for storage and add soft pads covered with fabric for comfortable seating.

● Old kitchen or office chairs—there are always some in second-hand and junk shops—look fine stripped and painted in a variety of colours, some red, some pink or purple, for example, or all white with perhaps a coloured strut or leg, or all black.

● Dreary reproduction chairs can be given a thoroughly modern look, smartened up with paint and the seats covered with a strongly textured fabric like tweed or corduroy. Paint plain wooden chairs a dark or vivid colour and try your hand at painting a scene, birds, flowers, a ship, on the seat. Old dressers and chests of drawers, if you

can still find them, can be stripped and polished or painted and decorated. Have fun with them—paint each drawer a different colour or do a small 'mural', perhaps of clouds or trees, across the front. Or stencil or lacquer them.

Once you have got into an improvising state of mind almost any piece of furniture will begin to develop potential.

Above: This bed-sitting room has been furnished to great effect at minimum expense. The floor is simply polished, sheeting-covered floor cushions serve for seats, while the bedhead bookshelves are made from planks balanced on bricks.

Right: Elegant bookshelves either side of a mirror-lined opening form a dividing wall between two rooms.

Everything in its place

Books, records, compact discs, cassettes, stereo, tv, video, papers, files, stationery, typewriter or word-processor, decorative objects, sewing-machine, sewing things, magazines, directories, drinks, glasses, ice bucket. . . . The living room has to house some or all of these things and if it's used for eating has to come up with storage for china, glass and cutlery too. Where do you put it all? Obviously good, well planned and ample living room storage is a must.

Highly sophisticated storage

A wall of storage units will make provision for most of the paraphernalia you own and might either incorporate a bar and a desk flap to let down, or a permanent table set at right angles to shelves and cupboards for work, games, sewing and hobbies. There are many versions and permutations to choose from in all price ranges and many finishes, so again it boils down to a question of taste, style and pocket, although here, unlike upholstery, expense does not necessarily indicate worth. Some of the German, Scandinavian and Italian built-in units are particularly smooth and luxurious with inbuilt fridges and mirror-lined bars but cheaper versions can look just as good, if not better, depending on finish and the final arrangement of possessions on shelves.

You can build in your own

LIVING ROOMS

bookshelves. The breakfront version is useful; this has cupboards below and a deep shelf at waist height to hold drink trays, stereo turntable and so on. The cupboards could be deep enough to hold filing cabinets and a tv set which would be concealed when the doors were shut. You would then need a separate desk or work table.

You would get a different sort of feel again by installing a big armoire or bureau bookcase if you could afford one or the other. Both pieces of furniture would be handsome additions to any room and would provide necessary height as well as being very capacious. A good substitute might be one of those huge Victorian or Edwardian wardrobes which you can often find cheaply in second-hand shops or junk yards, because they are too big for most bedrooms. These can be stripped, re-polished, painted, lacquered, decorated or mirrored to form decorative and useful pieces.

Or something simple

A little lateral thinking pays dividends here. Simpler storage items could include a drinks trolley by the side of a sofa to hold glasses, trays, ice buckets and so on. Industrial or hospital steel trolleys could just as well store stereo, files, tv, video, sewing or hobby equipment. Even good-looking baskets set side by side on the floor can hold a good

Above: Glass shelves are lit from above by concealed downlighters, which focus subdued attention on the books and ornaments.

Above right: The straight, clean lines of this floor-standing shelving unit make an excellent contrast to the rounded, sweeping lines of the foregound cane chair.

Right: Imaginative use of shelving, which also acts as a side table with a built-in storage cupboard. Colours have been carefully matched.

deal of paraphernalia–including bottles or books–with a certain panache.

Look at unusual sources and suppliers when searching for storage systems. Industrial outlets offer metal shelving systems, office-equipment stores yield brightly coloured drawers and trays.

Don't always think in terms of hiding things away. Some hobbies and interests use equipment or materials that are fascinating or colourful in their own right and these can often lend character to a room if they're left out on display. Skeins of wool and silk used for tapestry work or embroidery, lace-making pillows and bobbins, can look highly decorative. Plans and drawings or maps can be stored in neat rolls in large baskets or drums or laid flat in thin drawers set into a wall of storage; these can look interesting in themselves with their severe and narrow horizontal lines. Today's tv and hi-fi equipment is small and beautiful by design, so display your systems on open shelves or custom units.

Above left: The long, low and decidedly elegant lines of the sideboard allow functional elements, such as the tv and stereo speakers, to become part of the design.

Above: The space under the stairs in this house provides room for a meticulously stacked wine crates.

Left: Vertical panels between shelves in this crowded book wall are faced in mirror to give an illusion of space. Note the door which has been painted to look like walnut.

Living rooms that also have to act as office or work room by day (and more and more people elect to work at home if they can these days) can still perform both functions with comparative ease. For more information on study/living rooms, refer to the chapter on *Home Offices* (pages 184–99).

DEVELOPING AN EYE FOR DETAIL

Once people have got the framework of a room together – the walls, floor, ceiling, windows, lighting and furnishings – they often run out of ideas for what to do with smaller objects and any family treasures they possess. Good arrangements and an eye for detail can only be achieved with practice, so it may help to have a few guidelines to follow in the first place, if only to act as a spring board for producing interesting and unusual ideas of your own.

Whether you are starting to decorate a first home, have just moved into a new place or are redecorating an existing room, the problem is often much the same: not so much how to arrange things as how to fill up big blank walls and table or shelf surfaces when you don't seem to have very much to use and certainly very little to spend. If it is any consolation, the whole question of arrangement seems just as much a problem for people with enviably rare and valuable collections as it is for those with hardly enough to call a collection of anything. And the same thing applies to people who have collections of quite valueless things: baskets, keys, hats or whatever. How do you arrange what you have to its best advantage? And where is the best place to display these objects?

All kinds of things look good on walls. It doesn't have to be artwork like paintings, drawings, etchings, prints or even posters. Consider any of the following: pieces of framed fabric or even beautiful wrapping paper, particularly if they accent the background colours or furnishing themes in the room; framed arrangements of dried flowers or grasses or corn on a dark background; collections of framed cigarette cards (from old cigarette packets still available in many antique markets), or postcards; rugs, of course, and any sort of interesting quilt whether old or new.

Then too, any flat decorative thing – a fragment of embroidery or lace or part of an oriental rug – can be clamped between thin glass and hung up. You can buy corner pieces or special flat screws at most art shops. They also supply small metal clips to secure items between picture glass and a sheet of hardboard or thin plywood.

Right: Objects of different styles and eras can successfully be grouped together if you can find a common theme to link them. Brass predominated on this backlit, marble-topped window shelf, but even the patina on the bronze figures is in natural sympathy with the unrelieved green surroundings.

Finishing touches: a miscellany of objects (left) makes a charming still-life in front of stained glass.

LIVING ROOMS

If you decide on hanging fabric from the wall consider what sort of fabric will suit your room best, the choice is large – cotton, silk, felt and many others. Then work out what sort of design is most appropriate for the fabric and for the room. With wall hangings you can choose a bold, vivid effect that will be the focal point of the room; or you might prefer a subdued pattern that will tone in with the surroundings.

One of the easiest methods of making your own wall hangings is by cutting dyed fabrics into angular shapes and then stitching the pieces together to form a large, striking abstract design. This technique has the advantages that you don't have to paint or draw anything; nor is it necessary to tidy up the edges of the wall hanging as this can add to the haphazard effect. However, you do need a clear eye to pick up recurring patterns and themes in the room.

If you want a more definite pattern or motif the easiest method to achieve this is to use a stencil. You can either buy a ready-cut type or make your own, tracing the design from a pattern elsewhere in the room, such as the curtains or the carpet.

Another bold idea is to fix long coloured fluorescent tubes to the wall in a pattern of diagonals or V shapes. Lit up in their various colours against a white wall they can look spectacular; unlit they take on

an almost sculptural quality.

Arranging pictures and prints

On the whole, people are divided into those who want to make room for a serious collection and those who want to use wall space to its most decorative advantage. The first school thinks of a wall as a means to an end, a support, a mere background. The second thinks of it as a canvas to be made the most of; yet another surface to decorate or ornament. The big problem with this latter group is to find some sort of unifying factor that will make sense or give a theme to a miscellany of oddments that are less than distinguished.

A collection of nondescript prints, for example, can be given a sense of unity if each is mounted with the same distinctive colour: camel or chrome yellow or red, whichever fits in best with the room, and then edged all in the same way with a thin strip of wood or chrome or brass.

Try not to hang things too close, too high, or too far apart. Do not fix anything so low over a sofa that people can knock their heads on it when getting up or even leaning back; all the same, try to place everything at a reasonably flexible eye level. Obviously vertical arrangements will make walls look taller; horizontal will make them

Above: The soft, subdued shades of blue, grey and white in this pretty composition of objects is complemented by green foliage

Right: A pleasing arrangement of different sized paintings on the wall beyond this centrally placed sofa, looks particularly effective against the plain light walls.

Above right: Very convincing are these print-effect flat papers. Print motifs, borders and decorative features, such as the bows, are all available in kit form.

Far right: A common theme, here framed posters, always makes the task of arranging pictures far easier.

look longer. Most paintings look good against dark walls but if a wall is strongly patterned, try mounting prints against a deep matt or ground of the same background colour. In this way, a subject is becalmed in an area of its own and does not get lost in the richness of the surrounding background.

In order to avoid making nasty marks on the wall when you are experimenting with the hanging, it is best to decide on the overall shape of the arrangement first—a square, oblong, diamond or triangle—and on a painted wall mark out the area with light pencil which can easily be rubbed off, or with chalk on a paper wallcovering. Mark out the same sized area on the floor, then lay out the various items, juggling them around until you are satisfied with the positions. Draw a rough sketch and then translate them all in a permanent fashion to the wall.

Table-top inspiration

Still-lifes on tables, dresser tops, window sills and mantelpieces can be improvised just as successfully as those on walls. Old bottles, minerals, stones, shells, tiny baskets filled with dried flowers, old wooden or papiér mâché boxes, miniature bottles in different shapes, pretty dishes containing pot-pourri, an assortment of small vases stuck with single-stem flowers or leaves. . . .

Once you start, all sorts of possibilities will present themselves and you'll find real inspiration in some of the unlikeliest looking things.

Gather and group

Collections of small objects should always be gathered together and arranged in a group rather than being thinly spread around the house. Very small things like pebbles, marbles, polished beach stones, old buttons and so on, can be put into large glass goblets or jars and displayed on window ledges (against the light) or on shelves. Slightly larger objects, however different and unrelated, should be grouped so that they have something in common like colour or

national origin. Or if they're placed significantly with larger things, the impact and interest of the contrast will give harmony to the group.

If the arrangement is on a table, add a plant or dried grasses or flowers and perhaps one taller object to give balance. Since most tables are also used for dumping, leave space so that the arrangements aren't continually being disturbed.

If an arrangement is on a glass table try lighting it from underneath with an uplight. If it's on a solid surface you could light it from above with a downlight or spot.

Cheerful little odds and ends arranged with flair can often make a room seem far more interesting than much grander collections.

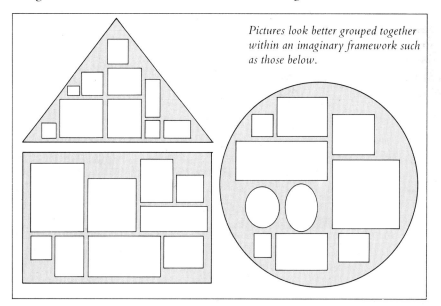

Pictures look better grouped together within an imaginary framework such as those below.

One-room living has come a long way from the old bed-sitter image with its general note of poverty and desperation. Today, some people actually prefer to live in one room: they even choose to take down partition walls in two- or three-roomed flats or apartments to make one big open-plan space.

But most one-roomed flats or studio apartments are box-like spaces with little to commend them in the way of interesting detail or character. And generally they are small. Since they are going to be not just living room but bedroom, dining room, and very often office as well, this means that every inch of space has to be dual-purpose if not multi-functional, and every activity has to be properly catered for and duly compartmented. To work efficiently this sort of room needs discipline, neatness and, above all, imagination. Successful one-room living is more an attitude of mind than anything else.

Everything is something else

The sofa bed or studio couch has made a great difference to one-room living. Beds that fold down from the wall when they are needed have lost their makeshift image and have been updated to a new smooth efficiency and now come complete with a wall of closets or wardrobes. Even double beds can be piled and piled with cushions to make an in-viting couch for yourself and guests by day.

Tables can be used as desks; end tables can be used for dining; chairs can fold up and be hung from large colourful hooks, or be stacked up into a tiny space; armchairs can become spare single beds; well thought-out storage will take care of clothing, books, files and china.

Manufacturers are now geared to one-room flexible living as never before. But if the room is not to look a complete jumble you have to try to create distinct areas for relaxing, sleeping, eating and work. Since you very often cannot physically divide the space, you have to divide the 'look' with different lighting or rugs or colour to make separate visual areas. A successful solution can sometimes be found by making an extra level in the room. Beds and work areas can often be accommodated in this way, and the effect can be neat, stylish, and space-saving. It will work best in a high-ceilinged room or a long, narrow one.

Left: A change in level helps to delineate the living room area, while a pierced wall creates a strong visual link with kitchen and bar areas.

The area on the right relies upon changes in level to define different functions.

LIVING ROOMS

Living at different levels

One of the most impressive examples of one-room living that I have ever seen was in a long, narrow space approximately 7.5 m by 3 m (24 ft by 10 ft). Sleeping, sitting, eating and working areas had been divided into 2.4 m (8 ft) steps, each 23 cm (9 in) higher than the other. Colours had been kept to a minimal dark grey and white with black and the occasional flash of green in plants and cushions. Storage was behind flush doors concealed all down one wall. The table did for working and eating; the mattress (put straight on the floor and covered in black tweed) did for sleeping and lounging; and the steps made extra seating areas as well, with the help of large flat black or white cushions which stacked like striped playbricks when not in use. Transparent fold-up perspex chairs were at the table.

Another successful room had a large floor to ceiling panel about 2.4 m (8 ft) wide set in the centre of the room. On one side was a desk/dining area; on the other, a sofa and easy chairs. At night, part of the panel was let down, revealing a bed with concealed lighting behind. Cupboards and shelves were built all round the room and concealed behind neat panels of canvas-covered wood, with touch-opening mechanisms so as not to break the continuity of the limited space.

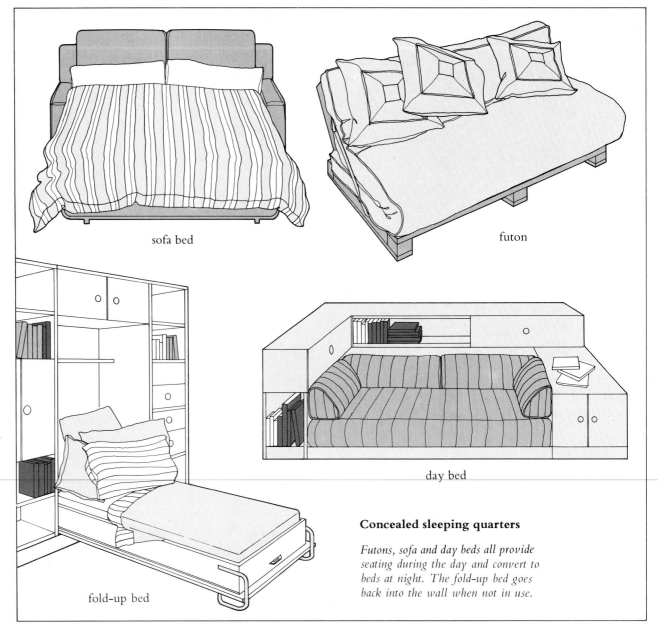

sofa bed

futon

day bed

fold-up bed

Concealed sleeping quarters

Futons, sofa and day beds all provide seating during the day and convert to beds at night. The fold-up bed goes back into the wall when not in use.

Above left: Strong horizontal lines of tables and seating bound by bookshelves and the kitchen counter sort out the various functions in this spacious area.

Above: An off-the-floor bed frees the floor space. Clothes are stashed away behind curtains.

Left: A dramatic change in height is provided by the high kitchen counter and bar stools, making a very effective room divider.

LIVING ROOMS

Disguising the bed

Nowadays, it is more a question of fitting in adequate storage as well as a good size sofa bed, than trying to disguise a bedstead. Almost every shape of sofa can now conceal a full-size mattress, and many ordinary beds can be bought with space-saving drawers underneath and be disguised with fitted covers and back cushions. One way of fitting in closet and sleeping space together, apart from the fold-up bed idea, is to build wardrobes or shelves around a bed-size area to form a bed alcove. The back of the recess can then be mirrored to enlarge the sense of space or covered with art or fabric according to taste.

An interesting room I saw in New York made ingenious use of its space. It measured 4.9 m by 4.3 m (16 ft by 14 ft), and had full length storage at one end, and low level storage—for files, journals and papers—under a window at the other end. Floor to ceiling book-shelves and low level cupboards were built about 1.6 m (5–6 ft) in front of the full-length storage to form a kind of corridor or ante-room, and a large double bed was placed in the middle of the room, tight covered like a sofa. In the middle of the bed, across its width, two substantial bolsters were set next to each other. In this way the bed became two back to back sofas by day and reverted to its original function at night. A round table served for working and dining, and there was still room for various arm chairs, occasional chairs and side tables.

How to decorate it

Much the same ideas about decoration apply to one-room living as to small spaces (see pages 27–33). Mirrored walls are obviously useful; so is good lighting–particularly up-lights in corners–and anything that takes the eye out and along like diagonal patterns, trellis, pale colours, to add a sense of perspective.

Right: In this extremely clever arrangement of a long and minutely narrow space, the owner has managed to squeeze in a double bed, storage, seating and dining table. Note how the bed is set on a stepped platform, carpeted to match the floor, which serves both to provide extra seating and to make room for storage drawers below. The bed itself can be cut off from view for extra privacy by matchstick blinds which match those on the window. The simplicity of the objects within the room and the light colours prevent any feelings of claustrophobia.

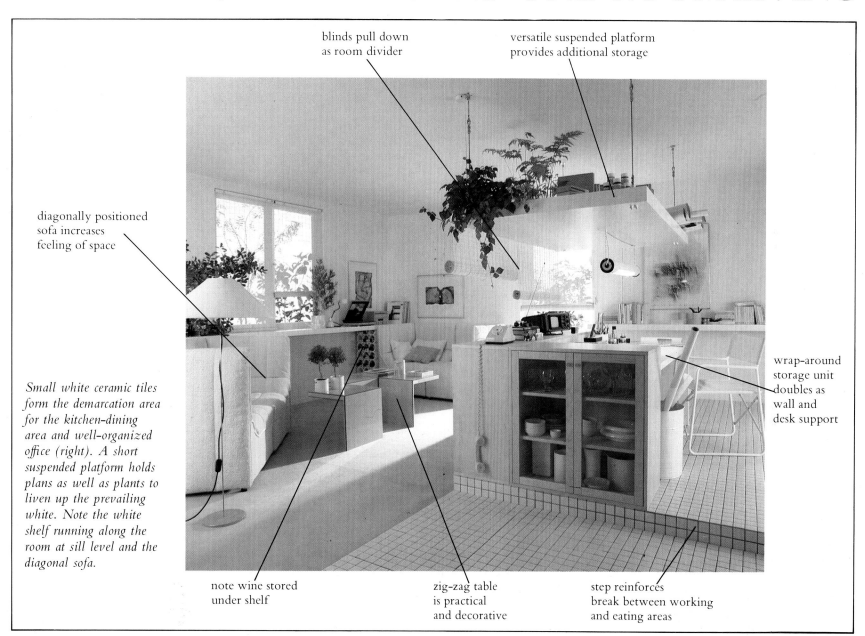

blinds pull down
as room divider

versatile suspended platform
provides additional storage

diagonally positioned
sofa increases
feeling of space

wrap-around
storage unit
doubles as
wall and
desk support

Small white ceramic tiles form the demarcation area for the kitchen-dining area and well-organized office (right). A short suspended platform holds plans as well as plants to liven up the prevailing white. Note the white shelf running along the room at sill level and the diagonal sofa.

note wine stored
under shelf

zig-zag table
is practical
and decorative

step reinforces
break between working
and eating areas

HALLS

It might seem odd to talk about entry halls as a postscript as it were but in practical terms most people put decorating their living rooms first. It is nevertheless the first part of your home that you and your visitors step into, and the last part that you leave. Obviously when you budget you have to allow the most money for the rooms you are actually going to live in, but once you have decided on what cash is available you must turn considerable thought and care – if not money – to making your hall as warm and welcoming and practical as you can. It might come last on your list of necessities, but there is no need for it to look the least.

Theoretically, halls should be easy to design, since there is generally little to purchase in the way of furniture and accessories unless you are blessed with the luxury of a wide, spacious and well-lit area. But whatever its size, you need to plan for convenience as well as impact, wear as well as warmth; a space that fits the feel of your home as well as it fits you.

The necessities

There should be at least one chair and a capacious table to take all the paraphernalia that inevitably collects in this clearing house for the home. If the hall is too narrow for this – and many entrance ways are barely more than a corridor, try to get in a long bench or a very narrow console, or at the very least a stool and a shelf.

If you have any built-in cupboards or closets you are home and dry – literally – as far as storage is concerned; if you have not, and there is really no room at all for any sort of full-length closet, have a hat stand or, failing this, a row of hooks to take not only your own family's coats, but those of visitors.

Mirrors are unfailingly useful in halls so that you can check your own appearance going out while visitors can check theirs coming in. They are also useful for reflecting too small a space and exaggerating every last bit of light. The best place to site them is over the table, or shelf, or other handy surface.

Many people install a telephone in the hall. While this is less common now you can fit phone sockets all around the house, the hall still provides a useful central place for a phone, and if you decide on this option, you will need a chair, table and space for directories.

Making an entrance – the unusually spacious lobby on the left has been used to advantage by the inclusion of a desk area complete with telephone in the small recess. In the much smaller hall to the right, bookshelves have been neatly fitted into the space under the stairs.

85

HALLS, STAIRS AND ENTRANCES

Suitability

What sort of furniture you have depends very much on the style of your home, your tastes and your pocket. Obviously if you have an essentially period home it is good to keep at least within the spirit of the place, although conversely, one old piece in a very modern hall can look stunning. Obviously too, if you have a country hall you will want to keep it as countryish and as relaxed as possible. Town halls should make an all out effort for interest and warmth to counteract the pervasive greyness outside. And houses by the sea should be well-prepared for sand and wet.

Durability

Any surface you choose should be as tough and durable as you can afford. People coming in from outside will bring in dirt and dust and damp as a matter of course so it's advisable to have both an outer and inner door mat. The most practical idea is to have a slight well let into the floor in front of the door and to fill it with coconut matting. This way, the mat will not shift, slip or kick-up, will not get frayed around the edges and cannot be by-passed.

The rest of the floor should be easily cleaned whatever material it is. Country halls look well in quarry tiles or French or Mexican tiles, flagstones, slate, brick or good old fashioned pavements. If you cannot have any natural material for some reason, keep your bare boards, scraped, sanded and sealed, or painted if the boards are in bad condition or have vinyl or composition tiles. Carpet is acceptable in town houses or flats but it must be the best quality you can afford because hallways take a lot of through traffic. Add rugs to hard floors for softness and interest, but make sure they will not slip and cause accidents. Secure them to carpet with gripper tape or use the sticky weave that is sold especially to keep rugs in place. This is also good for rugs on wood or hard floors. Otherwise tack a rug down lightly. Hallways are at constant risk of getting scratched, marked or chipped, so wall finishes must be highly durable. Paint and wallpaper could be protected and hardened by a final coat of polyurethane. Vinyl wallcoverings are always practical in halls since they will withstand all sorts of rough treatment.

Decoration

Ideally, walls on halls, corridors and staircases (if any) should be decorated with the same colour or treatment unless they are in quite different parts of the home and cannot be seen, one from another. Whatever the colour chosen, make sure it leads naturally into the rooms leading off it. Warm-coloured walls like apricots, yellows, terracottas,

Above: A hall should be both welcoming and practical. This room achieves both objectives. Warmth is provided by a radiator, while pictures and fresh flowers give colour and character. The quarry-tiled floor is hard-wearing, easy to clean and echoes the country look of the white walls and natural timber. A row of hooks and a stand take your family's and any visitor's coats and umbrellas.

Right: This long corridor-like hall has become something like a mini-gallery. Floral wallpaper, table, chairs, plants, pictures and oriental rugs all add to the cheerful feeling it manages to impart.

deep roses, plums, reds, tawny browns and marmalades all look good in city homes with moderate climates and in country homes too, come to that, but hot climates benefit from the reverse treatment: whites, cool blues and greens, pale yellows and creams.

Quite apart from mirror, the hall, corridor, landing and staircase walls will take any number of pictures, and general memorabilia. If there is space, you can line walls with bookcases to enormous advantage, and use an alcove for a desk to make an extra-mural study. Odd corners, window sills, ledges and shelves might take plants, and if you have a wide enough hall, you might well be able to make the hall an extra, if not a permanent, dining place by adding a small table.

Playing with the walls

If you have partition walls and not much space or light you can try playing around with the walls a little. For example, in a narrow town or terrace house where the front door opens directly into a corridor-like space, you could either take the wall down alto-gether, or make an arch going into the living room, or take the wall down to seating level, literally making a seating ledge. This way you will get all the benefit of the extra light and space and still have the suggestion of a division.

HALLS, STAIRS AND ENTRANCES

Above: A hall table strategically placed under the stairs offers a useful resting-place for bits and pieces that need to be close to hand.

Right: In a small space like a hall repetition of a theme makes for strong impact. Here, the square balustrade repeats the square glass panel of the front door below, but in larger scale.

Far right: A large healthy plant and a mirrored wall add interest and a sense of space to a cramped stairwell.

Another possibility, in say, a flat or an apartment where the living room door opens off the hall, is to cut two narrow floor-to-ceiling slits in the wall to give both extra light and interesting glimpses of the room ahead. Or you can cut out a large square or arched opening instead of a conventional door, and if the wall is big enough, a couple of openings or 'windows' either side—again to give different perspectives to the room ahead. Inset downlights into the top of the openings to light anything that you might care to place in these openings—a plant perhaps, flowers, an interesting object—and you will instantly dramatize the space.

Lighting

Lighting in halls, corridors and staircases should be clear and bright for reasons of safety as well as aesthetics. Downlights—recessed, semi-recessed, or ceiling-mounted—are good-looking and functional whatever the style of furnishings and collect fewer flies and less dirt than bowl-shaped or pendant fixtures. If you do not have many outlets, or cannot add extra lights, think of adding track-lighting to the ceiling since you can fix as many spots onto a track, trained to as many angles as you think it will take. If you have a lot of pictures on the walls this will light them beautifully as well as providing all the light you will need for comfort and safety. If your telephone is in the hall, a good light is essential for looking up numbers and writing down messages.

It might look particularly inviting to put a lamp on the table, chest or shelf and of course, if you have found room for a desk, it will certainly need a desk lamp. Very dark halls with little or no natural light will benefit from what the Americans call 'Plugmold'. This is a strip fixed with points on to which you can attach any number of bulbs that you like. The strip is placed behind a pelmet or soffit of some kind – a piece of wood or moulding running all round under the cornice, if there is one, or ceiling angle if there is not – and you then achieve the lighting expert's dream: light without a visible source.

Windows

Look carefully at any windows in hallways, corridors and on stairs to decide whether you should curtain them, blind them, shutter them or leave them alone. In general, unless you have very long and gracious windows, I think such windows look neater and let in more daylight if they are covered with blinds or shutters or even some sort of grill or trellis work. Very small windows are usually better just left, and given a plant, vase of flowers or object to cheer up the sill.

KITCHENS & DINING ROOMS

INTRODUCTION

If kitchens are the most complicated rooms to plan they are also the most rewarding to get right, the kitchen, after all, is primarily a working room and although good looks are an integral part of its design, easy function should be the prime consideration. If it is a machine for cooking, as design writers are fond of saying, it must be a well oiled one.

A kitchen tends to fall into one of three categories depending on its physical limitations and your life pattern: it may be designed purely as a work room when all the other family activities go on in other rooms; or it may be a room where the work is done and some or all family meals are taken; or finally it may be the real centre of the house, where work is done, meals are taken and where the family congregates.

Over the decades since the First World War, with the introduction of new forms of energy, the development of labour saving devices and changes in food and menus, there have been radical changes in kitchen design. By the 1950s, designers had turned kitchens into streamlined boxes with aseptic, clinical, easily wipeable finishes. It looked as if all traces of the cluttered, lived-in, homey kitchen, the heart and hearth of the home, had gone for ever. The appliance manufacturers, the frozen food kings, the canners and food merchants exploited to the hilt the female desire to get out of the kitchen just as quickly as possible.

But that was before the great cooking revolution which has restored the kitchen as a family room, if not *the* family room: warm, friendly, relaxed and comfortable. Nevertheless, if it's going to work at all, a well planned kitchen has, first and foremost, to suit the cook.

Given all this, a chapter about kitchens and kitchen decoration would be illogical to say the least, if it failed to take into account the room or area where food is served, which should be as pleasant a place as possible. Not only is the one space the inevitable extension of the other, but as often as not these days, the kitchen and dining areas are in the same room anyway. Today's dining rooms are defined by *where* you eat, not by the furniture. How you arrange these cooking/eating functions in your home depends on your life style as well as the space and money available.

Unless you have ample funds to hand, it is of the utmost importance to think ahead when you are planning a kitchen. You might not be able to afford all the appliances you would like from the start, but if you think you will need them and will be able to afford them later you must leave the space and supply utilities for them. That is to say, if you want a dishwasher but know you won't be able to afford one for, say, three years, then make sure the plumbing is available and that there is a niche for a new fixture before you install your worktops and units.

If you are planning on a family and intending to stay in your present home, then allow for much more storage space than you need now. And whatever your current needs, try to get as much worktop or counter space as you possibly can. You always need far more dumping/preparation areas than you could ever imagine.

Finally, make sure that you have ample power points or outlets. They are much easier to fit earlier than later; wires can be more easily concealed and circuits worked out at the start of kitchen planning. Again, you will probably need more than you think at first reckoning, so there is no harm in thinking ambitiously from the start.

Practical, warm and inviting, this country kitchen with dining area has all the ingredients which make it as attractive a place in which to eat as it is to prepare food.

If you are in the happy position of being able to plan your kitchen from scratch, rather than attempting to revamp existing layouts and equipment, it is worth giving the matter considerable thought.

It may even happen that you are able to choose *where* your kitchen will be, in which case bear in mind the following criteria. If your dining room is to be separate from your kitchen there should ideally be easy access from one room to the other. Long passages or stairs between the two make for difficulties in keeping food hot and clearing tables. Ease of access to the garden, especially if you grow your own herbs, vegetables and fruit, is also important, as is minimising the time you spend answering the front and back doors. Good natural daylight and attractive views are less important but should certainly be taken into consideration.

Once you have decided where you want your kitchen the next decision to make is what sort of kitchen you want. This will depend very much on what sort of cook you are. If you entertain a lot you may well prefer to have your kitchen separate from the dining area, unless you opt for a large and deliberately-for-dining kitchen. A dedicated cook with a demanding job outside the home will probably need their kitchen to be that much more functional than someone with more lei-

sure to shop – at least in the sense of providing good storage and extra-quick cooking facilities, such as a microwave oven and a freezer.

A single person, or a couple without children, extremely busy and not overly fond of cooking will almost certainly prefer a functional, working room that looks and is efficient. Again, facilities for rapid cooking will probably be important, plus easy-to-clean floors, work surfaces and cupboards. Although a lot of space may not be available, a small area set aside for dining is always useful.

If you really enjoy cooking you will probably want to be able to take at least some meals in the kitchen and to have as much space as possible for herbs, spices, pots and pans, cook books and all the other impedimenta collected by the keen cook, quite apart from generous food storage and good kitchen aids.

If you cook constantly, have a

With its generous work surfaces, storage and uncluttered feel, the kitchen on the left would be ideal for tidy-minded people. Others, especially dedicated cooks, might prefer the more casual-looking wood finishes and busier feel of the kitchen on the right, which, though unfitted, still has masses of storage space.

KITCHENS

family and are forced to spend a lot of time in the kitchen, you will probably want to make it much more of a family room where people can sit around and talk, have a drink, do their homework, write notes, lists, letters, pay bills, and do a lot of eating.

Fit your space to your life style
If you are not quite sure of the sort of kitchen that will best suit you, ask yourself the following questions:

● Do you think your present situation will remain static or are you likely to have children and more children (their friends), guests and more guests to feed in the ensuing years?

● Do you know what kind of meals you are most likely to cook, for how many, and how often? (Remember that the *kind* of cooking you do is very much to the point, for if you only cook simple meals you will need far less preparation area than a more ambitious cook – though here again your aspirations may change with experience.)

● Do you work all day, and are you likely to go on doing so?

● Do you live far from a good shopping area so that you will need more than the average amount of food storage space and a large deep freeze?

● Even if you cannot afford them now, are you likely to acquire extra equipment in the future like a dishwasher, microwave oven, washing machine or freezer?

● Will there be more than one of you cooking or working in the kitchen at any one time? Kitchens that work really well for one, very seldom do for two (or more).

● Are you lucky enough to possess space for a utility or washing room? If so, you can hive off washing machine, dryers, ironing equipment and probably cleaning appliances and accessories, which is a great help when you are short of space.

● All these points should be thought about and considered in relation to the space you have to play with (a square room, rectangular room, cramped galley, and so on) as well as any existing appliances, and should certainly give you a clearer idea of the sort of room that will answer your needs.

What do you need? What can you afford?
Having decided that point, you should next make a list of the kitchen furniture and utensils that you would like, if not now, then later when you can better afford them so that you can plan your kitchen around specific objects.

FURNITURE AND EQUIPMENT

Write down the items you need: basic essentials, then optional extras, then any luxuries. For the major items, make a note of the makes you would like, the price, and the dimensions, if relevant. Work out how much storage you will need for smaller pieces of equipment, serving equipment and foodstuffs: will one shelf in a cupboard be enough for tins, or do you need several? Can you hang saucepans on the wall near the cooker, or do you need cupboards or drawers for them? Will serving dishes, cutlery, table linen be kept in the kitchen or is there space for them near the dining table? Does cleaning and washing equipment have to live in the kitchen, or is there a utility room/cupboard under the stairs, or even a large bathroom where they can be stored?

*Left: This purpose-built
kitchen/dining/living room is
unashamedly utilitarian, clean-cut and
neat. It is also quite luxurious with
its built-in tv and stereo units vying
for place with rather more normal
kitchen equipment.*

*Right: There is a totally different feel
to this multi-purpose space viewed
from the kitchen area. The kitchen
equipment and utensils are used as
homely decoration while a sofa and
chairs provides comfortable seating in
the living/dining area.*

KITCHENS

Left: It is often the compact, internal kitchen that lends itself best to the perfect work-triangle, with the cooker, sink and refrigerator evenly spaced from each other for easy accessibility.

Above: Neat and perfectly adequate cooking space for a couple has been squeezed into this compact and corridor-like area.

When you have completed your list, think about the basic services you will need: how many electrical appliances are on the list? Where will each one be plugged in? New tracking devices are coming on to the market to make this stage of planning easier, but most of us still have to plan where we want our socket outlets and lighting long before any kitchen equipment can be installed.

It might sound elementary, but it is only too easy to leave out quite obvious necessities in the trauma of getting everything done and easier still to discount the quite alarming final costs. This way, you can at least work out the essentials and plan from there.

How to plan your space

The chief rule for any successful kitchen plan is that it should always follow a work diagram based on the sequence of operations. Because food preparation generally involves a good deal of doubling back to and from the refrigerator, sink, stove and different work surfaces, the walking distance between all the main work areas should not be excessive. And each work area needs careful thought to ensure that all necessary equipment and ingredients are conveniently to hand.

The three principal work areas—preparation, cooking and washing-up—are centred on the fridge, the cooker and the sink. Professional

kitchen planners use the term 'work triangle' to describe the imaginary lines linking the three areas. While you must allow enough space in each area to work efficiently, they must not be spaced too far apart, or you will be walking backwards and forwards much more than is necessary.

Consider the operation involved in cooking something as simple as frozen peas:

1 Take pan to sink and fill.
2 Take pan to cooker. Add salt. Bring to boil.
3 Remove peas from refrigerator. Open bag with scissors. Add to pan. Discard bag.
4 When cooked, take pan to sink. Use colander to strain.
5 Tip peas into serving dish.
6 Get butter from refrigerator. Use knife to add a knob of butter.
7 Return butter to fridge. Put dirty utensils in sink or dishwasher.
8 Take peas to table.

Even a task as simple as this involves two trips to the sink, three trips to the refrigerator, and two trips to the cooker (more if you warmed the serving dish first). You also need to visit the cupboards and drawers where the pan, salt, scissors, knife and colander are kept, and dispose of the bag in the rubbish bin.

So the distances between the work areas are crucial: each side of the work triangle should be between 1250 and 2150 mm (4–7 ft). If its

perimeter is more than 6.6 m (22 ft) you will be walking around more than necessary. If it is less than 4 m (13 ft) you won't have enough room to be able to manoeuvre yourself comfortably.

You must organize your storage around the work areas according to what is needed: knives near the preparation area; spices between the preparation and cooking areas;

wooden spoons near the cooker; coffee, tea and mugs near the kettle and so on. It may not be possible to get everything precisely where you want it, so think about the things you do most often (such as making a cup of tea, cooking a casserole) or in most of a hurry (preparing breakfast) and try to make the work flow for these tasks as simple and streamlined as possible.

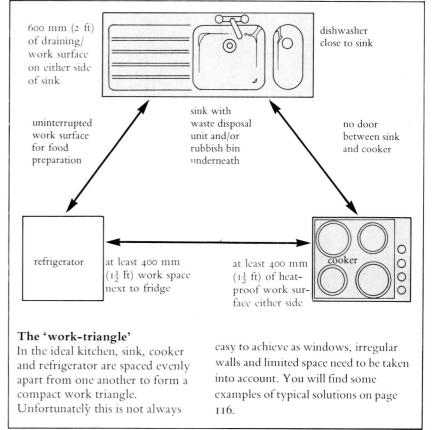

600 mm (2 ft) of draining/ work surface on either side of sink

dishwasher close to sink

uninterrupted work surface for food preparation

sink with waste disposal unit and/or rubbish bin underneath

no door between sink and cooker

refrigerator

at least 400 mm (1½ ft) work space next to fridge

at least 400 mm (1½ ft) of heat-proof work surface either side

cooker

The 'work-triangle'

In the ideal kitchen, sink, cooker and refrigerator are spaced evenly apart from one another to form a compact work triangle. Unfortunately this is not always

easy to achieve as windows, irregular walls and limited space need to be taken into account. You will find some examples of typical solutions on page 116.

KITCHENS

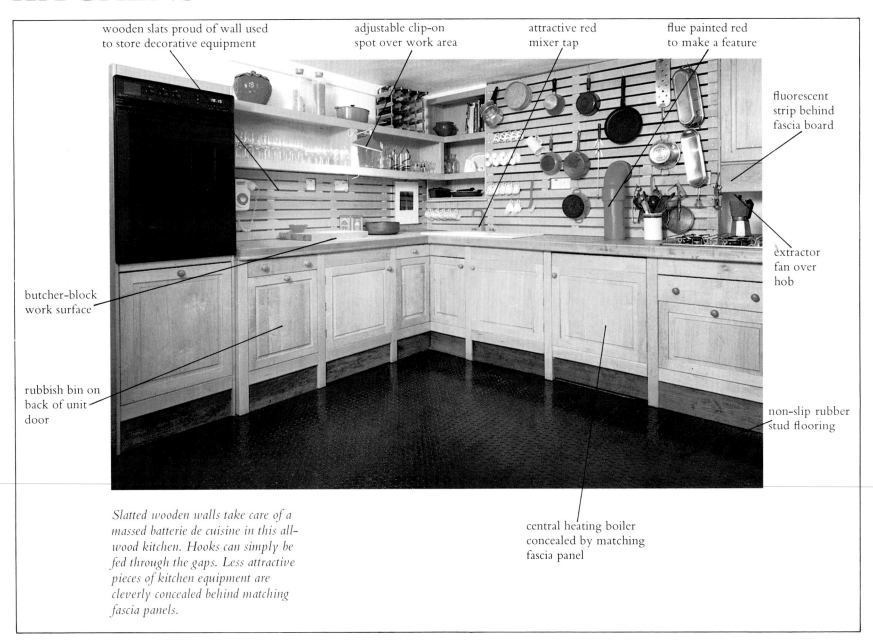

wooden slats proud of wall used to store decorative equipment

adjustable clip-on spot over work area

attractive red mixer tap

flue painted red to make a feature

fluorescent strip behind fascia board

butcher-block work surface

rubbish bin on back of unit door

extractor fan over hob

non-slip rubber stud flooring

Slatted wooden walls take care of a massed batterie de cuisine in this all-wood kitchen. Hooks can simply be fed through the gaps. Less attractive pieces of kitchen equipment are cleverly concealed behind matching fascia panels.

central heating boiler concealed by matching fascia panel

Put it on paper

Obviously, the actual dimensions of your particular work triangle are going to be determined by the basic floor plan of your kitchen. So, following the instructions on pages 18–19, you need to draw up a plan of what you've got already, then you can work out how best to improve it. This is the procedure to follow, whether you're planning a new kitchen entirely from scratch, or reorganizing an existing one.

The slightest error can be disastrous when you have to fit in appliances and units. If you have awkward pipes, low windows, a hatch or power points already in position, mark them on the plan, and measure up and draw elevations of the walls as well.

Measure up any items which have to stay in the kitchen, and cut out shapes from graph paper to represent them. If they can't be moved (for example you may prefer not to call in a plumber to move the sink), stick them down. Try to be as flexible as possible: it may be well worth moving, say, the cooker as little as 1 metre (3 ft) from its existing position in order to create a better work flow. Play around with the shapes and don't stick things down on your plan unless you are sure they can't be moved.

Work out the best way to organize your work triangle, then connect the points of the triangle. If the

triangle does not seem as efficient as professional planners would like, see if you can move the appliances or work surfaces to give a better arrangement. For example, to increase working and manoeuvring space in an existing work triangle you could set up a second food preparation or cooking area with perhaps a microwave oven outside your main work area. To lessen the distance between, say, the refrigerator and the sink, you could add an island unit to the centre of the room, or a free-standing butcher-block work surface, or even a mobile work trolley.

Your particular triangle may well be unique, as it results from a combination of your particular space and your particular needs. But there are some standard arrangements which may give you a few helpful ideas. You can look at these in more detail on page 116.

Once you have traced out your basic floor plan and work triangle you can develop the rest of the kitchen to include more work space (like a pastry or baking preparation area), more storage, other appliances, an eating area (if there's room), perhaps a desk area (see *Home Offices*, pages 184–99), and look into more technical details like electric outlets, and lighting. Finally, you will be able to add the finishing touches with decoration. If you cannot do everything at once,

or want to start making staged improvements, either concentrate on your first priorities (leaving space for the next stages) or your worst problems–depending on whether you are planning a first-time kitchen or updating an existing one. If you are starting from scratch, get the basics right – plumbing should be correctly sited and there should be plenty of electrical sockets. If you are updating, you may have to compromise with expensive changes such as new plumbing.

Corridor or galley kitchens are often particularly easy to work in – as long as there are not more than two people. This one is a model of its kind with clean lines, red and white scheme, wire grid hanging areas and careful use of every bit of space. Note the shelves across the window and over the door. Vivid red sinks, red and white checked vinyl flooring, red-topped stools, and fine red edging to the door frame to match the accessories, all contribute to the scheme.

KITCHENS

The importance of lighting

The same rules for planning light fittings apply in the kitchen as everywhere else in the home: general light to see by; work light to work by; an accent light to show off anything particularly worth looking at. The special rule of the kitchen is to make sure that there is light over every work surface so that you never work in your own shadow.

Insert general pendant lighting or inset downlights or wallwashers for the overall light; fix baffled light below cabinets to shine directly onto the worktop, and try to install special lights over stove and sink. If you are going to eat in the kitchen make sure overall lights are on a dimmer switch and that there is enough light over the table—use a rise-and-fall light fixture for example—which can, of course, be substituted for or combined with candlelight at night. Independent switches for each light will make it easier to create the appropriate atmosphere.

Fluorescent tubes are best for under cabinet/worktop lighting. They last much longer than incandescent tubes, offer more light per watt but need to be carefully chosen in the right colours for the most accurate presentation of food. That is to say, choose warm white de luxe (not just warm white) or cool white de luxe (not just cool white). There is no point in dimming fluorescent

Top left: Lighting, albeit slightly unconventional, is placed exactly where it matters in this kitchen; that is over the cook top and over the work surface, where spotlights are intertwined through a suspended wire grid.

Left: An angle-poise type fitting is used to maximum effect in this kitchen. The angle-poise lamp is adjustable so that it can shine on eating or cooking areas.

Above: In this deliberately old-fashioned and eclectic-style room with its prettily stencilled walls, a series of pendant lights is hung above the butcher block and dining table.

light; although it is possible, it is extremely costly and unnecessary. Mount tubes as close to the front of cabinets as possible and shield them with a baffle or small valance or cornice attached to the bottom of units. This will subdue any glare.

Sinks will need a minimum of two 100 watt incandescent bulbs or two 75 watt reflector floodlights which will focus light directly onto the bowls and draining boards.

If you have a hood over your hob or stove you should see that bulbs are enclosed to protect them from spattered grease and heat. Most manufacturers recommend a 60 watt maximum; or use fluorescent tubes.

Island work areas can be lit by general light, a rise-and-fall fixture or a fluorescent fixture containing at least two 30 or 40 watt tubes. Alternatively, try recessed or surface-mounted downlights using, say, 75 watt reflector floods. Good results for considerably less money can be achieved with clamp-on work lights.

Almost all light sources are concealed in the working area of this good-looking Hi-Tech kitchen. The exception—the long tubular green-cased fluorescent suspended from the ceiling—is as much sculptural decoration as lighting fixture. Note the large green-painted galvanized steel extractor fan over the cook top and supporting green columns.

KITCHENS

If you find your kitchen hard to work in, tiring, cramped for space, uninspiring, or shabby, you can at least take comfort in the fact that you are not alone. The trouble is that the majority of kitchens in the majority of homes were designed years ago with appliances, storage cabinets, work surfaces and lighting that is now either inadequate or unsuitable. Alternatively it may be that your kitchen actually functions with great efficiency and is relatively modern but simply lacks character. Whatever the problem, there is always a solution, so long as you are prepared to use your ingenuity, be flexible and remember that rules were made to be broken – or at least bent a little.

Unfortunately some solutions rely on structural changes for effect, but these don't always have to involve vast expense. For example, if you are short of wall space and have a door off the kitchen leading to a room which can also be approached from another door, block off the kitchen door. This could either involve removing it altogether and blocking up the space with bricks and mortar, or simply locking it and putting furniture against it on both sides.

Similarly, if your problem is one of poor ventilation leading to a steamy or smoke-filled room in which it is difficult to see anything, the solution is obviously an air ex-tractor. This could be let into the wall, which would mean taking up valuable wall space and also involve duct work. You could, however, if there is a window in the room, replace a pane of glass with one heavy enough to resist the weight and pressure of an air extractor. This will save on time, convenience and expense. If more drastic action is called for, some alternatives are outlined on page 115.

It may be that all that is required is a little lateral thinking. For example, if you are short of storage space, a perennial complaint, perhaps you could consider the ceiling. You would be amazed at what can be stored at this level. For example, if your wall units don't meet the ceiling, little-used dishes can be rowed up along the tops, or you could build extra cupboards in the gap.

Other storage solutions include hanging objects from hooks attached to the undersides of shelves or wall cupboards; suspending objects from wooden slats on the wall using S-hooks; and using wire baskets beneath shelves to give additional storage capacity.

The charmingly rustic kitchen on the left could scarcely be called custom-built; but it does have good storage facilities and refreshing touches like the yellow window frames. Even more decorative treatment has been given to the all-wood kitchen on the right.

KITCHENS

Luckily, as most of us have neither the money nor the time to undertake major remodelling, it is quite possible to make significant changes without going to the bank for a loan or calling in a builder.

If you have not really thought how you could improve your space, or can't quite place what is wrong, ask yourself the following questions:

● Do you find you are walking around a lot, even to prepare the simplest of meals?

● Do you always seem to be shifting things along on your worktops in order to make room to prepare something?

● Do you have to keep looking for things? A particular knife perhaps, or some other essential-at-the-time utensil?

● Are you constantly having to move things around in your cabinet in order to find what you need?

● Are all your cupboards or closets crammed full?

● Can you see items on your shelves or in your cabinets which you have not used for at least a year?

● Has the size of your household changed since the last time you bought a kitchen appliance?

● Do people tend to stand around in your kitchen when they are eating a snack or drinking the odd cup of coffee because there is no place to sit?

● Is your kitchen the sort of place where family and friends congregate for chats as a matter of course. If not, would you like it to be?

● Would you like to change the whole look but don't think you have the money?

● Are you in rented property so feel you just have to put up with what you have?

If you have answered yes to at least three of these questions, some sort of change is certainly due, if not overdue. Here's how to achieve it.

The answer to the first problem is obviously to try to do something about your domestic traffic problems. If you do seem to be walking around a lot during meal preparations try to count the number of times you walk to various work areas and even the number of steps you take. You might well find that another work counter will help a good deal. If there is no room to add any extra counter space try importing a free-standing butcher-block worktop or a trolley or cart. Again, if you find you are always walking back and forth to a larder or pantry, or to shelves at the other end of the kitchen, a storage trolley or cart which you could wheel up when necessary should help.

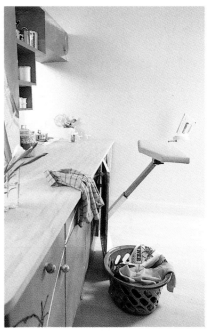

Far left: A free-standing butcher-block worktop adds useful extra working space in just the right area. The walls, stripped down to the bare brick, could accept more shelves in the future. The use of light wood on all surfaces unifies the eclectic mixture.

Left: Extra pull-out worktops have been built in to this run of units. The deep pelmet adds interest.

Above: If space is really at a premium, this pivotting, telescopic ironing board could be a winner.

KITCHENS

Make good use of storage space. Top left: Industrial shelving and wire grids have been used to excellent effect for high-visibility storage. Above: Pull-out vertical shelving makes maximum use of even the most awkward area. Far left: Open contoured corner shelves provide an opportunity for you to display your favourite bits and pieces. Left: A plate-drying rack and storage shelves suspended over the sink.

Sensible storage

Several more of the problems are clearly to do with your current storage or methods of storage. People are always complaining that they do not have enough work space/dumping space, but it may well be what they really need is better organized storage. Look at the work spaces at your disposal. Are you using them to their best advantage? Or are they so cluttered up that there isn't any real space to work on? If clutter is your only problem, be ruthless and get rid of anything hanging around that you have not used for the last six months, and put anything else away in a cupboard, cabinet or closet somewhere.

If there does not seem any room to get rid of storage jars, canisters, cook tools and so on, you might need to add more shelves and hooks. You can often use the space between the bottom of wall-hung cabinets and the counter top to put up small shelves which will take a variety of objects; this is often a good place to stand your collection of dried herbs in small pots or jars—it keeps them together, clearly visible and to hand. And if you add cup hooks to the edges you can hang things from them as well. Another useful extra storage space is behind cabinet doors where again you might fix narrow shelves or hooks. And don't overlook the exposed sides of end base or wall-hung cabinets.

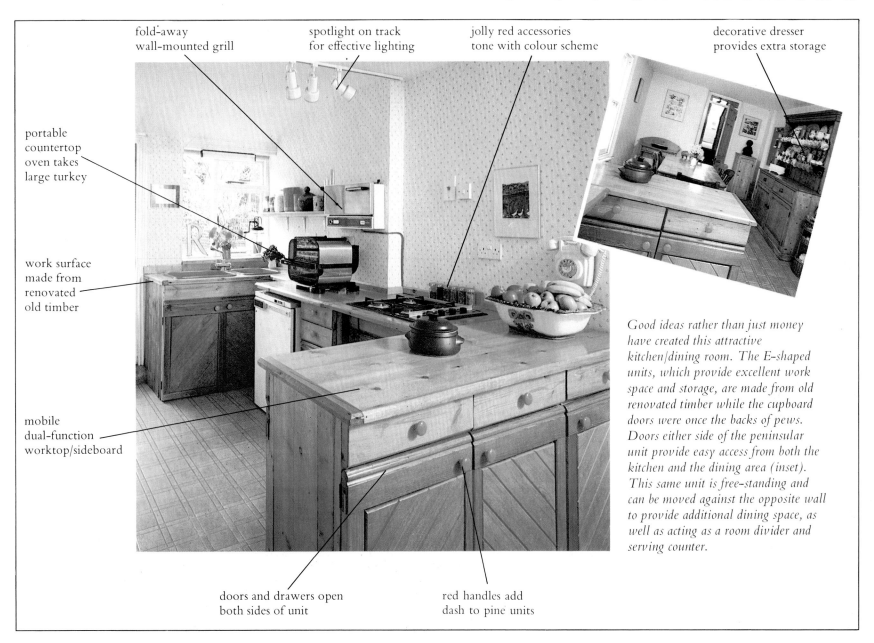

fold-away
wall-mounted grill

spotlight on track
for effective lighting

jolly red accessories
tone with colour scheme

decorative dresser
provides extra storage

portable
countertop
oven takes
large turkey

work surface
made from
renovated
old timber

mobile
dual-function
worktop/sideboard

doors and drawers open
both sides of unit

red handles add
dash to pine units

*Good ideas rather than just money
have created this attractive
kitchen/dining room. The E-shaped
units, which provide excellent work
space and storage, are made from old
renovated timber while the cupboard
doors were once the backs of pews.
Doors either side of the peninsular
unit provide easy access from both the
kitchen and the dining area (inset).
This same unit is free-standing and
can be moved against the opposite wall
to provide additional dining space, as
well as acting as a room divider and
serving counter.*

KITCHENS

Streamlined surfaces

A quick way to re-vamp a tired looking kitchen is to re-cover or replace the work surface.

Butcher-block, though expensive, will turn your food preparation area into one long chopping board. Oil it frequently, sand it occasionally and it will last for years. But avoid using it near the sink (where it might warp or the surface might rise) or close to the cooker (unless you have tiles and trivets for hot pans).

Tiles are a popular choice in country-style kitchens, but not to be recommended if you are heavy-handed with pots and pans. You can lay them on chipboard or plywood, or use them to cover your existing work surface. Rub down the surface with sandpaper, stick the tiles down with a suitable adhesive and grout in between them with a synthetic plastic bathroom or kitchen sealant (which won't pick up stains). Or use special coloured pigment (food colouring works too) to darken it. Edge the new surface with wooden beading, painted or varnished to suit the style of the kitchen.

If you have access to woodworking equipment or are employing a handyman, you can use planks of beech or hardwood, butted together and edged with rounded beading. Give the surface at least three coats of yacht varnish, rubbing down lightly with steel wool between coats.

Plastic laminate surfaces can be renewed: round-edged surfaces will have to be taken out and replaced. Square-edged surfaces can be re-covered with laminate, using edging strips of the same material, or lipping the edge with wooden beading.

If your kitchen is made up of separate units, each with its own worktop, you may be able to get a more streamlined look by installing a long run of worktop joining the separate units. If the units don't match the length of the wall, you can create a tray or vegetable storage area by leaving a space between units or continuing the worktop beyond the end of the unit, butting it up to the wall.

A cheerful but cheap way to renovate a worktop is to cover it with some sort of self-adhesive plastic. Smooth it tightly over the work surface, then give it a couple of coats of polyurethane for protection. It won't be as tough as plastic laminate, but it will be fairly hardwearing.

Many professional kitchens have stainless steel work surfaces, with wooden chopping blocks and marble sections (for pastry making) let into them. But stainless steel is expensive, and unless it is properly cushioned underneath it can be very noisy.

A complete work surface in marble would be impractical: cold, hard and expensive. But it might be worth topping one part of your work area (a single unit or a free-standing refrigerator) with marble for pastry making. But remember that it is easily stained by wine, acids and lemon juice.

Synthetic marble is an alternative: this new, durable material for work surfaces is proof against most stains, reasonably heat resistant, non-porous, and cuts like wood.

Sealed cork flooring tiles may also be used to re-cover a surface, but like butcher-block, they are not suitable for areas exposed to great heat or water.

Pale butcher-block makes a most elegant counter in this handsome room.

Slate is useful for pastry-making and also provides a decorative top.

This synthetic marble worktop comes complete with recessed sinks.

Extra work space

If you are satisfied that you have spirited away all possible clutter and still do not have adequate preparation space you could cover a sink with a portable chopping board, or turn a drawer into an extra work surface by fitting runners to a block of wood the same width as the drawer, so that it will glide in and out of the unit, resting on the top of the drawer when it is pulled out.

Cleaned up cupboards

If your cabinets seem to be constantly overcrowded, open up all the doors and look at the contents with a critical eye. If there are items around that you hardly ever use, remove them to more remote storage areas away from your work areas. Seldom used or once-a-year items like ham boiling pans, turkey roasting pans, fish kettles, picnic baskets etc, might well be parted from the day-to-day items. Or you can hang pot racks from the ceiling; and put up areas of peg boards to hang colanders, sieves, whisks, graters and so on.

If you have not bought any new appliances since you first moved into your home, or if your family has changed in numbers, you might be due for some updated versions. The sort of choice available is explained on pages 125–131, but a new refrigerator or fridge-freezer, the addition of a microwave oven, or purchase of a portable dishwasher if there is no room for a plumbed-in version, might make all the difference to your own work load.

Another salient question to ask yourself is: are you really using your space to its best advantage. I am not talking here about your work surfaces, or work triangles or the general space/work efficiency of your kitchen, but rather if you could use your kitchen as more of a family room—the sort of room which friends as well as family tend to migrate to at the first available opportunity. Obviously this is not relevant if you have a tiny galley kitchen, or a slit of corridor space, but if you can add a chair or two, or at least a couple of stools where there were none before; and some sort of bar, or at least an enlarged counter top if you can't fit in a decent table, then you are well on the way to making your kitchen a more welcoming place.

Another kitchen where every surface is made to work to maximum advantage. The counter top provides space for eating as well as cooking and preparation. Baskets, bowls and a fish kettle are hung on the stone wall. A suspended iron bar just under the ceiling holds a mass of decorative copper pans attached by butcher's hooks. Other walls have hooks for more equipment and still there is room for further expansion, if necessary, along the remaining walls.

KITCHENS

You might also think of adding a desk top somewhere: against a small wall; across a corner, as an extension of a worktop. A wooden counter with a couple of filing cabinets underneath, preferably on castors for easy manoeuvrability would be one excellent idea; or just a flip-down panel from a wall would be another. Try to have some shelves above for files and cook books, add a telephone, writing implements and note books, even a typewriter if you can, and you have a mini office to hand whenever you need it. See the chapter on Home Offices (pages 184-99) for further details.

Finally, you should remember that it really is not necessary to totally re-vamp the kitchen or call in a decorator in order to give it a face lift. There are all sorts of comparatively small changes you can make which will transform your kitchen's looks out of all proportion to the time and expense.

Right: Painted blinds repeat the cherry pattern of the wallpaper and combine with the red accessories to set off the dominant pine.

Left: A compact galley kitchen with many of its original fittings has been given a totally fresh look by painting the units and appliances the background green of the bird-covered wallpaper.

Changes for the better

● Cheer up dull-looking cabinets by painting them in a high gloss or eggshell finish. Or cut a stencil and re-spray the doors adding a simple motif – which can be repeated around the splashback, or around the top of a plain painted room.

● Take off cabinet doors: leave them off altogether for an open shelved look; replace them with new louvred or wooden doors with beading; replace them with glazed doors, or hang curtains in front of shelves instead (PVC fabric curtains won't pick up dirt so easily but cotton is cheaper and easier to wash).

● Re-tile the splashback between counter top and wall-hung cupboards. Plain white tiles are the cheapest: brighten them up with coloured grouting, or mix them with other plain tiles to build up an eye-catching pattern

● Paint everything white: walls, ceiling, units, and add new tiles as well. Even the floor can be painted (see page 379). The whole place will look amazingly different. Add colour and interest with brightly coloured or prettily patterned kitchen accessories–tea towels, canisters, cook books.

● Cover walls with a vinyl wallpaper (which can be wiped, or even scrubbed), in a pattern to suit your style–an all-over floral pattern for a soft, country look; splashy flowers in cheerful colours for a more lively country mood; a sharp grid or smart stripe for a more clinical style. If you can't find the pattern you want in a vinyl, you can protect paper wallcoverings with a polyurethane varnish, but it may yellow the pattern slightly.

● Change your window treatment: café curtains instead of a tired roller blind; glass shelves stretched across the window to display bits of china and glass or a collection of old stone and glass bottles; or paint the wooden surround in a pretty colour to frame a crisp new roller blind.

● Either arrange trailing plants in hanging baskets slung from a brass or wooden pole fixed across the window, or intersperse them with herbs and African violets on glass shelves (see above). Some plants like kitchen windows, especially if they are over a steamy sink, but always check first. In a window which does not get much light, a single, showy. Boston fern will make a focal point.

● Do the unexpected. 'White goods' (fridge, freezer, washing machine) needn't stay white: respray them (in a well-ventilated room) with cans of auto paint – by using masking tape you can easily create simple but eye-catching patterns in bold stripes. Cover surrounding surfaces for protection from paint 'drift'.

KITCHENS

● Change the walls. Make the room look warm and cheerful by panelling the walls: fix ordinary wooden lathes on the diagonal. Leave them natural or paint them to suit the rest of the decoration. Or cover the walls with tongue-and-groove panelling. Or do away with wallcovering altogether: strip away the plaster to expose the bare brick underneath. (This solution is only suitable for older properties—investigate the structure of the wall in an unobtrusive corner before setting to work.)

● Transform the floor: quarry tile it, or lay new ceramic tiles, Mexican tiles or bricks; put down a well-varnished wood block floor; or lay sheet vinyl, linoleum or vinyl tiles. Sealed cork tiles will create a warm atmosphere. Check the subfloor (is it solid concrete or suspended wood?) before you make your choice, as not all coverings are suitable for all subfloors.

Right: A radical transformation has been achieved in this room by stripping the walls to the brick beneath. The ceiling was tongue-and-grooved, the floor bricked and lights added in the right places.

Top right: Units here were wittily painted to match the upper walls.

Bottom right: Old dresser bases are used instead of modern units.

● For a really economical new floor, add a coat of paint. Lino paint is suitable for virtually any surface, and comes in a range of colours. Wood, cork and well-laid vinyl tiles can be painted with gloss paint and given extra protection with a few coats of polyurethane or yacht varnish.

● Add character and charisma: if the room is quite large but lacks personality, simply change some of the existing pieces of furniture: replace the table with an old pine one and add some old pine chairs (available in most junk shops); swap some units for a pine dresser; paint chairs cheerful colours; replace posters with a cork or fabric-covered noticeboard.

● Don't forget details: particularly in rented property, where you can't make substantial alterations, you can still make an enormous difference with carefully chosen accessories: sets of matching storage jars, wooden spice racks, kitchen roll holders, pretty tea towels, bunches of herbs, onions or dried flowers, interesting canisters—old or new; plants; posters; prints; and last, but by no means least, good-looking cookware.

I inherited one kitchen which had lemon yellow units with aluminium knobs, lemon yellow walls, a false flagstone vinyl floor and speckly plastic laminate worktops. I re-moved the units from one short wall, replaced them with a huge old pine dresser and painted all the walls, the ceiling and the rest of the units white. I changed the aluminium knobs for some more cheerful brass handles, covered the wall space between worktops and the bottom of cabinets with some blue and white Mexican tiles (which didn't cost the earth), re-topped the counters with butcher-block and changed the vinyl flagstones for quarry tiles. Result: a total change of character.

For other instant transformations you could jazz up an all-white kitchen say, by adding red and white tiles and red handles, or by just painting a stripe all along between drawers and cupboard doors. Another white kitchen could be given a totally different look by adding green plastic handles and importing masses of plants and some green painted bamboo blinds. Equally you could add wood counter tops to an otherwise all-laminate room, together with wooden slatted blinds, or the plain bamboo or matchstick variety, or some red and white or blue and white check gingham curtains or café curtains.

Once you really start to think of the components that can be changed in a room without too much ado you can come up with any number of ideas for a change of style, or more important, for adding style where none existed before.

KITCHENS

When you come to re-vamp your kitchen on a more major scale, your choices are wider. You probably have a good idea of the atmosphere you want to create in your kitchen, and you will find some simplified pointers to style on the following pages. First, however, you have to look at how to make the best use of existing space.

Making sense of your space

The great advantage of starting from scratch in a kitchen is that you can, for very little extra cost, make major improvements by repositioning services (gas, plumbing, electricity), doors, windows, even walls.

Since kitchens tend to be positioned at the back of the house, they are often in an ideal situation for extending into the back garden, or knocking through into a corridor or back room to create a more useful space. If you are planning major changes to your kitchen, it is worth finding out how neighbours with the same layout have solved the problem.

One of the first points to consider when reorganizing is the basic floor plan and convenient work triangle mentioned on page 97. There are several tried and tested arrangments of units and appliances which will give an idea of the use you can make of a given shape: The one-wall kitchen, the U-plan kitchen, the L-shaped kitchen and the galley kitchen – for details see page 116. The shape of your room will probably dictate the arrangement, although if you have a generous-sized room, you may be able to change the shape of the actual work area with room dividers. These can be full-height units giving extra storage space, or counter-style fittings, providing more work surfaces or space for a fitted hob.

When you get down to more detailed planning it is useful to know that in a standard European kitchen, base units are 600 mm (24 in) deep; wall units 300 mm (12 in) deep; most appliances are 600 mm (24 in) wide; units come in widths of 300, 500, 600, 1000 or 1200 mm (12, 20, 24, 39, or 48 in), counter tops are 900 mm (36 in) high, the bases of wall-hung cabinets 405 mm (16 in) above that. These dimensions have been tested ergonomically, and are designed to fit in with standard appliances, so they provide a useful guide if you are building your own units instead of buying ready-made.

The joy of starting afresh with a large budget shows on the left in marbled counter tops, built-in appliances, plenty of storage, elegant blinds and flooring, and a capacious skylight. Another high budget kitchen, right, with tiled floor, central cook top/eating counter, in clean red and white.

KITCHENS

The U-shaped kitchen

This is usually considered the best shape for any kitchen: the triangle idea works well, everything should be within easy reach, and there should be plenty of counter/work space and plenty of storage. It does depend, however, on having a rectangular room.

Still, the U-plan has been proved efficient in both large and small rooms though it's as well to remember that a minimum of 1500 mm (5 ft) and a maximum of 3000 mm (10 ft) is necessary between base cabinets. If your room can take a U-shape and is reasonably large, one side of the U can form a natural dividing line between work and dining space, whether formal or informal. Raise and cantilever part of the counter top on this dividing line and it can act both as a breakfast counter by day, and a barrier against kitchen debris for diners by night.

The L-shaped kitchen

L-shaped kitchens make good dining areas because by locating appliances and cabinets on adjacent walls you create both a compact work space and still have room for a decent-sized dining table. Once again, this sort of arrangement works in a large or in a long narrow kitchen but can waste space in a smaller room where there isn't the same scope for counter and storage space as in a U-shaped plan.

The one-wall kitchen

This is a good idea in a small space, or in a family room or kitchen-diner where the emphasis is more on a general living room than a kitchen. The whole kitchen may be screened off with sliding or folding doors if necessary. Again, it can be useful for a kitchen area off a living room where work and leisure space are divided by a counter or island unit. Unless the wall is very long you do, of course, miss out on storage space if this isn't taken care of in other areas.

The corridor or galley kitchen

As its name implies, this can be as neat and effective as a well-organized ship's kitchen—but can also be a disaster if the corridor or galley is open at both ends. When this plan works well it saves a great deal of wear and tear on the cook. However, it will not work for a family or dining/kitchen.

Since space will inevitably be very tight, planning should be as ingenious and imaginative as possible. Slide-out shelves, pull-out work surfaces and storage bins, revolving shelves, pot racks can all be brought into play for maximum effect. For manoeuvrability, there should be at least 1200 mm (4 ft) between the base units on either side. If space does not allow this it might be better to treat it as a one-wall or an L-shaped kitchen and build in narrow shelves down

the other long wall. You can even use 300 mm (1 ft) deep wall-hung units as base units, surfacing them with a narrow counter top, or you could combine a counter top and stools to make a breakfast bar, with storage space above.

The island kitchen

An island unit in a kitchen (if there is room for one) immediately adds extra work space, storage and interest. It is excellent in a large room which might otherwise lack focus and efficiency but it can also hinder the triangle work flow if the kitchen is not big enough to take it.

The usual function of an island unit is to hold a cook top (which can be self-venting or topped by an extractor hood), closet, shelf and extra work top space, but it can also incorporate an extra small fridge, an extra sink, dishwasher, wine storage, a bar, or an eating counter. If you do not have a cook top and extractor hood, the space above makes an ideal place for a pot or basket rack.

The peninsula kitchen

In a way, this is much the same as an island kitchen except the larger rectangular area is usually used to divide working kitchen space from a family or dining area. Again, you must have enough room for this arrangement but it is a neat way of getting extra storage, breakfast bar, work and buffet space.

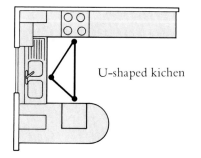

U-shaped kichen

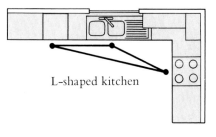

L-shaped kitchen

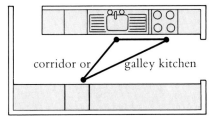

corridor or galley kitchen

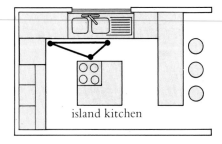

island kitchen

Left: This island unit in an immaculate kitchen-dining room holds dishwasher and sink side by side as well as providing a good counter top/serving space for the table. It also provides a useful focus for the large space. Note how the colours of plants, accessories and food come singing out against the all-white framework, including the stainless steel trim to the table and door.

Above: A one-wall kitchen with a difference—the addition of loud speakers nicely integrated with the back-splash between the units and the pop art displays of groceries. Not a cook's kitchen—more an efficient module for fast food service.

KITCHENS

THE FAMILY ROOM

Creating a family room

If you are prepared to invest a lot of time and money in your new kitchen you might consider making a sort of kitchen/living or family room; a real 'heart of the home' area, more casual than a living room, more cosy than a working kitchen. If you would like to have this sort of feel but don't think your existing space is big enough, or light enough, or for one reason or another, does not seem to lend itself to such treatment, then consider the surrounding spaces.

What sort of room do you have next door? Is there a scullery for example? Or a lobby of some sort? A sun lounge, verandah or covered porch? A little used dining room or even a corridor or hall? If the walls separating the two are of the partition rather than supporting variety you could take them down and incorporate the space into one much larger room which will make more family sense.

Far left: Both sides of the space are used for this homely kitchen which manages to incorporate a desk/eating counter as well as worktops and appliances.

Left: With thoughtful planning, and just a few carefully chosen accessories, this kitchen almost approaches a living room in style.

Right: An ideal kitchen/dining/living room for an active family.

KITCHENS

Sometimes, too, it might make sense to turn most of a ground or basement floor into an open-plan kitchen/living/family room/study. As long as you consult the professionals, a surprising number of walls can be taken down with ease and the resulting increase in light and space is clearly amazing.

In a case like this, it might be best to keep most of the kitchen part of the room to one wall and hive it off from the rest of the area with a long island unit which could incorporate extra work and storage space and possibly a cook top, sink and refrigerator as well. A long dividing wall like this would make a good serving unit for every day and a splendid buffet area for a party.

Looking at style

Whatever the shape of your kitchen, it is worth giving some attention to the decoration and accessories to create a distinctive style. The choices are unlimited, but here are some of the characteristic elements which help to give a kitchen a particular atmosphere.

Mediterranean style would be designed to give a cool, smooth working atmosphere, with long slate or marble worktops, terracotta-style tiled floors, and large, walk-in cupboards with thick walls—lined with marble shelves for food storage or racks for pans and crockery.

Roughly plastered walls, shuttered windows and wall-mounted lighting typify this style, with open storage under the worktop and little wall-hung storage. Strings of garlic and bunches of herbs hang from the ceiling, and extra preparation space is provided by a solid table with upright, rush seated chairs around it.

Farmhouse style kitchens are typified by stripped pine, bare brick and perhaps a dresser. Many manufacturers produce pine or pine-effect units, but none will give the easy-on-the-eye, mellow effect that you can get from old pine. Worktops, where they exist, should be in natural materials—wood or tiles. But by using old pieces of furniture of odd shapes and sizes you may well sacrifice the conventional work surface to retain character. A pine or oak refectory table, forming an island unit in the middle of the room, would make up for this. Quarry tyles, brick paviour or wooden boards are typical choices for the floor. For real farmhouse style, you'll need a traditional range (or one of the newer versions). Back up the cooking facilities of the range with a modern oven, and you'll have all the character with the advantage of modern technology. Go for pretty floral fabrics, patchwork or fresh ginghams, and dot farmhouse chairs and rockers round the room to encourage visitors.

The fresh, country look has evolved over the last few years as people have begun to paint wooden units and replace solid doors with glazed doors to create a lighter atmosphere. Keep to pale colours, even for work surfaces, and choose pale, pretty floral patterns or plain cream for walls and accessories. Coloured tiles or sheet vinyl are ideal for country flooring, or a wooden floor looks equally at home. Use the glazed cupboards to display attractive china and to provide storage space for attractively packaged dry goods.

Period look kitchens have warm mahogany units, deep butler sinks and brass taps. Traditional style ranges can be fitted, or buy a modern oven and hob that have a matt black and brass finish to give a nostalgic feel. Choose white tiles with black or deep coloured diamond insets for the floor. The best material for worktops are marble, slate, and natural wood.

City slick sytle can add life to a dull urban kitchen. Go for strong colours and simple geometric patterns. All-white units are cheap, and can be brightened up with coloured tiles and accessories. Or be bold and use more dramatically coloured cupboards. Efficiency is essential in the fast food world of city life, so storage has to be well organized and cleverly designed to leave worktops clear and uncluttered.

Top right: This kitchen can only be described as not typical (but none the worse for that) with its long sweep of a table incorporating both gas and electric rings and a griddle, its amazing roll-top desk-cum-dresser with its pull-out shelves and enormous storage capacity; its old Raffles Hotel-style rattan long chair and its well stocked wooden shelves.

Bottom right: This is a deliberately Farmhouse-style kitchen. Note all the ingredients: the old pine dresser and well-used refectory table which can also do duty as a preparation area; the capacious old plate rack which holds so much more and drips so much better than a modern version; and the slightly haphazard but practical notion of curtaining the bottom part of the work top rather than filling it in with conventional units. Note too another decorative touch: the frieze of old produce advertisements.

Far right: By complete contrast, this kitchen has gone the modern route. An extensive range of floor and wall units and floor-to-ceiling cupboards give ample storage space. Lighting is localized over the work surfaces and suspended over the built-in breakfast table.

KITCHENS

High-tech is characterized by the use of functional glass and metal. In its extreme form, the domestic Hi-tech kitchen is indistinguishable from a professional kitchen in a good restaurant. Long runs of built-in stainless steel worktop, with hob, sink, chopping board and pastry board built in. Separate cooking areas for different types of food: a pastry chef's corner, a vegetable preparation area and so on. Cupboards are replaced by open steel shelves, lined with glass storage jars. Flooring is usually synthetic but essentially practical – stud rubber tiles for instance.

Of course, it is possible (even desirable to draw the best elements of each of these distinctive styles together, to form a perfect, hybrid kitchen, adapted to your needs. They are not to be looked at in isolation and followed to the letter, but if you're not sure about style, they will give you some useful ideas.

Left: Perfect for cooking in and entertaining in, everything about this kitchen is practical as well as stylish. You should always consider including an area for eating when planning a spacious kitchen.

Right: Hi-Tech par excellence . . . . with plants and flowers adding just the right sort of contrast.

Very few of us can afford all of the appliances we would like all at the same time. What we can do, however, is plan for them. Whether you are designing a kitchen from scratch or updating an old one you must think in terms of priorities, define your most pressing needs, and start from there. Do remember that, contrary to the cynics' vciew of built-in obsolescence, most major appliances – refrigerators, stoves, dishwashers and so on – are built to last for years, so, as far as possible, you should keep future changes of circumstances in mind as well as your present needs. If your household is likely to expand in any way it might be cheaper in the long run to buy a larger model than the more modest affair you had thought of first.

In any case, it is perfectly possible to buy second-hand or re-conditioned models at a fraction of the price of new ones as long as you are prepared to accept the risk that they might eventually develop faults which could prove expensive. Still, they can make good stop-gaps till you can afford new models.

Obviously existing kitchens can be made more efficient with more up-to-date equipment – bigger freezer and/or fridge, a dishwasher, waste disposal unit and so on – but only if the appliances work hard for you, save time and labour and generally make your particular way

of life easier and more enjoyable. A new cooker or whatever can be a tremendous boon and investment but before you go out and spend money ask yourself questions about the way you live: is the pace hectic or leisurely? how many and what sort of meals do you have to provide? are you far from a good super-market or freezer centre? how much time do you have for shopping? are you out at work all day? do you grow your own vegetables? how often do you entertain? can you spend time on cooking and food preparation or is it always meals in a hurry? The answers will help you decide whether you need say, one vast freezer, or a large one in the garage and a small one in the kitchen, or a microwave plus freezer.

If space is limited, buying a larger model may not be possible. But consider other areas of the home. Is there room for a freezer in the garage or for a washing machine in the bathroom? Or can you fit in a fridge-freezer or a miniature washing machine?

There is plenty of excellent equipment in the kitchen (left), and plenty of room for more to come. For example, an extra fridge or small deep freeze cabinet could be tucked underneath the breakfast bar, and a microwave or grill could stand on the worktop. On the right, however, maximum effct is made with the very minimum.

KITCHENS

Gas or electricity?

This is really a matter of personal preference and the sort of facilities available in your building (or area – because, of course, nearby gas can be piped in at some cost, or use gas from cylinders if you really prefer gas). If you have the possibility of both services in a kitchen, you could opt for a gas cook top and an electric oven; or vice versa; or a mixture of both gas and electric plates to hedge bets should anything go wrong with one or other service, or to take advantage of both sorts of energy for different cooking needs (slow simmering; fast boiling etc.)

Stoves and ovens

We've come a long way from the free-standing stove with four burners and an oven with maybe a separate grill or broiler. Now you can get models to suit every size, shape and style of kitchen from separate hobs and ovens, to catering-size free-standing models and makes that can be slid or dropped into your work run or counter top for maximum sleekness. Ceramic cook tops can give the semblance of an almost unbroken work surface, and so do the new magnetic induction units that look like tiles, but do not heat up because they use magnetic energy to cook food by energising molecules both in the food and the pan. Both types of cooker top are very smooth in appearance and easy to clean.

Some cook tops combine both gas and electric burners, other have interchangeable parts including a grill, a griddle and a rotisserie. Some tops have built-in deep fryers, and there are stoves which combine conventional and microwave or high-speed cooking in a single unit. Some British cooker tops still tend to be niggardly in size and don't make sufficient allowance for four large pans. Other countries seem to manage this better – British manufacturers please copy.

But there are plenty of other refinements to look for: self-cleaning ovens, automatic timers, automatic meat thermometers for perfect roasts, capacious drawer space underneath for plate warming and storing pots and pans, and tops with built-in grills and their own surface-venting systems.

Check the size Many free-standing cookers are 550–600 mm (22–24 ins) deep and extend slightly beyond most cabinets. Standard widths are 510–600 mm (20–24 ins). If you have the space and the cash, you will find that American and some continental cookers are much larger than this. You will be able to choose between a single or a double oven, with an eye-level grill or a grill at waist level, often set into a small top oven. New American models often feature a small, eye-level oven.

Built-in ovens may be designed to

Far left: If you have space to store the fuel, why not consider a wood-burning cooker? This design has been proving its worth in country kitchens for many years.

Left: This handsome room with its white hexagonal tiles and interestingly white-stained wood units is extremely well off for cooking power with two full-size wall-mounted ovens and seven burners. With this number of working rings you would certainly need the enormous extractor hood and its inset powerful lighting. There is useful laminated counter space around the cook top and lots of extra cupboards built in underneath. In fact there is as enviable an amount of storage space as there are generous cooking facilities.

KITCHENS

Hob design depends to a certain extent on the type of energy used. Top left: This wall-mounted oven and grill has been built into a substantial brick unit and is close to the stainless steel gas hob. Far left: This electric halogen hob has been slotted into a run of units. Bottom: The tray-like electric cook-top here has been neatly fitted into a corner of a small kitchen.

go under the worktop (built-under), either beneath the hob or away from it, or they may fit into housing units so that the oven(s) are more accessible. Built-ins are usually just under 600 mm (24 in) wide, to fit neatly into standard units. Heights vary from about 500 mm (20 in) to 1000 mm (39 in). When you select a model, the literature which comes with it will tell you the exact size of opening and amount of ventilation space you need.

Compact hobs are about 550 × 450 mm (21 × 17 in) but if you have space, go for a large hob to take awkward-sized pans: you don't have to limit yourself to a simple, square configuration—there's no reason why you shouldn't have two or three small hobs in different places.

If you lead a hectically busy life, a microwave oven can be a real life —and time—saver, cooking food in a fraction of the time required by a normal oven. The snag has often been their lack of browning capacity—pale food doesn't look very appealing. But now there are special browning versions that take care of this. And the introduction of a turntable means that food is cooked evenly. Microwaves may be portable (but bulky) counter top models, wall-mounted, or built-in. Their measurements are less than those of standard ovens, although built-in models are the same width as built-in conventional ovens.

Above: A matched pair of ordinary-seeming kitchen cupboards slide forward to reveal cleverly hidden refrigerator and freezer housing units. Stencilled and panelled fronts and brass drawer handles complete the effect.

Left: Another housing unit, this time in white and blue, conceals a well-fitted fridge and freezer. Note how units have been cleverly fitted all around the small window.

Refrigerators and Freezers

The model of refrigerator and freezer you choose should depend on the size—or potential size—of your family and your work and cooking habits. Generally speaking, a 140 litre (5 cubic feet) refrigerator and 140–170 litres (5–6 cubic feet) of freezer space is ample for a couple and you should add another cubic foot per person in your household. If you can shop only once a week for example, you will need much more deep freeze space than if you can shop every day. If you cannot have a separate freezer you should look at a refrigerator with maximum freezer space and capacious food storage compartments. A good many of the latest models have sealed meat and vegetable drawers with adjustable temperature and humidity control to keep food fresher for longer.

Obviously frost-free models which mean you never have to defrost are as useful as self-cleaning ovens, and additional luxuries include iced water and crushed ice dispensers, automatic ice makers *and* the kind of American model with almost instant (that is to say about an hour) automatic ice cream and sorbet or sherbert-makers.

Separate deep freezers come in chest or upright models and are ideal for people with large gardens and plenty of produce to store and also for stashing away bulk buys and supermarket bargains.

Dishwashers

Really good dishwashers will clean everything from fine china and glass to encrusted saucepans and casseroles with settings that range from gentle wash to super scrub cycles. If you are a small family, look for models with the sort of controls that allow you rinse-and-hold cycles—a short cycle which rinses dishes for a short time to get rid of dried-on food and any smells so that they can then wait till you have a full load to put through. If you are a large family, or cook a lot, you should definitely look for a machine with a scrub cycle so you are not always hand-scouring pots and pans. Look too, for models with the sort of shelving that allows you to programme the machine to start work hours later and will make the operation a whole lot quieter, and the kinds that have soft food disposal units to prevent blocked drains.

If you do not have space for a build-in model beside or under the sink, there are portables available that sit on the worktop, where they can be connected to the taps and drains for washing. If you move and have more space, many portables are convertible and can be built-in.

Most models are 60 cm (24 in) wide to fit in with average counter tops. Slimline built-in types 45 cm (18 in) wide are also available.

Most models are 60 cm (24 in) wide to fit in with average counter top measurements.

KITCHENS

Top: Washing machine and dryer below a purpose-built work surface are conveniently located just off the kitchen.

Above, left and right: The same pair of sinks, set into a tiled worktop, has been photographed twice to show its

versatility. The rounded sink on the left is fitted with a drainer in one and with a wooden chopping block top, complete with cut-out for rinsing, in the other which has the effect of increasing the work space.

Sinks

If you have space (and the money) it is useful to have two and even three sinks: one for soaking dishes, one for preparing vegetables and one smaller one for a waste or garbage disposer. A waste disposer can, of course, be fitted into a single main sink, but do make sure your building or house has the sort of drainage system that will not be fouled up by liquid refuse in bulk. Some sinks come complete with extra cutting board surface to fit across the top when necessary and so provide extra work space; others have small spray attachments at the side to aid cleaning. If you are short of space do not forget the inch-saving corner varieties.

Materials are generally stainless steel, porcelain-covered cast iron, or the new plastic substance which looks like marble and makes a neat and effective all-in-one counter and sink. The most common choice for taps is a single swing spout with either one or two handles.

Waste disposers and rubbish (trash) compactors

The newest waste disposers can handle up to 1 litre (2 pints) of waste food at a time very much more quickly than the old bone-chilling (and bone-crunching) models. Rubbish or trash compactors can squash up cardboard boxes, cartons, tins, cans and bottles to a quarter of

their original size. They may be worth considering if you live in a high-rise flat, or have infrequent refuse collection, but they do take up space. They can be located almost anywhere in the kitchen and attached to the same sort of outlet as an electric stove.

Cooker hoods

Although some stoves have built-in self-venting outlets, there is an enormous market for hoods of every description and style with built-in fans for ventilation and to remove cooking smells. Most units need to be on an outside wall or ducted to vent outdoors but others can be bought which are ventless, recirculating the air through activated charcoal filters which should be changed regularly.

All of them have incorporated light bulbs to give extra light over the work top.

Washing machines and dryers

If there is any possibility of placing washing machines and dryers away from the kitchen you should consider it. Detergents and dirty clothes don't mix very well with food preparation and in any case the most sensible place to position both appliances is somewhere near the bedroom/bath area. Standard machines measure 600 mm ($23\frac{5}{8}$ in) deep by 595 mm ($23\frac{3}{8}$ in) wide, to fit between units and can be stacked one above the other. But, unless you have a separate utility room, that does not leave much space nearby for storing laundry supplies and accessories or setting down the just-cleaned laundry. If there is room for a 1300 mm (5 ft) cupboard or closet just outside the kitchen, bedroom or bathroom, say in a corridor, or lobby, this would be a better solution. It would give room for a washer and dryer to stand side by side under a convenient counter top. Better still, if there is room, would be a 2500 mm (8 ft) wide louvre-fronted closet which would give you space for washing machine, dryer, clothes hamper and general purpose cabinet with a metre wide (3 ft) double door wall cabinet above and a clothes rod to hang out just dried permanent press clothing. The units could have a counter top and there would need to be efficient lighting.

If you really cannot find the space anywhere else in the home you will have to try to squeeze space in the kitchen (or go to a launderette). In this case, you may want to opt for one of the newer washer/dryers that combine both facilities. Do not forget that most dryers need to be vented to an outside wall.

Appliances and units alike in this modern kitchen/dining room are all fronted by an interesting closed louvre finish which resembles an updated version of the old roll-topped desks.

KITCHENS

glass-fronted cabinets become decoration in their own right

spotlight over cooking area with blue-grey shade

stove flue enamelled blue to match range

blue-grey painted frames tone with stove

blue and white accessories all add to the general effect

refrigerator concealed behind aerated cupboard door

two corner doors open together on hinge for easy access

well-designed and generous drawer and cupboard space enables only good china to be displayed.

This charming blue-grey and cream kitchen combines the appeal and solidity of traditional fittings with the convenience of modern appliances. The stove-enamelled cooker is gas-powered for ease of use. The base units both conceal items like the refrigerator and provide sufficient storage to enable only the more elegant objects to be stored in the glass-fronted cupboards (inset) with their clever slotted shelves.

slots cut in shelves to hold plates

Kitchen units and cabinets

If you are handy yourself, can employ a good carpenter, or go to a custom cabinet maker, you can make or obtain literally any size or type of unit to fit the most awkward spaces. Another ploy is to buy unfinished or whitewood cabinets and fit them into your space, finishing them off yourself with paint or stain.

If you are going for a fully fitted kitchen, you will find the units are made up of three elements: the carcass (basic cupboard and shelves), the doors and drawer fronts, and the work surface which runs along the top. Usually, all can be bought separately. In some ranges, you can buy decor panels to fit the front of specially designed built-in appliances, making them match the cupboards.

Ready made cabinets come in a huge choice of finishes, colours, and measurements. Heights for wall cabinets range from 300 mm (12 in) –good for the space over a refrigerator–to 1000 mm (39 in). The depth from wall to face is a standard 300 mm (12 in) and widths run from 230 mm (9 in) to 600 mm (24 in) for single door cabinets to 1000 mm (39 in) to 1200 mm (48 in) for double door models. Corner cabinets with a single door and either fixed or revolving shelves can be mounted diagonally across a corner to use every inch of available space.

Base units generally stand 900 mm (36 in) from the floor if you count the worktop as well and widths match the wall hung cabinets, though the depth is generally twice as much. You can buy them with doors, drawers, or both, and with different depths for different drawers. Again, there are many refinements to choose from: glide-out vegetable storage equipment, wine racks, slide-out chopping blocks, bottle drawers, silver storage drawers, pot lid holders, tray storage, sliding trays for linens and cutlery racks. Alternatively, you can buy standard but empty units and fill them with your own choice of such 'organizers' from other sources.

Pantry or food storage cabinets are specially made to accommodate cans and dry goods (breakfast cereals, jams, flour and other packaged goods). Often they are heavily hinged with one can deep shelving from top to bottom of the doors for maximum use of space. You can buy them in wall, floor or full length sizes.

Utility or broom cupboards are generally 300 mm (12 in) or 600 mm (24 in) deep, 1950 mm (7 ft) tall and from 500 mm (22 in) to 600 mm (24 in) wide. They consist of one tall space with an upper shelf for brooms, vacuum cleaners, mops and cleaning supplies. Similarly-shaped cabinets can be bought as housing units for particular models of wall oven and for refrigerators.

All these four pictures show the sort of variations and refinements that you can expect to find in the various ranges of units currently on the market. Top left: Swing out stove-enamelled (for easy cleaning) trays for corner units. Top right:

Open-shelved corner unit–ideal for better-looking possessions. Bottom left: Pull-out trash container drawer which neatly holds rubbish bin. Bottom right: Deep drawers have aerated wire racks for saucepans and their lids.

The central fact to acknowledge about any sort of storage is that there is rarely enough of it, and this is certainly true in the kitchen.

Be ruthless

The kitchen is the one room where you should literally use every inch, nook, cranny, piece of ceiling, window, door or side of cabinet; in fact the key to successful and efficient kitchen storage is to use every possible surface, and to assemble equipment and accessories by the places where they are the most needed. Start your kitchen reorganization with a drastic sort-out and throwout. Don't weaken. If you do not use an object once a day, or at least once a week, it does not deserve prime storage space (that is within easy reach and somewhere between knee and eye level). Put it instead at the back of a base cabinet or high up on a wall cabinet, or in the space, if there is one, between wall cabinets and ceiling which you can always turn into a second tier of cabinets by adding fronts to match your other units. Things which are used once or twice a year – turkey roasting pans, huge party casseroles, picnic baskets, should be rigorously stashed right away, if possible out of the kitchen altogether – under the stairs, in an attic, in the basement or garage in a house; in some more remote cupboard in a flat or apartment. And what about all those

gadgets lying loose in drawers? Would they be tidier and more accessible hung on pegboards?

If you have not used something for literally years the chances are that it won't come in useful for a rainy day (the hoarder's excuse) and that you probably won't *ever* use it. So give it away, send it to a jumble sale, sell it if you can, or just throw it away. Whatever you do, be tough . . .

Don't keep it. If you do, it will almost certainly be the beginning of the end and you will never get properly organized. Perhaps one should keep a picture of hideous confusion pinned to the kitchen door in the same way as slimmers keep a fat photo taped to the fridge as a deterrent to snacking.

Once you have eliminated superfluous items in this way, you can prioritize the rest of your storage so that the most useful items come most readily to hand. The result – a more efficient and pleasant room.

In the kitchen left, storage space has been used to maximum effect, particularly in the form of open shelving. (Even the space around the extractor fan has been used to optimum advantage.) Shelving like this, where everything is on show, will probably only suit the tidy-minded, however. If you are less tidy, you may prefer the totally concealed storage units of the kitchen on the right.

Far left: A clever pull-out unit the full height of the run of cabinets makes day-to-day necessities clearly visible and easily accessible.

Above: Two wood plate drainers flank the window here to provide excellent storage. A shelf across the window connects the racks and gives further storage space. A wooden rod suspended from the ceiling holds yet more equipment.

Left: Even the space between these handsome units has been used for storage.

Right: The staggered top cupboards of these good-looking units allow more wall space for hanging equipment that is decorative and functional.

Be logical

This simply means that instead of bending and scuffling around for saucepans stacked up in a dark base unit, try hanging them from hooks near the sink (where you are going to fill them with water) or near the stove. Keep herbs and spices on small racks just above or by the cook top. Store pulses, rice, pasta, sugar, flour and condiments by the worktop or preparation area. Stash old plastic or paper shopping bags near the rubbish or garbage bin and then you can re-cycle them as bin liners. Everyday plates can be stored upright in a wooden plate rack above the dishwasher or by the sink. This is much easier than keeping them in piles in a cupboard or closet. Similarly, mugs and cups used regularly can be kept on hooks near the stove top, and glasses can be kept in a cabinet near the washing machine. Store wooden spoons, whisks, colanders, sieves in containers or from hooks by the worktop or cooker top, wherever you need them most, and keep oil, vinegars, condiments, herbs and garlic near salad bowls.

Be ingenious

Once you have thoroughly reorganized your existing storage you can look around for new surfaces to conquer. Bunches of herbs and pot and saucepan racks can be hung from the ceiling. You can fix tiny narrow shelves or racks to the inside of cabinet doors; attach spice racks, hooks, more shelves (to take cook books?) to the sides of cabinets; add further shelves just above worktops on the splashback areas, and add shallow shelves 300–450 mm (12–18 in) above cook tops and sinks with hooks attached to the edges for various bits of equipment such as measuring jugs and ladles.

As usual in most rooms, corners are often a wasted area. You might be able to build a corner unit across the angle of two worktops for cook books, or more spices and condiments, with more storage space for jars on top. If there is not room for this you might utilize the space by making slots in the counter top to take your cooking knives, or you could suspend them from a magnetic bar just above out of reach of children. Think too, about using the underside of your cabinets for kit-chen paper holders, more suspended spice racks, or for hooks to hang just about anything.

Spare bits of wall which are too small for conventional cabinets can be used for mounting peg boards for small implements and utensils; or pin-board for recipes, bills, receipts, reminders to the family and to yourself. Make better use of your base cabinets by fixing slide-out towel racks to the doors, and by installing swivel storage shelves to do away with all that groping around for things at the back. Shallow alcoves can be used for yet more narrow shelves just the depth of one can or bottle or for mounting a magnetic knife-rack; awkward spaces, say between stove and storage cabinets, can be used for trays.

Only when you have made your plans, decided on your work sequence, bought your appliances and thought about the style of room you would like to create, can you focus on the treatment of the rest: the framework of walls, floor, window and ceiling as well as the sort of tiles, splashback and worktop you would like. This, of course, is the actual decoration of the room, the process which comes first in most areas, but certainly last in the kitchen planning squence. Last, but *never* least: colours, surfaces and embellishments have their own particular and important role to play in kitchen comfort.

Walls

By the time you have put up an appropriate amount of cabinets and storage there is not usually much wall left to cover. It is often possible to tile a large proportion of the wall for guaranteed ease of maintenance. Paint, however, should always be washable – do not use emulsion because you will not be able to wash grease and smoke off easily, but rather use gloss or eggshell finishes.

White or earth colours – tobaccos, umbers, sand, sludgy green, pine green – are particularly appropriate with food, while blue and white, green and white, red or pink and white and a sunny chrome yellow, always look good and fresh. Try painting walls white and colouring

woodwork, or vice versa. It depends very much on the units you choose. Obviously, if they are a colour as opposed to white or wood, you shold choose a background that blends with them.

If you decide on a wallpaper, try to use a paper-backed vinyl, a vinyl impregnated fabric paper, or a PVC wallcovering. Or else paint the surface of ordinary paper with a coat or two of eggshell or gloss polyurethane for a practical protective finish.

Stripped or new brick makes a good kitchen background, so does tongue-and-groove wood panelling or panelling of wide wooden planks. Bricks should be sealed with a masonry stabiliser, while wood should be waxed, varnished or painted.

If you have a kitchen/dining room and want to make it look particularly warm and comfortable you could make a visual division between working and eating areas by stapling the dining walls with a cheap cotton treated with a protective spray. Or you could give your

In the large loft left, the units are in place, the floor is stripped, sanded and polished and there is still plenty of scope and general living space to play with. The elegant cream trim of the kitchen doors and drawers (right) is picked up in the walls and blinds and there are even matching polished resin handles.

KITCHENS

shelf unit suspended
from ceiling provides
additional storage

glossy red diagonal
tongue-and-groove
boarding adds space

charcoal-filter
extractor hood

light
positioned
over work
area

double sink
unit with
drainer rack
fitting

*The warm and cheerful
look of this small kitchen
has been achieved with a
fairly low outlay.
Tongue-and-groove
boarding set on the
diagonal has been given a
coating of brilliant red
paint. The suspended shelf
over the worktop holds
plants and spices and also
supports a charcoal
extractor hood.*

mosaic-
tiled work
surface

curtains conceal
food and utensils

room an interesting old country look by adding a 'wainscot' of boarding to a free wall, or at least some moulding at dado level.

Ceilings

Unless you have a particular pretty beamed or coved ceiling it is often a good idea to lower the ceiling area in a kitchen. This enables you to put in recessed lighting, or to add an acoustic or tongue-and-groove wood finish. Acoustic tiles are used for ceilings rather than walls and are made to absorb sound. They have to be suspended from battens and are most often made from pre-finished, slotted insulation board, polystyrene or fibreglass. Tongue-and-groove pine boarding looks good; it should be sealed with polyurethane to protect the wood and needs hardly any maintenance–just wiping over occasionally. In America, the virtues of the old pressed metal ceilings have been rediscovered and re-deployed. But if you do not want to add a ceiling covering, simply paint the surface with white, or very pale emulsion to reflect as much light as possible.

Floors

Kitchen floors need to be tough enough to withstand all sorts of spills, grease and damp, comfortable enough to stand on for long periods, and handsome to look at. The choice of covering in fact, very

Above: Mini-print hexagonal tiles and floor tiles that match in shape if not colour, are nicely offset by the strawberry print curtains in this wood-trimmed, friendly little kitchen.

Left: The beamed ceiling in this kitchen blends admirably with the wooden units to create a country atmosphere that is even further enhanced by the choice of kitchen furniture.

KITCHENS

much depends on the sort of style you have set yourself. If you want a rustic kitchen, then quarry, brick or Mexican or French terracotta tiles look very splendid. Slate is marvellous to look at but at a marvellous price, and there is an enormous choice in ceramic tiles which can be mixed in among the terracottas for an ethnic Mexican or Provencale, Italian, Spanish or Portuguese look. Terracotta tiles, brick, flagstone, slate, terrazzo and non-slip ceramic are all durable, impressive, good to look at and easy to clean. They generally come in a range of beautiful colours and pleasing shapes. Most are heavy and therefore only suitable for laying at ground-floor level or where floors are exceptionally strong. All of these treatments are as hard on the feet as they are easy on the eye—but sometimes, as I have said, good appearances win over practical considerations. If both price and hardness bother you, there are acceptable alternatives in

Left: A bright cheerful kitchen where vivid colours are carefully balanced. Red/white/yellow checked vinyl flooring co-ordinates the red and white checked tiles and red stripes with the yellow in the accessories.

Right: Brick-shaped terracotta tiles have a country look to them and nicely bridge the gap between rusticity and modernity in this pleasant kitchen.

KITCHENS

vinyl, and cork coated with vinyl which can look very good too. Both vinyl – in sheet or tile form – and vinyl-coated cork are easy to maintain.

Hi-Tech and more sleekly designed kitchens look good with white tiled floors whether ceramic or vinyl, but again you could use cork and vinyl, or composition tiles or even limoleum which has taken on a new lease of life now that people have realised how well it can

look inlaid with other colours. Wood treated with polyurethane to withstand spills and grease can look very handsome, especially in a dining kitchen, and old floors can be spruced up with paint, various painted finishes and stencilling, protected with extra coats of varnish (see page 379).

If it appeals to you, the new stain-resistant kitchen carpet, available as tiles or in sheet form, is very warm and quiet, making it particularly

suitable for a kitchen-diner.

When choosing flooring for a kitchen/diner, make sure the surface is suitable for both functions, or delineate one area from another by using different types of flooring. For example, if you have quarry tiles in the kitchen, they may be rather cold on the feet for dinner guests lingering over coffee, as well as being noisy when chairs scrape across them. You may find that people are encouraged to use the

room as more of a gathering place if the floor of the dining area is covered with colourful rugs, and even with practical vinyl flooring

Above left: Polyurethaned wood boards are a handsome contrast to this mainly white kitchen with its distinctive blue and white tiled border. Note the repetition of the boarding on the ceiling – here painted white – and the linear effect of the blinds.

Emphatic flooring. *Top left: Brilliant blocks of primary colours set into black make imaginative use of composition tiles. The bold colours are picked up in the accessories. Bottom left: Neat herringbone parquet makes a warm-looking expanse in an otherwise fairly austere kitchen.*
Above right: Practical, comfortable and noise-absorbent, the carpet tiles in this kitchen not only provide an interesting textured flooring, but tone well with their surrounding units.
Left: Crisp, clean lines are achieved with dramatically contrasting yellow and white colours that have been picked up even in the grouting around the tiles.

KITCHENS

you can create a change of atmosphere around the table by changing the colour of the floor or simply by adding a rug.

Windows

There is no point at all in elaborate window coverings in the kitchen. They only get dirty, greasy and in the way. It is far better to use café curtains, short, tied-back curtains, or blinds. Fabric should be easily washed or cleaned cotton, or vinylised cotton (for roller blinds). Otherwise use Venetian blinds in plastic or wood which can be easily wiped, or wooden shutters, or no covering at all. Shelves look good and are practical across a window and can be made of glass, or wood, or metal grid for a Hi-Tech look. Alternatively, just hang plants from hooks above the window, or stand small pots of plants along the windowsill, making sure that the ones you select are going to be happy with the kind of light, temperature and humidity you are providing. Used this way, with massed greenery, or collections of glass on glass shelves, the kitchen window becomes a strong focal point.

If your kitchen has a whole wall of window, this needn't be a problem. Either treat it as a feature in its own right, with a striking blind or shutters; give it as much impact as possible and let the view and the light pour in. Or, if you think it steals too much potential storage space you could consider sacrificing some of it. If you're desparate for storage space it's often possible to build units right around a window so that the window acquires a recessed effect and becomes an essential part of the arrangement. In this case, the simpler the window treatment the better; plain blinds, café curtains or just left bare.

Worktops

Worktops have to be as durable as floors, able to withstand chopping, hot utensils and spills, and still be good to look at. The plastic laminated top is very popular but you must be careful not to chop directly on to it (use a chopping board) or to put down hot pots and saucepans. Once ruined it is extremely difficult to put right.

Ceramic tiles—which can be continued up the space between counter top and unit to make a handsome splashback—come in a huge range of colours and designs and can look spectacular, gentle or fresh depending on the effect you want. However, the grouting can easily get discoloured and dirty-looking, so it might be better to start off with a dark grouting from the beginning. Also, you should be wary of putting down pots and pans straight from the stove; this might cause the ceramic to crack.

Butcher-block and wood counter

Left: This terracotta-tile effect vinyl floor is almost indistinguishable from the real thing and makes a smart contrast to the white tiled units and brilliant yellows and greens of the rest of the kitchen/dining room.

Above: The red sink fits neatly into the white-tiled counter top and blends with the dotted wallpaper.

Right: This continuous work surface with its moulded integral sinks and generous depth, not only looks good with its marble appearance but could hardly be more practical. It is hardwearing and relatively stain-resistant. Damage, like scratches, can be removed with reasonable ease.

147

KITCHENS

tops are sturdy and look good but they are not very practical near the sink surrounds or anywhere where there is water because they can warp and the grain can rise up. If you are using wood as a continuous work surface, introduce some variety; let in a square of marble or ceramic tile for making pastry; surround your sink with stainless steel, tile or plastic laminate rather than wood, which tends to lift up and warp.

There is a new plastic substance that feels like marble but is immensely more practical. This material is ideal for countertops and pastry surfaces since it is very durable, resistant to most stains, and does not burn or warp. It comes in white, cream and a slightly veined beige. It may be cut and glued to give a virtually seamless surface.

For more ideas on renewing or replacing worktops, see page 108.

Splashbacks

These can be made of plastic laminate, synthetic marble or, the most popular, ceramic tile. They can be plain, patterned or flowered, bevelled, or a mixture. Tiles can be laid on the diagonal or in a basket weave design to produce handsome effects.

A calm, pretty pink and white kitchen. The laminate top to match the units beneath, contrasts happily with the pink tiles, painted ceiling and ceiling-mounted spots.

Safety rules

Statistics reveal the horrifying truth that there are more accidents in the home than on the road and that most of these take place in the kitchen and to children. So safety should be a priority, whether starting from scratch, or just re-vamping.

To avoid all possible causes of accidents take the following precautions:

Always unplug small appliances when they are not in use, and don't let appliance cords dangle over the edge of counters where they can be reached by children. Keep flexes as short as is convenient to avoid a spaghetti of cables.

Choose non-slip flooring and always mop up spills immediately.

Treat food processor blades with the greatest respect. Handle them gingerly; wash them carefully; don't ever leave them soaking, submerged in water in case someone else unsuspectingly puts their hand in. They can be lethal. Equally, if they are in the dishwasher, pick them out very carefully.

Whenever possible, cook on the back burners of cook tops or stoves, especially when children are around. Make sure pot handles are turned towards the back of the stove and that the oven door is firmly closed.

If you have small children around cover electric outlets with safety caps or tape.

Never pull any appliance—kettle, mixer—out of its socket without switching off first.

Never add dishwasher detergent (which is toxic) until the last moment, then close door immediately. Make sure that dishwasher doors are always latched tight. Left down they are a temptation to children who might climb onto them and tip the whole appliance.

Place all poisonous, potentially poisonous and toxic household cleaners, detergents and scourers on the highest possible shelf. Never keep any of these in innocent looking old lemonade bottles particularly if the original labels are still on.

Keep all trash and garbage out of children's reach and place any old container which held a toxic substance into the outside dustbin or garbage can as soon as it is finished.

Don't ever leave your children alone in the kitchen; they have even been known to get trapped inside fridges and freezers.

Never leave an iron on if you leave the room, and never let young children near an ironing board while you are ironing.

When you are serving up hot dishes make sure that toddlers and young children are well out of the way.

Keep sharp knives well out of the reach of children—either on a magnetic panel set back and above the worktop; in slots made at the back of the worktop, or in a knife block set well back too.

Try not to use long tablecloths, or at least tablecloths within the reach of a yank from small hands.

If you have high shelves keep a proper, solid stepladder within easy reach and do not climb on chairs or worktops.

Always keep a first aid and burn treatment kit in the kitchen, near the stove, ready for emergencies.

If you possibly can, keep a small fire extinguisher to hand near the stove and make sure that everyone knows how to use it. It's too late to absorb the instructions when the kitchen is in flames. Ensure it is suitable for fat fires and electric fires. A fire blanket, hung to one side of the cooker, may also be useful, as long as you understand how to use it.

Do not keep any fabrics near the stove or cook top: if the window is near the stove top do not use curtains. Nor should you keep drying up cloths or oven gloves in the sort of position where they could drop or drag on a burner.

short curly cable

cooker guard

cover for electric socket above work surface

knife-block

fire extinguisher

WHERE TO EAT

DINING ROOMS

Cooking and eating go together, so naturally the next step is to decide where and in what sort of style you are going to serve and eat meals. It really hardly matters if this happens in a room of its own, in the kitchen, the living room, or even the hall. Dining rooms today are wherever the food is served.

If you do have a separate dining room, you're lucky. It need contain no more than a sideboard, table and chairs and can be decorated in its own individual way. If you do a great deal of formal or business entertaining then this sort of dining room is essential. But these days, with space at a premium, a room kept solely for dining is rare; the chances are that it has to double as a work room, say for hobbies like model making, or as a quiet place where the family can get on with homework, studying or other paperwork. And far more likely is the dining room which is no more than a corner of another room. This, of course, makes it simple to furnish; all you really need are a table and chairs which fit in well with the rest of the room. A kitchen-dining room is ideal for a family; it's cosy, convenient and economical since it saves heating another room. In tiny flats and bedsitters it's more often the living room that has to make space for dining, in which case it's a good idea to separate the two functions with

either a physical division – like an arch, trellis or shelving – or with visual treatment like different lighting or flooring, or perhaps a change of colour or mood created by wall coverings and soft furnishings.

If you can define the area with a different floor level or use one arm of an L-shaped room, so much the better. You may still be able to emphasize the division by decorative changes, to give your dining area its own atmosphere, as you would if you were trying to divide a simple rectangular room.

But whatever your dining area consists of, organizing it, giving it character and interest can be challenging and stimulating. In fact, the dining room should be a particularly interesting room to decorate, because, like the bathroom, it is generally used for comparatively short periods of time, and then mostly at night. As long as its main purpose is borne in mind – that of providing a relaxed, comfortable and enjoyable area for eating which is also an attractive, unobtrusive background for any food served – it can,

Two contrasting styles. Left: Dark red walls, dark polished wood furniture and formal place settings combine to create an elegant and moody, traditional atmosphere. Right: A fresher, more informal look is achieved with lighter colours, wooden floors, and a profusion of spring flowers.

DINING ROOMS

theoretically, be as inventive, curious, and as experimental as you like.

Before you embark on the decoration, however, you need to have the practical considerations firmly in mind. Decide exactly what functions the room has to fulfil. Ask yourself these questions:

● How many people will eat in the dining room regularly?

● What is the maximum number of diners which will have to be accommodated at a sit-down meal?

● How much storage space is necessary for china and cutlery; for dining accessories; for other items not related to eating – books, papers, sewing equipment and so on?

● Is the room the only dining space or are family meals usually taken elsewhere?

● Will it be used mainly at night, or does it need to look fresh for breakfast, serviceable for lunch and intimate for dinner parties?

● Are your needs likely to change over the next few years – will you have children to cope with; are you likely to entertain more often than you do at present?

Consider whether a very bold, outrageous, or dramatic look would be too overwhelming in a dining room which all the family are going to want to use at different times. I remember an all-black room I saw years ago which has always stuck in my mind: black velvet walls, black carpet, ebony table and chairs, black lacquer side table. The only relief was in the tablecloth, napkins, china and flowers which varied from spanking white, to black and white, to brilliant yellow or green. The lighting was subtle: concealed behind pelmets, inset into the ceiling, bounced up from uplights on the floor, flickering from candles. And the room always looked beautiful, except on a gloomy winter's day, when it was frightful. Such rooms are definitely not for breakfast.

Another room I remember for its verve was all shiny dark green lacquered walls, gilded carpet and *trompe l'oeil* painted walls which looked like real draperies: a theatrical, stunning experience. But the fact that so few rooms stand out in my memory is not so surprising. On the whole, dining rooms fall into pretty familiar categories, furnished with pretty familiar types of furniture, colours and accessories. And perhaps that is as it should be. The serious diner likes to feel comfortable, at ease, to have a sense of well-being, but does not want his attention to be distracted.

Having worked out how your room will be used, you should consider what sort of finishes are going to be suitable. With food

Left: Built-in bench seating round a corner-placed table provides a lot of seating in small space. The continuation of the white and blue colour scheme also ensures that the dining area is in tune with the kitchen.

Above: An intimate dining area has been created here in the alcove beneath the stairs. The magnificent beamed ceiling reinforces the enclosed feeling.

Right: The kitchen area is one convenient step down from the dining room with its nice use of pine, well-stocked bookshelves and gleaming wood floor. The kitchen area is tiled to continue the rustic effect.

DINING ROOMS

Getting seated

Dining tables come in a vast range of shapes and sizes—square, round, rectangular or oval: but there are some basic rules to follow when it comes to choosing a table for a room of a particular size.

Each place setting (with an armless chair) takes about 66 cm (2 ft 3 in) with 5 cm (2 in) added to the width for chairs with arms. A long table should be at least 75 cm (2 ft 6 in) wide if both sides are to be used. Each person will need at least 75 cm (2 ft 6 in) to give space for getting in and out. And, of course, there must be an ample passageway around the table: 100 cm from table to wall is really the minimum allowance.

When buying a table and chairs, if possible spend some time sitting in the chairs *at* the table. Make sure they are a good height for the table, that any chairs with arms will fit under the table, and that seats stay supportive through long sitting sessions. If cushions are used on chairs, remember this may change their height.
Further equivalents of the measurements given opposite are:
25 cm (10 in); 32 cm (13 in)
35 cm (14 in); 50 cm (20 in)
73 cm (29 in); 90 cm (35 in)
100 cm (39 in); 110 cm (43 in)
115 cm (45 in); 130 cm (51 in)
150 cm (59 in); 175 cm (69 in)
210 cm (83 in); 250 cm (98 in)

Place settings

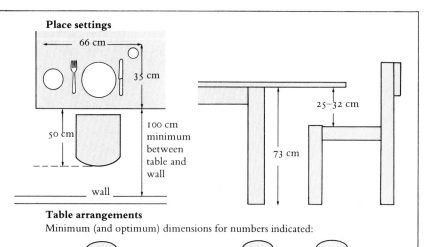

Table arrangements

Minimum (and optimum) dimensions for numbers indicated:

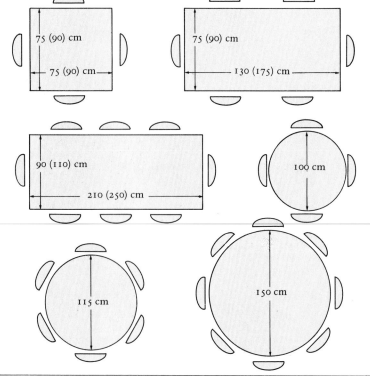

around, surfaces should be as practical as possible: choose flooring which will not show crumbs and can be mopped up easily; sideboards should be provided with protective covers if they are not heatproof; traditional polished tables might look good, but with children around, you may be better off going for a heatproof, scrubbable surface which can be wiped over quickly; upholstery should be washable; wallpaper need not be as tough as the vinyl-coated varieties.

In short what you should aim to create in a dining room is a special atmosphere within a very practical framework, so when you've provided for the basics you can add to the mood with window treatments, interesting lighting and decorative tricks to make the room as comfortable, as functional and as good looking as you can.

Eating in the dining end of this extremely pretty dining-kitchen is like eating in a conservatory. Floor to ceiling glass doors and window open directly onto an equally charming paved garden. It all looks beautifully casual until you notice the careful transition from dining area tiles to garden paving with the fresh grey and white blinds as a demarcation point. Wine racks are tucked neatly and accessibly under the marble serving top with its vaguely rural wood supports.

When you know where your dining area is going to be and what size table and chairs will fit best into the space, you can start thinking about how you plan to treat the other important elements in the room – the walls, floor and windows.

Walls, floors and windows

There are any number of suitable treatments for walls in a dining room: there is not going to be much wear and tear, and no need for waterproof surfaces, as in kitchens or bathrooms, so you can afford to have some fun. Paint them deep matt, eggshell or shiny gloss and hang them with pictures or a collection of some sort. Use one of the attractive paint techniques which are re-gaining popularity: sponging, rag rolling or dragging (see pages 368–79). Stencil a border round the ceiling, around the door and windows, and above the skirting boards. Wallpaper them or cover them with fabric: felt, hessian, sacking, lining fabric or printed cotton. Panel them with wood, line them with cork, strip the plaster back to the brick; the choice is endless. Tongue-and-groove panelling will make a complete transformation: stain it, varnish it or paint it. Or finish with *trompe l'oeil* painted murals. If you do a lot of entertaining and want it to look spectacular at night, then mirror tiles will gleam and sparkle and reflect candle-light

beautifully. In fact you can do almost anything with the walls of a dining room. But remember that above all it is going to be a place where people are meant to enjoy their food. Have interesting decoration by all means, but avoid anything too demanding on the eye. You will want people to relax over their meal, especially if you do a lot of entertaining.

If floorboards are in reasonable condition, they could be stripped, sanded and polished. Or they could be painted, or stencilled or both (see page 379). I, personally, do not think it a very good idea to have carpet in the dining room where it only picks up smells and gets dirtier more quickly than in most places, since people do, without fail, drop things. But there is nothing against rugs of any description. Bricks, old tiles, new tiles, quarry tiles, Mexican, French or Spanish tiles, ceramic tiles, slate and even marble facing all look spectacular – provided, of course, that you are prepared to put up with the clattering noise from chairs being pulled up to the table and pushed back. Vinyl is

A clever feature of this living/dining/ guest room, left, is that half the table top can be removed and pushed against a wall when not in use (see page 26). In another kitchen-diner, right, old linoleum has been painted a milky cream to go with walls, ceiling and units.

DINING ROOMS

Above: Cork tiles are given a smart black border to echo the lines of the octagonal table as well as the colour of the marble counter top. The arched windows are too pretty to be covered. Top right: Bleached boards are in keeping with the various shades of pine in a spacious country room.

Right: This diner conservatory has a real feel of the outdoors. Created by the stencilled wooden floor, where familiar garden flowers such as wisteria, old roses and bluebells have been dotted amongst the geometric shapes. The bold design and strong colours work well next to simple yet elegant furnishings.

practical, so is vinyl-coated cork, and lineoleum, which now comes in all colours and can be inlaid or arranged in a pattern in various shades with quite spectacular results. Black and white vinyl tiles can look particularly effective, and hardboard or chipboard, painted or varnished, make cheap cover-ups. I was always immensely impressed with the vinyl flooring we had in the dining room when my children were small. It seemed to withstand the onslaught of bicycles, tricycles and roller skates with scarcely a scratch to show.

Windows give you a chance to go to town. The obvious window treatments in traditional dining rooms are curtains on rods, or under pelmets, or hung from various headings, tied back at the sides, and used with roller, Roman or festoon blinds if you wanted to cut a particular dash. Blinds on their own can fit any atmosphere, particularly if windows are awkward, small or you did not want to lose too much light. Vertical or louvred blinds, pinoleum or matchstick blinds or Venetian blinds are more appropriate in modern settings. Add colour with roller blinds, atmosphere with Austrian blinds, or create an entirely different mood with cottagey patterned curtains. Match them with other patterns in the room.

Then there are shutters in natural or white-painted wood: if you have

Victorian shutters, strip them, and hang a pretty lace panel at the window. Close the shutters over it at night. Or have no window treatment at all except glass shelves full of plants, or plants hanging from the ceiling or from poles slung across the window. There are enormous numbers of possibilities when you get over the thought that you must have some sort of fabric at the windows.

Seeing to eat

Whatever the style of your dining room, traditional, modern or something in between, the same broad principles of lighting apply. People need to see what they're eating but the light must never be so bright that it kills any atmosphere you're trying to achieve. Although the fittings can be totally different according to the room itself, the effect should be the same: subtle lighting, capable of creating different moods but in plentiful supply over those places that need it.

Obviously the table and sideboard or carving table need to be well lit, but whether you use a light right over the table, a chandelier, candelabra or side lights, they really should be used in conjunction with a dimmer switch. If you do have a hanging light over the table it should not hang more than 85 cm to 90 cm (34 in to 36 in) from the table top. A rise-and-fall fitting ensures it will be right. This could be discreetly boost-

Window treatments for dining rooms. Top left: Grey walls, Roman blinds and a grey-covered table tucked into a panelled bay window makes a pretty dining oasis. Top right: Dinner for two among a symphony of nutmeg shades in the mellow dining hall with its romantic curtains. Right: Sheer lace curtains share the same flowing fern design as the wallpaper. The bare pine table set right by the window is a cheerful breakfast or lunch place. Far right: White ventian blinds add a stark, cool contrast to the black door frames, table and chairs in this elegant dining room.

DINING ROOMS

ed by concealed uplights in corners, or by strip lights running round the room just below the ceiling and concealed by a pelmet or valance.

There are, of course, all sorts of chandeliers available for traditional rooms in brass, iron, wood, wrought iron and crystal, but again the effect can be enhanced by recessed downlights set in the ceiling to light up the chandelier itself. This is especially effective with crystal.

To add special accent, use spots round the room to highlight pictures or fireplace, and take any collections you may have into consideration when you are planning lighting: a lit display is always very dramatic. Wallwashers, downlights or uplighters can be used to highlight areas of the room, or sculptural halogen floor lamps with dimmers can be ready to flood a room with sunshine-like light, or give a warm and cosy glow.

Setting the table

The table setting–china, glass, cutlery, linen–is as much a part of dining room decoration as the furniture and framework. There's no point in getting all the other decorative details perfect if your plates and knives and forks are all wrong. It doesn't matter whether they are family heirlooms or bargains from the market stall; if they're right for the setting, that's all that counts.

China, cutlery and glass all need to

Far left: A wide-brimmed pendant light adds sparkle as well as light to the transparent table setting of glass and clear plastic beneath. Flowers stand out with clarity against the see-through surfaces and floor. Note the upright radiator in the recess.

Left: An adjustable downlight has been lowered to give a dramatic yet subtle light to this stunning central table setting.

Above: Clever neon lighting above this table means that the whole feel –and colour–of the room can be changed at a touch of a switch.

DINING ROOMS

flowers repeat colours of room

red lacquer finish walls
make room look much larger

elaborate print
napkins remniscent
of oriental fabric

cool marble
table against
the riot of
colour

brilliant
mustard yellow
curtains over black
blind add dash

light carpet
to expand space

inexpensive bentwood
chairs painted black
add to oriental air

Red, mustard and black together add
dash and style to what is actually a very
small room. The glossy walls and
curtains help make the room look
larger than it is and combine with a
Burmese table and corner cupboard
to give a vaguely Oriental air,
which is even more apparent when
the octagonal marble table is laid
(above). Here the mood is
continued with the black straw
tablemats and the exotic napkins
fanned out into the tall glasses. The
chairs are basic bentwood simply
glossed black to achieve an expensive-
looking finish.

be useful as well as decorative. When you're choosing them think as much about shapes and sizes as about colour and pattern. Do they come in a wide range to suit all your needs? Are they going to be your serviceable everyday sets or only used on special occasions? Will they stand up to family wear and tear or look too sturdy for dinner parties? Are they all dishwasher/oven/freezer/microwave proof? Do they need to look equally at home in kitchen, dining room or living room? Do you want to be able to add to them over the years or is the

manufacturer likely to discontinue that particular pattern? Good table linen is also essential–to show off the food and add to the atmosphere. By changing cloths and napkins you can alter the feeling and style of the room quite spectacularly without going to a lot of expense–bright paper tablewear for children's parties, sophisticated damask or fine linen for a formal dinner party or cheerful gingham for casual or family meals.

One of my most favourite dining rooms was in an old country farmhouse with brick floors, uneven

nutmeg brown walls and a huge fireplace where there was almost always a fire. There was a long elm table, an old chestnut French provincial armoire, a rather well-worn 17th century velvet-covered Spanish chest and thick white cotton Roman blinds, edged with a brown and apricot cotton to match the tablecloth.

The matching or contrasting of tablecloths, napkins and window fabrics is always a pretty thing to do, and by changing them you change the mood effectively at little cost.

Left: Silky festoon blinds make a sumptuous backdrop for a nicely faded wood table full of sparkle and gleaming silver. Lace mats and velvet seated Regency chairs complete the traditional dining room elegance.

Right: Breakfast by the sea, and what could be more appropriate than the blue and white china on a blue and white tablecloth under a full vase of roses. The striped rug fits quite happily into the unashamedly romantic setting which even has a flower-filled fireplace.

DINING ROOMS

Once you have decided which facts you have to face, and whittled down the possibilities according to space, family and pocket, you can decide much more easily on the feeling you would like to introduce. Clearly, in a family dining room with several small children to cater for you are not likely to plump for any sort of exotica, or even the favourite splendours of velvet and mahogany. You are much more likely to go for old pine, or oak, tough lacquer or vinyl – at least for several years, but there is no reason why these cannot work just as well and create a feeling of their own. You may end up preferring these practical, hard-wearing materials in this well-used room.

Even if you don't have children, there may be other limitations that turn out to be more inhibiting than inspiring. Here's where it pays to borrow a little inspiration. Think which public places – restaurants in particular – have made you feel comfortable and at ease. Do you go for the opulent feel of linen, sparkle of cut glass and rich warm colouring, or do you prefer the more casual look of bare wood and brick? Do you like a clean-lined, pale wood, Scandinavian feel? The lightness of glass and wicker and white-painted plaster or brick? Or the softness of long print tablecloths and fabric-covered walls?

These days you do not have to go for matching suites of furniture in the dining room, any more than you have to go for three piece suites in the living room. No one will look askance if you have a makeshift wooden table disguised by a floor length tablecloth (with interchangeable overcloths), painted or lacquered ex-kitchen chairs, and an old dresser for a sideboard, or an old Victorian or Edwardian wardrobe for glass and china storage. Why would they? What you are achieving with such a happy mix is very much more personal and, therefore, interesting than the blandness of the careful match.

Set the mood
Colour is a useful tool to achieving a particular atmosphere: dark colours – shades of rust, deep green, the earth colours, and dark woods – create a warm, inviting atmosphere

Left: In this cheerful dining room, pale colours, light-coloured woods and a white-topped table combine to create a clean-lined look that is emphasized by the rather geometric alignment of the lamps. A different effect is seen, right, where a happy mix of pretty pine dresser and table, white-painted directors' chairs, old stove and cane side tables is still homogeneous.

DINING ROOMS

and show off food well. Bright, primary colours make for a cheerful, family room. Fashionable pastels are fresh and clean for daytime eating and cool and subtle for evening atmosphere. Whatever the colour scheme, there are certain characteristic styles.

Traditional with polished wood furniture and fine accessories to create a feeling of opulence. Walls in dark, warm colours, with rich fitted carpets or traditional rugs make for a quietly splendid effect. Panelled walls enhance the atmosphere.

Farmhouse follows the style of the farmhouse kitchen, and has a pine dresser or armoire as its focal point. Traditionally, flooring is of flagstones or quarry tiles, softened by rugs or matting. Old fashioned pine tables are expensive, but you could cover a modern one with a PVC cloth in a rustic pattern for everyday use and a more prettily patterned cotton cloth for special occasions. Window treatments should be fairly simple: floral or gingham curtains with tie-backs are ideal.

Scandinavian freshness is characterised by modern pine or beech and clean lines. Colour and design are all important; plants, clear colours (but not strong primary ones) and lots of white (paint, walls, floor or accessories) help to achieve this healthy non-fussy look.

Top left: Dark, warm-coloured walls and dark polished wood furniture – the epitome of the traditional look.

Above: Chunky furniture, black-painted bentwood chairs, matting and a cheerful garden view for a nice no-nonsense dining–living room.

Left: Up-dated traditional with slightly oriental overtones in the Chinese chairs, art, blossom trees and rattan blinds. Co-ordinated cloths, napkins and curtains owe rather more to the West.

Right: Farmhouse style furniture assisted by the charming rustic nature of the room itself.

DINING ROOMS

Above: A rather unusual combination of stripes and floral prints, combined with dark polished wooden table and chairs serves to create an updated version of the traditional look.

Right: Wooden dresser and furniture, poppy-patterned curtains and wallpaper matched by tablecloth and chair cushions all give this dining room an elegant, country feel that is far removed from the more usual, basic rustic style.

Far right: A touch of Eastern fantasy, with the Oriental flavour of the blue chair fabric being reflected in the prints and background screen.

Eastern fantasy runs riot with fabric decorations in either plain or delicately patterned style. Tented ceilings, fabric-covered walls, floor-length cloths and extravagant combinations of curtains and blinds at the window give a luxurious exotic feeling. Use lining fabrics for economy, trimmed with pattern border or edged with braid.

Thirties style cries out for a dining suite. Although this is generally considered a thing of the past, there has been a revival in the popularity of the solidly built, veneered Thirties suite with its square lines. You need panache to carry it off, with carefully selected ornaments and crockery from the period– fortunately, there's still quite a lot of it around; geometric patterned wallpaper or plain walls with a border pattern in peaches and rusts.

French café is reminiscent of the local bistro. The French are masters of restaurant cooking and atmosphere, so why not take a leaf from their book? Bentwood chairs, small circular tables and wall-mounted globe café lights are the key. Walls need to be mellow: dark creams, possibly sponged or rag rolled to give a textured effect. A dado rail, fixed round the room at the level of chair backs, with painted panelling below it will add more character.

Hi-tech says modern finishes and colours which give a bright, space-age feel. Go for angular-shaped chairs, softening them with brightly coloured cushions. Trestle tables of either laminate or glass are far more suitable than wood. Flooring should be non-committal: plain, functional cord fitted carpet, or rubber stud flooring. Simple window treatments, such as vertical louvres or slick Venetian blinds are the most appropriate, although you could also use cheaper roller blinds.

But don't be tied by necessity or convention to furnish all in one style. It is quite acceptable to mix, say, the feeling of the 17th century with the very modern; country pieces with glass and chrome; modern bentwood with early Victorian; a nice Regency side table with a scrubbed pine table. If you can't afford, or can't find, a good antique table to suit your style, get a second-hand, junk table, cover it with cloths, and invest as much as you can in comfortable chairs. Then again, you can still get a traditional feeling without having to spend money on a set of antique chairs. Old deal or pine kitchen chairs can be picked up reasonably in junk shops and painted or stained. Not particularly nice reproduction chairs can be lacquered in unexpected colours. And so on.

DINING ROOMS

Stylish transformations

As well as these pointers to distinctive style, there are many finishing touches which will add personality to a dining room, whether it is newly decorated, or a dining room you can't afford to re-vamp (or don't want to re-decorate, because it is in a rented home).

Put in a dado rail round the room, level with the backs of the chairs: it will protect the wallcovering, and change the proportions of the room. Polish it, or paint it to match the woodwork.

Fireplaces with real fires can be awkward in a very small dining room. Go for background heat, which is more controllable, and put an arrangement of dried flowers in the redundant grate.

Cover the walls with large panels of fabric—wall hangings, rugs or (appropriately) tablecloths. Staple them in place or stretch them on battens.

Add light to a room, and increase its apparent size by putting up mirror tiles (or fixing panels of mirror) in alcoves.

Make the room an extension of the garden by keeping potted plants by the window. Patio plants can be moved to 'winter over' in the dining room. Windowsills serve as greenhouse staging.

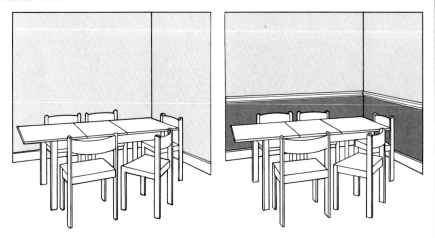

A plain dining room (above left) given character by adding a dado rail (above right) or covering the walls with panels of fabric (below).

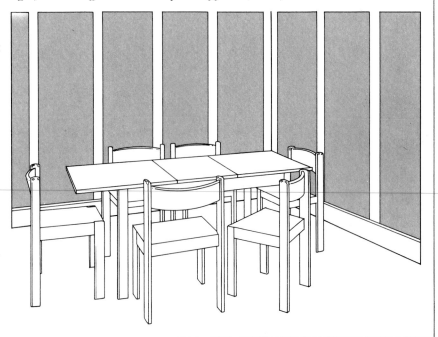

The collector's room

Because of the nature of the furnishings in a dining room (a large, flat surface, empty walls) and because it is needed to serve its purpose only at regular, specified times during the day (meal times), it is an ideal room to serve as a collector's library. Collections can be displayed and made into a decorative asset, and if you are a serious collector you can use the room as a quiet retreat to pursue your hobby, cleaning or mending plates, checking hallmarks on silver, valuing new purchases from relevant text books, cataloguing details—whatever might be involved in your particular field.

● Use wire plate hangers to hang a collection of plates on the walls, grouped according to colour, size or origin.

● Line the walls with shelves to house a library of books or magazines.

● Build storage cabinets and shelves to hold a collection of records.

● Display a collection of models—houses, soldiers, toys, cars—on shelves, carefully lit by strip lights behind baffles.

● Frame a collection of samplers—or something more unusual like lace collars or handkerchieves (or table napkins), and hang them in groups on the wall.

real candles in
candelabra and sconces

Regency column
and bust

wood glued
to produce
'gothic' shape

pediment is
actually hardboard

inexpensive
muslin curtain
with quality trim

'lace' is
cut out
paper

dado panelling,
door and cabinet
(inset) painted
for 'oak graining'
effect

Regency
fire-screen

genuine Regency
table and chairs

*A graceful Regency dining room in
which period features, such as the
dado, with its 'faux bois' oak-grained
treatment, have been restored for effect.
The candle-lit candelabra and chairs
are genuine but the curtains and
skirting board heating are welcome
modern introductions. The equally
modern cabinet (inset) is ingeniously
aged with paper 'lace' and a hardboard
pediment.*

DINING ROOMS

Above: Terracotta-coloured painted boards in this dining room make a spectacular background for part of a collection of blue and white china. There is more of it on the table which is given additional emphasis by the blue and white chair covers. Note too, the interesting barley-sugar twist candlesticks and the old chest. The russet colour is the perfect complement to the blue/white scheme.

Right: Everything about this dining room – the high skirtings, dark-blue walls and curtains, the magnificent black, gold and white dining suite – is redolent of a past elegance.

● Collect old kitchen equipment– bread boards, copper pans, jelly moulds–and hang them on the walls.

● Put up a pin board and start a collection of cards from restaurants. Each time you visit a new eating place, pick up a card, write your verdict on the back, and pin it on the board for future reference.

● Display your children's art lesson masterpieces round the room–it will encourage and gratify them and will certainly provide talking points.

● Certain collections–Mickey Mouse ephemera or period memorabilia need a range of different treatments to display them to their best advantage: dot pictures and plaques round the wall, arrange toys and crockery on shelves, lay rugs on the floor. Even the table setting can be part of the collection.

● Collect something that you can actually use: a collection of cruets is both amusing and practical; give each guest a different set to use.

Whatever your collection, display it thoughtfully. Try to give pride of place to one prized item: maybe the most valuable, or the most spectacular, perhaps the very *first* of your collection, or the one that was a special gift or heirloom.

Position it in the centre of the mantelpiece, stand it on a shelf on its own, shine a spotlight on to it, or hang it on an empty wall where it will attract attention.

Clever lighting can make all the difference to the look of a collection, drawing attention to it and showing it off to its best advantage at the same time. The kind of fixtures that are best for this sort of accent lighting are the various types of spotlights, wallwashers, pinhole or framing projectors, as well as uplights and candles. If you are lighting a single object, aim to place your fixture so that there is no distracting reflection. You need to experiment, lighting from above, or below or straight on, to see which gives the best effect. Glass shelves are often particularly effective, especially when set in a mirrored alcove, and lit from above or below, or both.

Above: Almost everything else is subjugated to the neatly arranged collection of art in this dining room where both decor and furniture are firmly restrained. The long glass table is dramatic but not distracting and the only other colours are in the plant life and the mahogany-finish arched door frame. Note too, how everything in the room–table, chairs, all the pictures–is framed in steel.

DINING ROOMS

I like to think that one can make provision to eat almost anywhere in the home, just as one should be able to move small tables about to different parts of the garden. It is obviously nice to be able to eat in the kitchen or in the living room. But why not the hall for a change? The bedroom for a breakfast *à deux* or cosy supper? All you need is a table and chairs that do not look out of place in whatever room they are put – though, of course, folding varieties of both can be brought out for the occasion.

In any case, in any home where space is at a premium, you have to learn to use that space for all it's worth. If you do not have the luxury of a dining room used just for dining – and most of us do not, the trick is to make your dining table look as if it is not a dining table most of the time. And that means that you do not have a table surrounded by chairs – except, of course, when you are actually going to use it for eating. For example, if you use what was the dining room for a work room/study as well, you should either have a round table which can be piled with books when necessary, a table set off-centre, or a drop-leaf table that can be pulled out and set up in the centre of the room as required. All of them can then double as a desk, homework table, sewing or drawing table.

Another great aid to any part-time dining area is the trolley or serving cart which makes a valuable link betwen kitchen and eating area, is useful for transportation of food and dishes, and in addition provides storage and an extra serving surface.

The problem of where to put all those extra chairs is not really so very difficult. There are several solutions. For example in a flat or apartment, you could buy chairs that would act as occasional chairs; have them covered in the sort of colour that will go in every room and they can then be distributed throughout the flat and brought together as and when needed. Alternatively, buy folding chairs that could either be put away in, say, a hall cupboard and taken out when needed, or hung on a wall. The clear perspex or plexiglass variety take very little visual space since you can look right through them and the brightly coloured wooden varieties are a decoration in themselves.

Left: With the use of attractive matching furniture and well-displayed ornaments, a corner of a living room can easily be transformed into a pleasant dining area, as in the room on the left. While white dining table and chairs blend happily into this chunky white living room, right, with its dividing chimney breast.

DINING ROOMS

Dining/guest rooms

Much the same suggestions can apply to a room that also acts as part-time guest room. Here, of course, you will also need to make provision for a bed and clothes storage. The bed could either be a sofa bed or a studio couch with, perhaps, extra drawers underneath, or, in a smaller room, an armchair that transforms itself into a bed. The bed/storage area could be neatly screened off with matchstick blinds.

If at all possible, you should provide a wardrobe either by having a wall of storage with shelves, drawers and cupboards to take both dining accessories and clothes, or by having a separate armoire or old wardrobe (which can also take silver, china, glass etc.). And there is almost no limit to the ways you can reorganize the space in some of those old Victorian and Edwardian wardrobes that can still be found. Even with dire shortage of cash and space, hooks fixed on the back of the door will take an overnight clothes hanger or two.

If you wanted to make the room seem more like a bedroom/sitting room than a study/library/dining room that will also accommodate a guest, you could make much more of the sofa bed and have a rectangular or drop-leaf table like a sofa table behind it. This can then be pulled out and opened out as the occasion demands.

Living/dining rooms

This is a pretty usual arrangement nowadays, and again the trick is to disguise the dining table when not in use for dining. Round tables and drop-leafs can be bought to act as library tables and sofa tables as described above, or there are large adjustable coffee and cocktail tables which can be raised to dining or lowered to coffee table height as desired.

Table tops can also be concealed within a storage wall in much the same way as fold-up beds, so that the leaf can be pulled down when wanted and shut up later to look like a piece of smooth wall. Or, more ingeniously, the underside can be mirrored so that when it is flipped up it will look for all the world like a large looking glass.

Obviously, tables can be a visible part of a storage wall, acting as either a desk or for dining, and some of them have an extendable top so that they can be pulled right out when you have company.

If you have a dining alcove in your living room you could make the division more complete by building a low storage wall of shelves or cupboards with plenty of room inside for all your dining equipment and serving space on top. Or you could line the walls with bookshelves from waist-level, with cupboards underneath to provide storage and serving space.

Alcoves like this can also be treated like separate small rooms and lined with mirror; or with the curtain or shade fabric; or painted or papered in a colour from the room scheme which is at the same time different from the main walls. Any cloths used on the table could be made from the same fabric as the main room curtains or upholstery.

Above: In this living room the round table under the large pine mirror is perfect for dining and looks just as good when it is not laid for a meal. The handsome 19th century chairs can be used as occasional seating in other parts of the room.

Right: A kitchen/dining room with a distinctly country feel.

DINING ROOMS

If the alcove is very narrow, use an upholstered bench with suspended cushions for back rests on one side of the table and chairs on the other.

If the style of the main room will take it, a dining alcove can sometimes be semi-curtained off as in a box at the theatre or in one of those titillating little areas off famous turn-of-the-century Paris restaurants used for discreet entertaining.

When there is no separate alcove or eating area allowed for, a distinct dining place can be made by raising a table on a plywood platform at whatever height is preferred. Again, it can be separated a little from the mainstream area with a low wall of cupboards and shelves, or, providing the main area is big enough, a high wall of shelves.

If, of course, the room is quite big, all sorts of divider devices can be used to partition off a dining area, from screens of one sort or another to large indoor plants or trees.

Another good solution for dining if the room will take it, is a long old refectory table which, like the library table idea, can be used for piling books and magazines on, for displaying flowers and objects and to provide both work and eating surfaces.

Dining halls

A nice wide hall is a natural for dining, and again, the table should be an object in its own right, in use for

Left: The dark gate-legged table at the dining end of this all-white living room looks just as charming devoid of chairs, which can be easily folded away when not in use.

Top right: A spacious kitchen/diner where elegance and practicality are combined in slate-grey melamine table tops and work surfaces. The position of the table and matching overhead lamp act as a natural division from the working area. However, when not used for eating, the table could just as easily serve as extra worktop.

Bottom right: Landings, if they're a reasonable size and shape, can make good dining areas too. This space, somewhat exotically divided from the living area by what looks like a christening font, makes a very pleasant place for eating, for sitting chatting or even for playing cards.

Far right: Sometimes, squeezing in dining space is more a matter of courage than anything else. One could hardly imagine a table for six in this tiny bedsitting room (the bed is up the other end), but it works. And pushed against the wall when not in use for dining, the table makes an excellent desk/work surface as well.

DINING ROOMS

display and general dumping space when not in use for eating. If you are lucky enough to have full length cupboards in the hallway, they can easily be reorganized to take china, cutlery, glass and linen and maybe even a trolley or serving cart.

Small tables for two can make very good use of the wasted space at the end of a corridor. Good lighting, a picture or two or a rug fixed to the end wall will give a whole new lease of life to what could have been a boring dead end.

Dining/kitchens

There is no doubt that eating in the kitchen has an attraction all its own. It is more informal, warmer some-how (both in fact as well as in atmosphere), and, naturally, there is no feeling of separation from the action or the cook, for whom, of course, it is also more practical. Many more dishes can be made that go direct from stove to table than could ever be produced for a separate dining room or area.

It's important to have enough space and a well-thought out ar-rangement that allows both eating and cooking to take place without the one interfering with the other. The cook needs room to get at the cooker, sink and cupboards without hindrance and to move around the kitchen comfortably. Lots of work-tops and dumping space is essential. It's more pleasant for the diners too

if the cooking paraphernalia – dirty pans and plates – can be kept out of sight

So if the kitchen is large enough to take any sort of eating surface – even if it is only an extension of a counter top to make a breakfast and supper bar, this is obviously a bonus. If

breakfast is a cut-and-run meal then a bar counter is a good idea and a nice compromise between setting a proper table and snatching a cup of coffee on the wing. And children enjoy perching on stools. But you still have to decide whether you want to make a kitchen you can eat

There is a very clever use of space in this kitchen-dining-family room. The central green tiled island unit, here laid for supper, acts as dining table and is also the main work surface. Every surface is used for cupboard space including the area over the island unit as well as beneath it.

The right setting for the right room. A round, skirted table makes a pleasant place for breakfast (and supper, too) by the window seat in a country bedroom, top, far left. Flowers, candles and matching tablecloths and chairs, bottom, far left, all make for a pretty, yet elegant setting, while the table's glass top adds a note of practicality. A stained glass window offers a dramatic backdrop for the stylish, coordinated table setting in the room top left. The whole is offset perfectly by the patterned plates on the walls. Once candles are lit the table becomes an oasis, as here in the room shown bottom left. Wherever there is space for a table and chairs there is space for a dining area. The landing below, by the French doors, makes a pretty indoor/outdoor dining space.

Above: The dining area counter top of this apricot and white room acts as a kind of visual partition.

Left: Two differently coloured rugs over a polished wood floor provide the necessary visual separation in this living/dining room. The sharp change in furniture style – comfortable, upholstered sofa and easy chair and clean-lined dining furniture – strengthen the duality of the setting. Light turquoise colouring, however, picked out on the dining chair rails, skirting, and window frames, as well as in some of the room's ornaments, helps provide a unifying framework.

Right: An uncluttered yet hard-working living-dining area in an attic room.

in, or an eating place which is also the kitchen. There is quite a difference.

Either way, you will probably want to put more emphasis on decoration than you would do normally. You could, for example, divide the table area off from the working area with a storage/serving wall or the sort of peninsular unit described on pages 107 and 116. Or install some sort of screen, dividing panel, a blind that lets down from the ceiling, and even a stack of wine racks which would make a substantial and permanent wall in themselves. You could too, choose rather different wall treatments for the dining part: flame-proofed fabric; wallpaper, a warm, dark paint, and add pictures, prints, objects, favourite collections, bookshelves, anything that emphasises that the space is as much for living as for working in.

Use pretty table cloths and napkins. Go for well-designed china that delights the eye and sets off the food. Pay attention to plants and flowers and make sure that you have your lighting on dimmer switches so that you can dim it right down for dining as well as drawing a veil over any kitchen clutter.

In fact, if you always bear in mind that once a table is set for dining, lights lowered, candles lit, that table becomes an oasis, complete in itself, you can make a dining room wherever the table is.

STUDIES AND HOME OFFICES

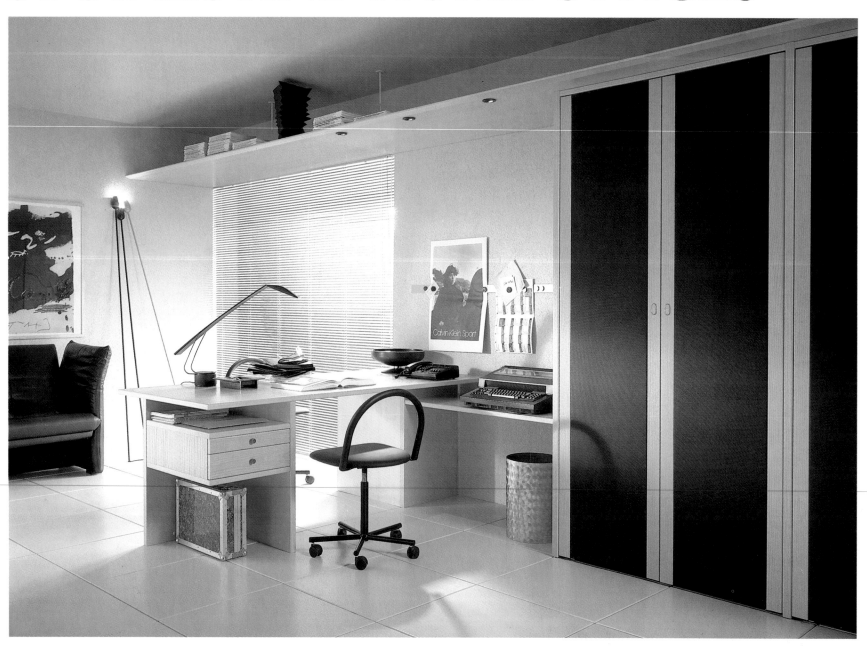

INTRODUCTION

Work spaces in the home are known by a number of names, being referred to variously as libraries, studies, dens, or simply home offices. Over the years these rooms have taken many forms, but all have their roots in what began as the hallowed eighteenth-century library. Before the advent of the shelf-lined library, people kept what books they had in closets, and presumably spent their quiet reading and contemplative moments in the bedroom, smaller sitting rooms, withdrawing rooms or boudoirs that abounded in grand houses. (The less fortunate, who lived in smaller houses and were trying to scratch out a living did not have too much time for reading and writing, nor was there much light for these pursuits after dark.) But as books and professions proliferated, and a reasonable standard of living began to be enjoyed by the professional and middle classes as well as by the aristocracy and the upper echelons of the church, libraries became increasingly popular, reaching their peak in the eighteenth century.

Already by the first quarter of the nineteenth century, however, the library had lost its hallowed, studious status and had become much more of a family room, where the occupants of the household played cards, charades and other games, listened to music and generally entertained themselves in a more relaxed manner than in the rather more formal drawing room. Thus the poor master of the house, if he wanted peace and quiet to pursue the gentler occupations of reading, writing, studying and managing the family affairs, was forced to retreat into a smaller, quieter room, which became the study – a room with panelled or warm, dark walls, comforting fires, deeply comfortable leather armchairs, club fenders, and capacious pedestal desks. This was essentially the male preserve – the inner sanctum, whose occupant was rarely disturbed without trepidation, and certainly not before knocking on the door.

In the twentieth century, as more and more houses were built where there simply was not the space – or indeed the need – for a library per se; where such rooms as there were had to become, by necessity, increasingly multi-functional while people's lifestyles became increasingly informal, there was still a need, where possible, for a smaller, more relaxed room which *could* be used as a study but where the family could also listen to music, watch television, relax and even work if needs be. This kind of room – adopted particularly in the United States – became known as the den: less library-ish and study-ish than either of these two rooms, it was nevertheless more casual and relaxed than a sitting or living room.

In the latter part of this century, several events have conspired to produce a new type of room that is yet another variation on the original library theme. Most importantly, perhaps, the advent of the computer and the Fax machine have made it possible for many more people to work from home and link up to head offices. This, together with the exorbitantly high costs of prime office space, and the time and expense of commuting, has made the prospect of working at home seem increasingly attractive – not least amongst working women with families. Thus, the whole concept of home offices has become steadily more popular, whether this be the luxury of an entire room given over to an office, or well-designed adjunct to a living room, dining room, bedroom, hall or corridor, not to mention converted garage, attic and basement space.

This section, while showing one or two good old-fashioned libraries, studies and dens, also offers helpful advice about setting up functional but attractive rooms, or parts of rooms, which will work efficiently as offices without disrupting the home too much.

Left: An uncompromising commitment to hi-tech fashion is the keynote in this office-cum-sitting room. A very practical arrangement and one designed to impress.

STUDIES AND HOME OFFICES

Right: The pull-out work table in the middle of this cheerful kitchen divides cooking and workroom space as well as providing an excellent sewing/writing surface with telephone conveniently to hand. Such bonus workspace means that one can take advantage of lulls in the middle of cooking and preparation to get on with other jobs—or catch up with bills, lists and letters and still keep an eye on the meal. After all, the table could just as well hold a typewriter, or drawing materials or any other working equipment.

Kitchen office

It is very useful to have some sort of desk in the kitchen where you can write lists, pay bills, file receipts, copy recipes, and take messages. There might be some odd space between kitchen base units that you could span to make a desk top, or you might add a swing-up flap at the end of a worktop which can be raised and lowered as required. Another alternative is to widen or deepen a counter top so that you can sit at it with a stool; or you can convert a drawer to a small pull-out work counter/worktop that doubles as a cutting board by fitting a block of wood on top which you can draw out and sit at.

Think about the benefits of a kitchen telephone installed on or near the improvised desk top within, if possible, easy reach of the stove. It is infuriating to have to run and answer the telephone when you are in the middle of preparing some intricate sauce or dish. To have a phone within arm's length of the cook top makes a world of difference to your general convenience so see that any kitchen phone has either a long cord or is a cordless type.

This kitchen/dining room, with its useful draughtsman-like table and mobile chairs, works equally efficiently as an office. Altogether a practical, useful room.

STUDIES AND HOME OFFICES

Guest room/Studies

If you are lucky enough to have a lot of books and the space for a proper library or study you should obviously take advantage of them, only bear in mind that since at one time or another there's bound to be an overflow of guests, it is probably a good idea to instal a sofa bed rather than an ordinary sofa, so that the room can occasionally double as a guest room. If your study is too small to fit in a double-size sofa bed, you could consider investing in a small 'daybed' style sofa, or a chair that converts into a single bed.

This being the case, you might also think of other simple conveniences such as putting a couple of brass hooks on the back of the door to take the odd coat hanger when necessary, and checking that there are some drawers or shelves available for guests' clothes – perhaps in a desk, secretaire or bureau-bookcase, a chest of drawers, or even extra shelves in cupboards that are under bookshelves.

It is also advisable to have a good reading light by the sofa which is positioned in such a way that it's equally useful for anyone wanting to read when the sofa is being used as a bed.

This study area, with its warm wood fitted units, is tucked into unused space under a mezzanine gallery in a double height living room.

Above: A traditional wooden roll-top desk is a good choice for a living room as its lid can be closed on clutter when visitors call.

Right: The area under a bedroom window has been fitted out as a small study space. The desk unit could double as a dressing table.

STUDIES AND HOME OFFICES

Dining-Room/Studies

If you cannot set aside an entire room for a library or study, don't despair – you may well be able to use part of another oom for this purpose. If, like many people, you use the dining room for a workroom/study as well, buy a round table which can be piled with books when necessary, a table set off-centre, or a drop leaf table that can be pulled out and set up for dining as required. All of these can double as a desk, homework table, sewing, games or dining surface. Bookshelves with cupboards underneath can take china, glass, cutlery and table linen as well as files, stationery, and normal workroom apparatus. It's just a question of organization.

Books and book-shelves are an integral part of most studies and book-lined walls will give a particularly nice feeling to a dining room. If you have cupboards below the shelves from waist height down, make sure that the top of the cupboard part is about twice as deep as the shelves above. That way you will have a ready-made serving area for meals.

If you have a lot of books bear this in mind when painting or papering blank walls. On the whole, brightly coloured book jackets will look best against plain, restful paint colours, or dense tone on tone papers. Plum colours, damson, aubergine, dark greens and blues, bluey-greens, rusts, terracottas, apricots, nutmeg or chocolate browns are all particularly effective.

Shelving and storage

Bookshelves themselves look good in woods that are natural, stained or grained to look like mahogany, oak or pine. Or they can be painted – either in the same colour as the walls, or in a contrasting colour such as white. Shelves can be custom-built and cover a wall, or walls, completely, even framing sofas or stretching around the tops of doors and windows. This will give a good sense of depth and perspective to the room – the eye is automatically drawn through to the view beyond the window when windows appear to be recessed.

Alternatively, the shelves can be part of modern wall systems which include built-in desks, cupboard units, bars, refrigerators, space for TV, video cassette recorders, stereo systems, records, tapes, discs and all sorts of other storage units. Further storage can be provided by desk drawers, cupboards under bookshelves, bureau-bookcases, secretaires or armoires without having to resort to office-like filing cabinets.

A glass-walled conservatory has been turned into a successful study. The Roman blinds at the windows are very necessary to shield the sun's glare.

Floors and windows

These can be much the same as in your sitting room, the deciding factors being personal preference and budget. For flooring, carpets and matting, with or without rugs, and plain, polished or painted floorboards with rugs are all possibilities. Windows surrounded by books will look best hung with Roman or roller blinds or shades. Otherwise they can be curtained or draped in whatever style seems to best suit the room. Long curtains can offer a useful way of concealing additional, unsightly storage shelves.

Lighting

Bear in mind that lighting will have to serve for all uses of the room, not just its time as a study. You will probably have to buy more lights than for a single-purpose room. If there is a desk in the room, there should be a good, adjustable desk lamp. A halogen-type fitting can be expensive, but will provide longer-lasting light than standard fitments.

Any seating, whether sofa, sofa bed, or armchair, should have a good lamp at the right height for easy reading – in other words, so that it can shine *down* on to a book from over either the left or the right shoulder. In general, lighting should take the form of table lamps set on small side tables, or adjustable floor lamps, provided with three-way switches or dimmer switches to vary the intensity of the light.

Shelves can be lit by wall-washers or downlights recessed into the ceiling about 75 cm (2 ft 6 in) out from the wall so that they graze the shelves with light, or, if recessing is impossible, by surface-mounted lights positioned in the same way. Alternatively, you can set downlights into an overhanging top moulding – again so that they graze the shelves under them – or set ministrips of light under each shelf to light the shelves beneath. For a more dramatic effect, try setting lighting in corners and at the bottom of banks of shelves to cast light upwards.

Although the large room above and right has been completely devoted to office use, it retains a homely feel – largely because of the soft floral blinds, comfortable sofa and the addition of ornaments and plants.

Left: A high tech wire desk works surprisingly well in a pastel bedroom as its light lines suit the soft, delicate scheme.

STUDIES AND HOME OFFICES

Home offices

Unless you happen to have a large home with spare room to make into a work space, finding the actual square footage for a home office may seem something of a challenge. This is not an insurmountable problem, however, for it's almost always possible to borrow space from existing rooms without destroying their character and original purpose. You can take a sliver off the sitting room, family room, kitchen or master bedroom, for example. Or you can make an all-purpose dining or guest room office. You might also be able to convert an attic, basement or garage space.

If, for any reason, you cannot do any of these things, there are still several possibilities for useful work spaces, such as, say, the area under the stairs, a bay window, a wardrobe or closet with the doors removed, or part of a corridor, landing or hallway.

To accommodate all these kinds of spaces, built-in modular furniture manufacturers are producing increasingly ingenious designs, such as the Murphy bed with folds up and away behind neat doors when not needed. There are also all sorts of work surfaces and desk tops that slide out from wall units, or fold down to reveal computers complete with accessories from modem to mouse. When shelves and tops are

pushed in or up, walls seem merely panelled, making these systems ideal for living rooms, family rooms, dining rooms and bedrooms. One moment the area is definitely a fully functioning work space, the next all is calm, serene and uncluttered.

Knowing what you need

Once you have decided where to put your work space – whatever its size – knowing *exactly* what you need is more than half the battle, particularly where equipment is concerned. The other important consideration, of course, is having the money to do it all, which means deciding on a firm budget so that you can work out what you can afford.

Evaluating your space

Before making a shopping list of your requirements, evaluate your chosen space by asking yourself the following questions:

● Does the space need remodelling or any sort of conversion? (For example, will any partition walls have to be put up or dismantled? Will you need any insulation/sound-proofing?)

● Are you planning to convert an attic, basement or garage? (If so, you will almost certainly need to insulate walls, create new windows,

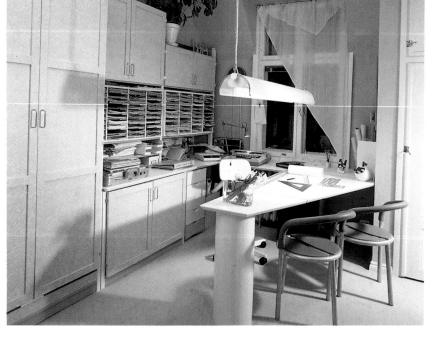

a good ventilation system, re-wire or improve the existing electrical system, put down new flooring, arrange heating/air conditioning.) If doing any structural work you must check with your local building inspector about building codes and requirements.

● Do you need to put in a phone jack in order to have a telephone on your desk? Will you need two lines or more? Will you need any separate lines for a Fax machine or modem? Have you space for an answering machine? Have you a convenient socket for it?

● Do you need to upgrade your electric circuit to accommodate new electronic machinery?

● Will you be using a computer? (In which case you will need anti-static flooring – at least around your desk/computer area, and plenty of sockets to plug in VDU, printer etc.).

● What condition is the lighting in? Will it need many changes? (You will obviously need good desk lighting and, if the space is large enough to entertain visitors, subtle background or general lighting.)

● What condition is the ventilation in? (This might well need attention if you are planning to convert a closet or wardrobe space, or the area under the stairs.)

● Will the space need re-decorating or decorating from scratch?

● Is there room for any special needs like storing plans, blueprints, fabric and paper samples, back numbers of magazines?

● Will there be a need (or the space) for a conference table and chairs? Or even a second chair?

For many of these factors you will need professional help of one sort of another (electrician, architect, telephone engineer). This help should be chosen, and estimates received for the work at the start of the project.

Opposite left: This home office is built into one corner of a large kitchen, using units that match the fitted cupboards. Fluorescent lighting (use daylight balanced tubes) over the work surface provides strong, even light.

Right: Converting the loft space is a very practical solution if you have no spare room elsewhere in your home. You should gain enough space for a desk, plenty of bookshelves and storage, and a seating area, as here.

STUDIES AND HOME OFFICES

Planning out a full-scale office

If you choose to employ an architect or designer, he or she will organize and supervise the whole project, including employing workmen and suggesting equipment. If, however, you decide to plan a full scale office – or even a dual-purpose room – by yourself, it's a good idea to draw out a scale plan, however small the area, since every inch will count. (Directions for drawing up plans are given on p.17).

Planning the most efficient arrangement of your desk, storage cabinets, and equipment in relation to fixtures like windows, doors and electric outlets, will be easier if you draw up elevations and floor plans (see p.17). They needn't be very professional – just good enough to give you a realistic idea of proportions. Once you have done this, you will have your chosen area all mapped out and ready to include your selection of units and equipment.

Next you must work out what will fit in the space you have allotted. To do this, first decide what would suit you best and then work backwards from there. You will, for example, almost certainly have to do a lot, if not all, of the following: telephoning, typing, writing, drawing, and computer keyboard operating. This means you will need a large desk and probably extra surfaces for a typewriter and answering machine, as well. You will also need

filing cabinets and storage space for stationery, etc., and possibly a printer, copier and/or Fax machine, and recording equipment. You may also need a conference table – or at least extra chairs for meetings – and perhaps, if there's room, a sofa, coffee and side tables.

Bearing all this in mind, your first priority might be the position of the telephone. If you're right-handed, make sure the telephone is on your left – that way the cord won't get in the way as you jot down information and notes. If you're left-handed, the opposite will apply. If you use a good deal of electronic equipment, you will need easy access to the various outlets and switches. You will not, however, want an obvious network of cords and cables, so ensure that they are hidden behind furniture as much as possible.

If you do need quite a lot of equipment, it is a good idea to make scale cut-outs of each piece and move them around your plan, as well as drawing up various alternative arrangements in elevation. You can also simulate arrangments *in situ* with old cardboard boxes, string, chalk or whatever comes to mind. Sit where you think would be most practical and comfortable; reach for handy file drawers, swing around to work at your keyboard, get up and go to where storage cabinets will be placed. In short, act out your work-

ing day until you find the best layout possible. Once you are satisfied, you can then proceed with getting all the electrical, telephone outlets and jacks in position, and can plan the framework of the room before finalizing the rest of the decor – lighting, heating, flooring, furniture, equipment, storage, window treatments, wall coverings, paintwork.

This modular furniture provides very efficient storage and work space in a study. A high level shelf holds little used books, saving space at eye level. Neutral colours are used to create a restful work environment, indoor plants provide a softening touch of green, and framed prints enliven a blank section of wall.

Lighting

Home offices need special attention with regard to lighting, in particular ambient lighting. It is very important to avoid a high contrast between your work area and its surroundings, particularly, for example, between the room and the computer screen. You should also avoid glare when using a computer, since this will detract from the visibility of the screen. All ambient lighting, therefore, should be controllable by dimmer switches, and all natural light (from windows) by blinds and shades.

Décor

One of the good things about having an office at home is that you can do away with the more subdued conventional ideas about office décor and do exactly what you want in terms of colours and style. It is a good idea, however, to keep the general décor of your home in mind, as well as upkeep, practicality and safety. And, of course, if your office is actually in part of another room, it is essential to keep to the same colours and general feel of the rest of the room.

Floors

Practicality and sound-proofing are the most important factors to bear in mind when choosing floor coverings, particularly where computers are concerned. Sound-deadening materials include carpet, vinyl and rubber tiles. Industrial rubber tiles have another advantage – used under and around a computer area they will prevent static. In the rest of the area you should think about having carpeting if you're expecting to meet a lot of clients in your office (though this will still not prevent you from installing rubber tiles around the computer area). Rugs are not so practical if there is likely to be a lot of traffic.

Windows

It is important to prevent daytime glare from windows, so whatever else you choose for window treatments, try to always use some form of see-through shades, blinds or shutters as well, so that you can control the amount of daylight at will. It is not a good idea to have long trailing curtains unless you are working in a bay window which is part of the main living room, dining room or bedroom.

Venetian blinds are very practical as you can alter the amount of light entering the room quite subtly, letting light in without glare.

A large table is ideal for art or design work, and vinyl flooring is a most practical choice. However simple your requirements, a good desk lamp and a bin for waste are essential accessories. This kind of minimal scheme won't suit everyone as it calls for a tidy owner.

STUDIES AND HOME OFFICES

Choosing your equipment

The range of office furnishings now available is enormous. Particularly versatile are the modular wall systems, where desk tops and work surfaces drop down and pull out to reveal computer stations and general storage and where you can even be provided with a pull-down Murphy bed as well. All these systems work like neat building blocks, and can be used in a number of configurations according to requirements and space available. Some retailers will even tailor a system according to your specific needs. One huge advantage of these systems is that they can be easily dismantled, should you decide to move house.

Computer work centres

Computer work centres are extremely useful in that they provide safe storage and easy access. Several types are available. The *roll-around table* type has a slide-out shelf that takes the keyboard, while the monitor sits above. It can be moved around within the limits of the electric cables. The *cabinet on castors* type with pull-down lid and cabinet door is particularly good for small spaces, since both the keyboard and printer can be slid out for use, then back for storage. *Stationary work centres* are large corner units that are L-shaped to give generous wall space. They have a triangular inset, and the smaller unit holds the printer. *Stan-*dard computer desks are smaller, more compact units. All are some 60 cm to 67.5 cm (24 in to 27 in) above the ground, which is considered the best height for working.

Desks

The standard desk height is 72.5 cm (29 in). The top can be anything from 1.5 m × 45.5 cm to 1.8 m × 91 cm (5 ft × 1 ft 6 in to 6 ft × 3 ft). Antique pieces and writing tables may be slightly higher or lower, but this won't present a problem – a good, height-adjustable desk chair should be able to accommodate to any height. It is usually more comfortable to type at a slightly lower level than the best height for writing, say 60–67.5 cm (24–27 in), the same as the recommended height for a computer keyboard.

As with computer centres, the range of desks available is extensive. *Working office desks* (as opposed to the more elegant variety chosen for a study, library, den or living room) have a right or left hand projection or return to accommodate a typewriter. The old style *roll top desk* and flat or slant-front bureaux look particularly splendid. The rolltop variety *can* be adapted, if large enough, to take a computer, etc. though they are used mainly for writing, being too high for typing. Their main advantage is their elegance and the fact that you can shut papers and

any mess away. *Glass top desks* look sleek and elegant but you have to be well organized and have a good deal of convenient storage space nearby, or not mind a mess. You will obviously need a separate computer centre and typing table with such a desk.

Filing cabinet desks. Cheaper desks can be made by simply laying a sturdy wood or plastic veneered top over suitably placed filing cabinets, thus saving space on storage as well.

Chairs

For many people, 75 per cent of a typical working day is spent sitting in an office chair, so it is very im-portant to buy the right one. The prime requirements of a work chair are that it should be *comfortable, mobile, flexible* and that it should provide *good support*. The ideal desk chair should move with you when you turn to type or use your computer (swivel chairs with castors are perfect). It should also support you as you lean forwards or back and should have a height-adjustable seat. Make sure that whatever you choose fits in with your desk.

If you do a lot of typing you should avoid chairs with arms as they can get in the way. An alternative chair made especially for back sufferers, is the Norwegian Balans

Opposite left: This L-shaped unit is purpose-designed for working with today's home computers. There is ample worktop for VDU, keyboard, printer and mouse, and plenty of storage space for computer and stationery supplies.

Above: A modern version of the traditional roll-top desk, ideal for a dual-purpose room.

Right: Here, storage is built into an alcove, and an ordinary table serves as a worksurface. A rubber mat protects the polished surface.

Making a pin-board

One of the simplest ways to make a pin-board is to buy a cork bath mat and mount it on the wall. For a more substantial board, fix unsealed cork tiles to the wall, and surround them with beading or picture framing (architraving to

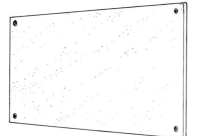

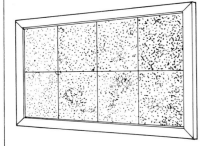

match your door surrounds is a neat solution), mitring the corners for a neat finish.

For a fabric-covered board, use coloured felt to cover a piece of softboard, wrapping excess fabric over the edges and glueing it to the back. Mount the board on the wall, using round-headed screws.

chair. With this, you sit on a seat that tilts your torso slightly forward and you rest your knees on cushions below. This eases pressure on the back even without any structural back support, since it keeps the spine straight and free from strain.

Storage and shelving

Whether you are using a whole room, or part of one, try to fit in the maximum amount of storage, otherwise your office will soon become a morass of papers, unanswered mail and stationery supplies. Obviously, an easily accessible filing system that enables papers and correspondence to be kept in some kind of logical order should be

a number one priority. There are many systems to choose from. *Standard filing cabinets* come with drawers arranged either vertically (most common) or laterally. Depths range from 35 to 62.5 cm (14–25 in) and the height will depend on the number of drawers. *Roll-out vertical filing cabinets* are useful for stashing under desks or counter tops. *Lateral filing cabinets* have an average depth of 47.5 cm (19 in), vary in width from 75.5 cm to 105 cm (30–42 in), and usually come in tiers of two or three drawers. Although they take up more space than vertical cabinets they can also be stashed one on top of each other to make useful room dividers – a particularly good idea in cases where an office is shared with

another room (though only one drawer should be opened at a time if you don't want the whole edifice to topple over).

Flat, horizontal filing cabinets

have deep, wide but narrow drawers. They are often used by architects and designers for drawings and blueprints.

Again, however small the space, you will almost certainly need some sort of shelving for reference books, telephone directories, etc.

Furniture for a home office can be simple or sumptuous in style. Above: A few planks of pine, a clip-on spotlight and cane chair have turned a bedroom corner into an occasional office for tackling home paperwork. Right: Altogether more grand, this antique desk and chair are the perfect partners for the solid mahogany bookshelves behind them.

CHILDREN'S ROOMS

INTRODUCTION

Planning a child's room may sound an easy enough thing to do. First-time parents can dwell romantically on such thoughts as cribs hung with sprigged muslin, nursery teas by a glowing fire, shafts of morning sunlight and a general happy-ever-after feeling. There's no harm in dreaming, but these ideas have to be juggled with practicalities, such as space available, cash in the bank and the fact that the babe in the cot is going to grow up, sooner rather than later. Between the baby in the crib and the teenager with the computer game there are going to be several major changes and stages, each of which is going to make very different demands on that room, and all of which will be upon you before you can make major plans to redecorate every time.

Children's rooms present more of a forward planning exercise than just about any other room in the house except for the kitchen. And so they should. After all, if you are hoping to make the space look good, and serve a useful purpose over the maximum number of years for the minimum expenditure, you're asking a lot and you won't achieve it without first giving very careful consideration to the problems involved.

Right at the beginning you must think far ahead and plan for modifications to be made over the years: how cribs must give way to cots, cots to beds, toy cupboards to wardrobes, play surfaces to desks. You can't anticipate every detail of games or electronic equipment that may be wanted in ten year's time, but you can ensure a degree of flexibility in the space they will occupy.

So, before you go overboard for that miniature paradise, stop and think. There are lots of ways to accommodate the necessary altera-tions over the years, to keep up with your children's progress and avoid having to discard too much of your original investment. That's what this chapter is all about.

The choice of decorative schemes for a child's room can be another stumbling block to parents who are concerned about the possible effect – good or bad – on their offspring. So much is written about the importance of environment to a growing child, the necessity for a stimulating background or a restful one, that some parents are afraid of making a terrible mistake over colours and furnishings. How can you make a room that is fun by day and calming by night? How can you create the sort of room that will help children to develop their creative abilities, give them all the stimulation they need, and still leave room for them to add their own stamp when they are ready for it? How can you be certain that everything you have chosen is safe? That there are no hidden pitfalls and traps? Above all, how can you avoid making mistakes when there is little money or time to set them right?

The purpose of this section is to reassure and inspire: not to promise miracles but to show good ideas at work and explain how they were achieved. There is no blueprint for the ideal children's room but there is plenty of good, practical advice that you can profit by and any amount of options to choose from. All of them are aimed at giving you some measure of confidence, for that is the most important element that you can bring to any sort of decoration. With confidence, you can plan a sensible, adaptable framework that can be dressed up or played down – a room that will successfully serve both you and your children for many years to come.

This warm and welcoming room provides the perfect environment for a child's early years. Bright primary colours provide an exciting stimulus for young, inquiring minds, and shelves and a chest provide ample room for storing and displaying favourite toys and possessions. The flooring is warm and safe, and the floor area suitably large for playing in.

The old-fashioned nursery had the right basic ideas. It was essentially a room given over to children for which most parents were content to provide, if they could, a well-ventilated space with somewhere to sleep, plenty of floor/play space, somewhere to sit, some sort of games, drawing, work surface and reasonable storage.

In a sense this sort of framework is still in force today – but with some big differences. First, many of the clever and colourful ideas produced for nursery and primary schools to provide intellectual stimulus for their pupils have begun to trickle back into the home in the form of educational playthings, body-building structures and early learning apparatus. And second, children today belong to a technologically sophisticated generation where the computer is becoming as commonplace as the television, and where audio-visual equipment replaces building bricks and snakes and ladders almost as a matter of course. As children grow older, the demand for computers, video games and similar hardware will increase. It is important to provide adaptable shelving and storage and to allow plenty of space.

This means that any forward planning at the infant stage should involve thinking at least about the probability of having to make room for such things. While it is impossi-ble to project several years ahead and visualize exactly what amazing new inventions are going to invade our lives, let alone what size and shape they are going to be or hor many extra electric points and out-lets they'll need, what you *can* do is think in terms of flexible arrange-ments in the home.

Parents of young infants will find it difficult to imagine anything at all beyond the immediate world of nappies and feeds, cots and baths. But this stage doesn't last for ever and if that's all they've planned for, they'll find the room soon out-grown and unsuitable for the next stage in their children's lives. The time, money and effort spent on creating a room the children don't want to use will be wasted.

So, when you are faced with this empty room that you want to take care of your children's needs for the next eighteen years, remember, as you make your plans, that adapta-bility is the name of the game.

The perfect teenager hideaway, left. The effect has been created by using an existing workbench as a dressing table, the shelves above it provide storage space, and the bright scatter cushions and a plain duvet cover turn the bed into a sofa when friends visit.

A trompe l'oeil window is fun in a small kid's space, right.

CHILDREN'S ROOMS

Clear contours, adequate storage, good lighting, sturdy flooring – these are the major considerations in any child's room. *Above left: Shelves and hanging space are useful for toys and sports gear. When the child is older it could easily be used for clothes. Above: In this pretty room a built-in unit under the bed is used for storing clothes. Far left: Flexible storage and warm colours will look right for many years. Cot can give way to bed later. Left: The abacus under the work surface is perfectly placed for a small child as well as looking decorative.*

Infancy

The first thing to plan in any room that is going to be both bedroom and play space is storage. Children, even babies, have a lot of belongings — toys, clothes and equipment of various kinds — that are going to accumulate with the years. Where are you going to put it all?

For an average, say 4 × 3 metre (12 × 10 ft) room that has no existing cupboards, either build in a full-length double cupboard, floor to ceiling, or buy a sturdy, roomy second-hand wardrobe. It really is false economy to bother with any of those specially built mini cupboards that may look rather sweet but become obsolete in no time at all.

In the very early stages, your basic cupboard/wardrobe can be divided in two. Use one side for hanging space, with perhaps one rail at waist level and either another rail or removable shelves above. These can be removed as the child's clothes get larger and longer. Fit the other side with well-spaced shelves and use it for toy storage; later on it will be useful for sweaters, shirts and a lot of chunky, bulky clothing.

You will also need at least two chests of drawers. Unpainted wooden chests of drawers are inexpensive and perfectly adequate. Set them against the wall leaving a knee-hole space in between (to form an eventual desk/dressing table) and top them with some sort of easily cleanable laminate surface. If these can run along the length of one whole wall so much the better: such an arrangement looks neat and tidy and these are words you are going to be using a lot over the next ten years.

The drawers can be used for nappies, night clothes, underwear, talc and all the other baby necessities in the beginning as well as for an overflow of toys. Later the same drawers will take clothes, toys, games, school work and general clutter.

The long run of work surface along the top of the chests can first be used for changing the baby, then for play (painting, drawing, cutting out) and later still for school work and displaying possessions. The actual chests can be painted, lacquered or otherwise decorated, many times over the years in whatever style happens to be in keeping at the time.

Against the wall behind and above these units it would be a good idea to build a series of shelves or

The same work surfaces that serve so well for changing nappies on, can later be used for playing on and, when the child is older still, they make ideal desks and dressing tables. Here, light grey and white wallpaper and curtains, combined with white furniture and bed linen, help to enlarge visually a relatively small space.

CHILDREN'S ROOMS

shelves and lockers interspersed with pinboards and space for the child's own drawings and the inevitable posters of pop stars. Make sure all drawing pins are out of reach of toddlers.

In the first instance, shelves can hold soft toys later giving way to books, records, files. The pinboard takes progress charts and nursery information to start with and can carry on into school years to provide space for homework timetables and general reminders.

Well planned lighting

The lighting should also be planned at this stage. Begin with simple wall lights on a dimmer switch. These

have two advantages: they can be turned right down at night and the fact that they are built into the wall means that there are no wires or cords for a child to tamper with or trip over. Moreover, this sort of light will be far pleasanter than that given by a central ceiling pendant.

At the same time, at least six other outlets should be provided: two of them above the work surface and the others in corners but placed above a crawling child's reach and safely fitted with shutters.

Simple Venetian blinds at the window will filter the light during the day at rest times — or use roller blinds backed with suitable black-

out material.

Flooring

This completes the background except for the floor covering which is discussed in detail on pages 227–30. At this stage it is enough to stress that the most sensible floors should be hardwearing and easy to clean but not uncomfortable or cold or noisy. Young children spend a lot of time on the floor, sitting, crawling, lying, playing, so the covering is important. Fortunately there are plenty to choose from: planed-down and polyurethaned wood, vinyl-coated cork tiles, cushioned vinyl tiles, linoleum.

If you are going to put rugs on hard floor surfaces, make sure they are held in place with a non-slip backing; on fitted carpet they can be prevented from rucking with strips of Velcro touch-and-close fastening stitched to the back – use only the hooked side of the strip so that it will catch on the carpet tufts or loops.

Free-standing furnishings

When the baby is very small you may want to use a crib or cradle for

him or her to sleep in. These should be abandoned in favour of a cot (which has greater stability) as soon as the child can sit independently – usually at about 5-7 months. A cot should be sturdily built and thoroughly safe, which means making sure that slats are not more than 6 cm (2 ⅜in) apart, that the top rails are an adequate height for protection (i.e. preventing the child falling out even when the side is lowered), that the drop-sides themselves are the sort that cannot be released by a child and that the mattress is firm and a perfect fit so that there are no dangerous gaps between it and the cot sides. Look for the British (or American) Standard when buying a new cot and see page 259.

Apart from the crib or cot you'll need very little furniture. At the infant stage a trolley is a godsend (especially if it has a wheel lock) because it is versatile and moveable. You can wheel it about to have it at your elbow wherever you need it; with a baby on your lap you can't be leaping up and down for things you've forgotten – the furniture has to come to you. Move the trolley by the crib or cot, use it as a stand for a baby bath or scales or general washing kit. Move it into the bathroom at bath time, if that is where you wash the baby.

Another useful item at this stage is a cane or old wooden rocker or other nice capacious chair which

The need to plan for the future has produced this inventive idea for adaptable work surfaces. As the child grows, so the desk top can be raised to an appropriate height. The blue paint gives a sense of unity to the odd assembly of furniture.

will last through all the stages and possibly only need re-cushioning occasionally as opposed to recovering. Do choose one which does not constrict your elbows, to make feeding easier.

Pre-school 2–4

Now the room has to cope with a bigger child who is up and around and into everything.

The window can be left much as it is (with Venetian blinds or blackout backed roller blinds) so that the day does not start too early for parents, daytime resting is made easier and any sun can easily be filtered. However, it is a good idea to fit some vertical bars not more than 6 cm (2⅜ in) apart (which can be removed later) to prevent any unsupervised adventuring and possible accidents. It is essential that these can be easily removed in case of fire. Bars with keys are available.

Because children at this age can't concentrate for long on any one thing they need lots of playthings and you are liable to have a great overflow of toys. Make a home for these in an old wooden chest which could later act as a coffee table, or with tough polyurethane or corrugated cardboard storage boxes which can double as play equipment and become trains, carriages, trolleys or anything the child likes to make them in his imagination. Stacking boxes and trays are also

Above: A trolley is almost indispensable in a baby's room, not only for storing all the necessary paraphernalia, but also for its ability to be moved where it's wanted. Later it can be used to hold a tv, hi-fi or general washing kit for children lucky enough to have their own washbasins.

Right: Totally secure bunk beds for very young children will enable you to sleep better at night too. There is no chance of little bodies rolling on to the floor from great heights here. The fresh pink and blue paint helps to relieve the rather cage-like atmosphere. The same colours are also used for the lights and bed linen.

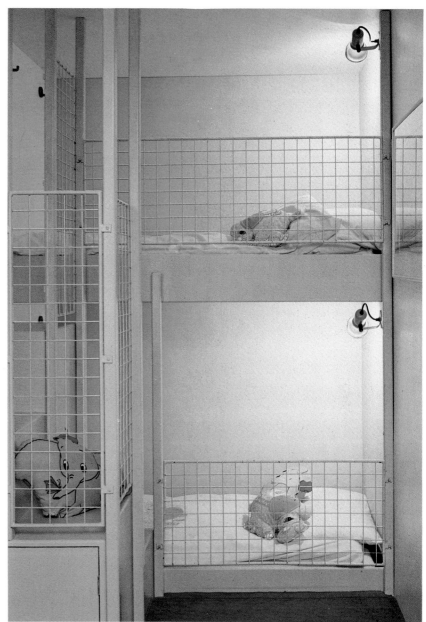

CHILDREN'S ROOMS

good ideas. And, unless there's another baby, the trolley, denuded of all the infant paraphernalia, can also help to cope with all the toys and games. A portable Moses basket or basket carry cot are both useful for storing soft toys. They can also be used for transporting toys into another room, if necessary.

About halfway through this stage the cot can be replaced by a pair of modular bunk beds of the kind that can be dismantled and turned into ordinary single beds. The second bunk will come into play either for a second child or for a friend and provide a two-tiered play area as well. Some bunk beds have a useful drawer underneath for even more storage; buy this kind if you are pressed for space.

School 4–12

Now the second rod can be removed from the wardrobe to leave full-length hanging space. You can dispense with window bars. The play top is going to do double duty as part-time work top so, to ease the transition, add an angled light for homework. A couple of upright chairs can come in at this stage. The pinboard can stay, and the trolley will now become useful for holding models, games, perhaps a tv set or a small home computer to amuse a child and to help with learning.

Teens 12–17

The bunk beds can now be dismantled and turned into two single beds. If space permits, place the beds at right angles to one another and put a small low table between them, to serve both. By day turn the beds into sofas by adding tailored covers, some bolsters and cushions.

The floor may need some attention too: it could be carpeted or covered with matting or painted and stencilled. Or you could simply add one or two rugs.

Window blinds can be changed for a new fabric roller or curtains and walls — decorated to the teenager's wishes.

Teenagers have very much more sophisticated needs than younger children. They will more than likely feel the need to make their room into a bed-sitting room of some kind. Extra seating, in the form of bean bags or floor cushions, is reasonably cheap and always seems popular since it is less formal. Or a spare armchair, if you have the space, makes a comfortable

A vivid, cheerful room, that fulfils all a child's needs. Shelves, chest and skirted area offer plenty of room for toys, there is ample floor space for playing and stacking pine beds offer accommodation for friends. (When not in use the second bed is stored underneath the top one, and its mattress is used as a backrest.) The bars across the windows are a good safety feature, and the brightly chequered squares on the floor might easily provide the basis for a game like hopscotch. Although at present very much designed with a child in mind, it is not difficult to see how this room might, in time, become a sophisticated teenager's bedsit.

place to sit and read. Cover the bed with a fitted cover and scatter cushions to turn it into a sofa by day. If space is short, provide a large kneehole dressing-table which can double as a desk. Otherwise, television sets, cassette players, computers and school books can be placed on the laminated work surface. A more extensive wardrobe, musical and electronic equipment (guitars, synthesisers and so on) will maximise the need for good storage.

With any teenager, it is a good idea to install a washbasin in the room, to discourage them from monopolizing the bathroom! Dressing-room style light fittings around a mirror will be particularly appreciated by girls for make-up practice.

The great thing is that, although the room looks quite different and fulfils changing needs at each stage, the furnishings remain substantially the same over a good number of years. No change of stage costs very much money, except perhaps for the final transformation.

As well as being very budget-conscious, such a plan is highly flexible. It allows first the parents and then the child himself enormous scope for adding, changing and indulging individual tastes and interests. As long as the original basic plan is simple and includes plenty of storage a room can go on developing along with the child it caters for.

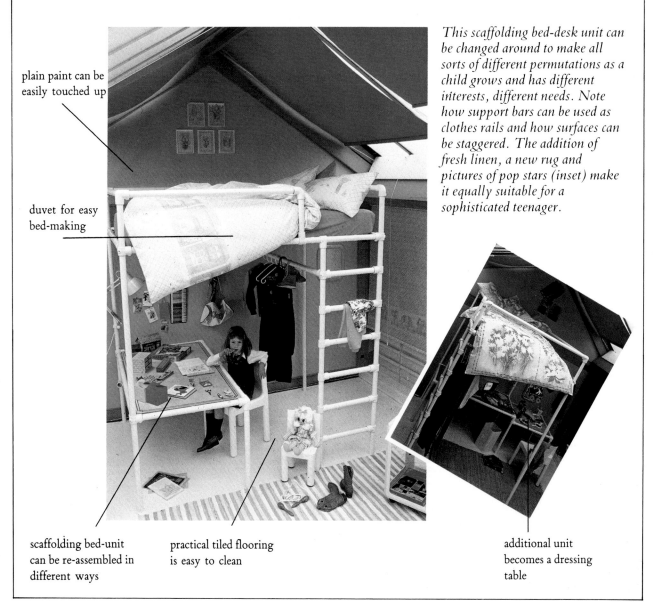

plain paint can be easily touched up

duvet for easy bed-making

scaffolding bed-unit can be re-assembled in different ways

practical tiled flooring is easy to clean

This scaffolding bed-desk unit can be changed around to make all sorts of different permutations as a child grows and has different interests, different needs. Note how support bars can be used as clothes rails and how surfaces can be staggered. The addition of fresh linen, a new rug and pictures of pop stars (inset) make it equally suitable for a sophisticated teenager.

additional unit becomes a dressing table

Before you actually start any decorating at all you must plan out the lighting for your child's room. Any re-wiring and re-routing of existing electrics should be done well before you put paint to wall, both for aesthetic and practical reasons. Aim to get rid of any trailing wires; apart from looking unsightly they are a safety hazard.

It is equally dangerous to overload too few outlets with too many appliances so make provision now for a generous number of points, ideally no less than six. You will need these in the early stages for bottle warmers, extra heaters and so on, and later for toys and games – trains, racing cars – and any equipment you might want to install such as tv, radio, stereo, video, computer, tape recorder, model-making equipment. Remember this is the age of electronics and it will become more so, not less. Sophisticated gadgets that might seem expensively out of reach now might well be commonplace and much cheaper in a few years.

It might also be an idea to wire in a baby alarm system with extensions in the master bedroom, the kitchen and outside the living room.

Children's rooms need a lot of light but the type and the amount will vary considerably at each stage of their growth. For example, you should have good overall light for nursing and bathing the baby and for him or her to play by later. In addition you will need lights that can be dimmed right down at night, as a comfort to small children in the dark and so that infants can have their night feeds in a gentle glow which will not disturb them or any older sleeping children; enough light by the cot to enable parents to read bedtime stories; a reading lamp by the bed later on for older children, and good light on the work surface for playing and drawing and later on for homework and study. Individual clip-on lights are a particularly good idea for children in bunk beds as they can read at night without disturbing the other child.

Two ultra-modern settings make the most of the latest technology and lighting effects. Right, plenty of outlets for stereo, television and general musical equipment have been provided, with desk and floor-standing lights for essential reading. Left, track spotlighting comes in useful for a young collector and model-maker.

CHILDREN'S ROOMS

If you can afford it, a separate circuit of low wattage lights is ideal for a child's room but it is expensive. Whatever you do, try to install dimmer switches so that lights can be dimmed at will. Not only is this comforting for the child but it will save running costs.

Task lights

This includes light for the play/work surface and light for reading. Get outlets installed in the appropriate positions so that you can introduce reading and work lamps later on. It's advisable to avoid any sort of free-standing lamps; toddlers can easily pull them over. Again, wall lights by the cot or bed could be preferable. If you had cupboards or shelves set over the play/work surface, you could install strip lighting behind a baffle or valance just below them and then later on supply a lamp that can be angled directly on to whatever work is in progress.

General light

Most electricians will automatically install a centre point in the ceiling but try to avoid this if you can unless you are going to use it for track lighting. The sun does not stay still in the middle of the sky all day, so why, if artificial light is meant to emulate daylight, should we always have this often harsh central light?

Evenly spaced wall lights are a much better solution; or recessed

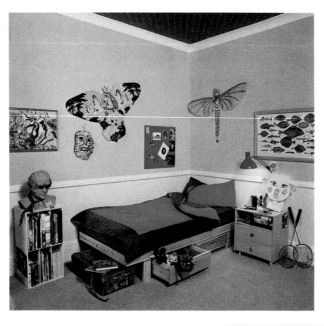

ceiling lights set all around the perimeter of the room. Track lighting may not fit your romantic idea of nursery lighting but architects often specify it if used with a dimmer switch.

Adjustable lamps and spotlights are especially useful: a large angle-lamp (top left) is ideal for play, with a shielded wall-light for reading in bed (top right). The small room uses shiny surfaces to reflect light from one narrow window and a row of adjustable spotlights.

Right: Overhead lights have been placed unusually above each individual bunk bed to ensure a perfect reading light.

radiator has been shielded with a cloud-shaped screen to protect child from possible harm

attractive canopy effect over the bed keeps off draughts and encourages a feeling of security

built-in safety rail on a higher-than-average bed is essential for young children

continuous roll of drawing paper and large blackboard save scribbles on the wall

bedside fabric pockets save the bed becoming uncomfortably cluttered with favourite toys

A central pendant light can be better positioned by using a long flex and ceiling hook. This bright, appealing room with handy storage bed (right) now has light where it's needed – over the bed. A row of spotlights highlights the painting and play counter, specially positioned at child height.

sturdy pine beds incorporate useful drawers for storage below

For the first few years of children's lives their own room (with the exception, perhaps, of the kitchen) is virtually their whole world. So, when it comes to designing any sort of space for them, the aim should be to create a warm and welcoming environment in which they can grow and develop and open up their senses.

For some people this is a signal to try and create rooms that are as full of fantasy and fun and humour as possible. But it is advisable, economically and psychologically to go for a purely temporary fantasy effect that can be changed to make quite a different sort of room as the child grows older. You cannot, after all, sleep in a train-shaped bed or underneath a castle headboard for ever. So rely on things that you can remove as your child develops. Posters, friezes, rugs and bedspreads can all transform a room without altering it permanently.

The same applies to the actual arrangement of the space in the room. When children are very small you can divide the space up in a way which might not work nearly so well once they grow older and taller. Then their needs will dictate quite a different sort of division. In addition, you have to realize, as one architect put it, that children naturally tend to create chaos and you have to learn to strike a balance between what they do and what you can live with. There are many colourful plastic stacking containers that can be used for storage, and to help alleviate the chaos.

Obviously not many families can afford to change their children's rooms around very often, hence the wisdom of the staged plan for the sensible basic room discussed on pages 203–9, but they can certainly change arrangments and emphasis within the room, and most easily of all, they can change the colours.

The two things that all child psychologists seem to agree on are the importance of a child's first environment and the fact that all small children respond to and are stimulated by colour. Infants also respond well to movement (they love watching mobiles above a cot), to noises (bells and musical box devices strung across the pram), to shapes, textures and smells, but colour is far and away the most important stimulus. Fortunately it is the easiest and most economical way to transform a room completely. Use this chapter for ideas.

Clever use of blue and white and kite-shaped light pep up a box-like room for very little expense (left). With a thought to the future (right) this small room simply needs a change of wallpaper and duvet cover to see a child from toddler to teenager.

CHILDREN'S ROOMS

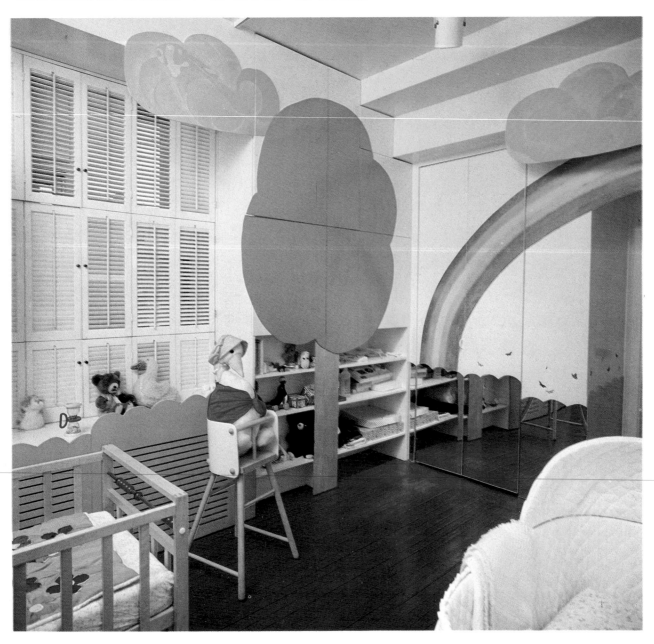

How to use colour

Once the framework of a child's room is settled, the inside can be altered at will simply by wielding a paint brush, pasting on paper, changing the window or bed treatments or, for that matter, applying paint-on or paste-up supergraphics like clouds, rainbows, butterflies, nursery rhyme characters, giant letters or numbers. Murals are only one step further on from this and the brave parent or willing artistic friend can transform walls, and thus rooms, into fairy-tale gardens, circuses, cowboy prairies, forests or whatever takes their fancy.

Quite apart from the many and varied decorative uses of colour in treating walls, floors, ceilings, furniture and windows, colour can also be used to form demarcation areas. It can be a purely visual way of dividing two sleeping areas or private play territories or marking off sleeping from play space simply by painting relevant parts of the floor or walls in different shades.

Colour used on walls can be put there to serve as a rich and varied background to set off other colours

Left: A fantasy room uses simple plywood cut-outs to make effective trees, hedges, rainbow and clouds, with the first two masking pragmatic storage. The bright red painted floor adds warmth; the mirrored wardrobe doors, more space and light.

in the room or it can be injected in vivid accents against an all-white, easy-to-clean form of decoration.

Colour can transform old furniture to make it work as part of a scheme. Or, if you have more than one child sharing a room, paint each child's own particular furniture a different colour. This colour zoning can also be applied to individual drawers in a shared chest, or shelves in a bookcase unit, or cupboard fronts. Even if the colour is just applied to the handles, it is enough to identify it to the owner of the space. This is a very good and easy way to encourage tidiness and respect for other people's possessions from a very early age.

Remember that paints used for children's furniture and equipment should be non-toxic.

How to use space
When we think of space we tend to think only of floor space and therefore miss many of its other exciting possibilities. There's an awful lot of unused space in every room and one way of bringing it into play in a child's room is to build in different

Right: A bedroom takes on a new dimension when the bed is a double decker London bus complete with wheels and plausible graphics. A wooden ladder leads to the play area on the top deck. Note too, vividly lacquered walls, ceiling and floor.

CHILDREN'S ROOMS

levels so that the space can be divided neatly for various activities.

You can build platforms making wide steps that use the available space twice over or you can elaborate on the bunk bed idea. There are endless ingenious variations you can achieve here using plywood sides cut into different shapes. You can take off into the realms of fantasy: for instance, with bunk beds turned into a double-decker London Transport bus; or a farmyard barn with 'windows' cut out of the uprights and the top bunk covered with a 'roof' complete with dormer window; or two-tiered space capsules (with the help of old sonotubes — those fibre moulds used for making concrete pillars and available from large building sites); or Punch and Judy-like theatres; or stables; a ship's cabin complete with portholes; forts and towers.

Or you can construct something along the lines of the playhouse/climbing-frame structures which combine sleeping, work, storage and exercise areas within one sturdy, workaday unit. It can include all sorts of parallel bars, swings, slides, steps, trapezes, ropes, balconies, mattresses, work surfaces, cupboard

A nursery looks especially pretty decorated in sugar almond colours: pink, blue and yellow (left). Old chests of drawers can be cheaply painted to match walls and fabric.

space, shelves and closets – a really intensive use of the space available.

On a simpler level there are the portable platforms of different sizes which can be placed together like huge steps. These have to be on castors so that they can be reasonably easily moved around. One large wide platform becomes the bed and cube-like structures behind it act as bedhead and extra storage as well as steps to open shelving behind.

The extra advantage of all these structures is that, once they have served their purpose, they can be dismantled leaving the essential ingredients like beds, shelves and so on to be re-situated separately somewhere else in the room, perhaps under a different or more conventional guise. While the framework of the room remains quite untouched, it will now have gained some space for more ordinary or classic furnishings.

The platform structures can also, of course, be moved from house to house if the family moves, or be re-used somewhere else for subsequent children.

More fantastic ideas

The sort of island unit fantasies that can be made out of bunk beds, plywood and a good deal of ingenuity are one way of putting a lot of fun into a child's room, but it is possible to make fantasy rooms

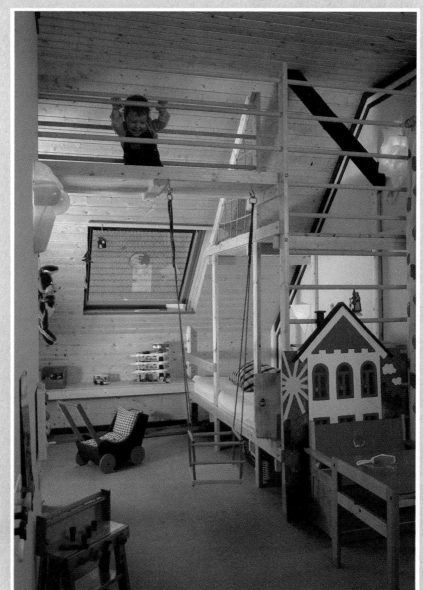

Let your imagination have free reign and you will be able to devise a multitude of unusual ideas.

Left: A wooden climbing frame/sleeping complex transforms a bedroom into an adventure playground.

Above right: Integrate special storage for small toys and a seating area below into a corner to leave the rest of the floor relatively free for playing. A sturdy ladder and well-fixed balcony rails are absolutely essential for safety.

CHILDREN'S ROOMS

simply by decorating the walls, ceilings and floors.

A New York designer, who specializes in children's rooms, developed a series of fantastic ideas for his son's room. When the boy was a toddler, his room was the end of the rainbow, with the rainbow painted on the wall and plywood cut-out clouds suspended from the ceiling to float above him (see page 216). Plywood was cut in the shape of trees and hedges, with the whole scene reflected in plastic mirror. Now, somewhat older, the child has a completely different room, fully wired for electronic hook-up to the family's central audio-visual system. It is also multi-levelled, with lots of built-in furniture in natural wood and practical plastic laminated tops, ceramic tiles, and only an authentic suit of armour adds a touch of fantasy. Yet another idea is to create a farmyard (see far right). A high-level bed is a sleeping loft, reached by a ladder, with an attached slide for quick exit. This sleeping loft rests partly on an old chest of drawers painted into the design and partly on hollow storage/play space.

To divide up the room a little as well as to make the yard more realistic, the designer built a shallow platform just beside the barn with its own real post-and-rail fence. He covered this raised area in an old remnant of green carpet to make it

look like a field and covered the 'earth' beneath it with another remnant of old brown carpet. A black and white vinyl cow lying sleepily in 'the grass' made a tolerably comfortable sofa, walls were painted sky blue with sun and occasional clouds, and a pair of plastic geese lights looked thoroughly realistic in the setting.

The effect of both these fantasy rooms was totally beguiling and enormous fun yet they were capable of being turned back into more everyday rooms when the time came.

Involving your children

As children grow up, encourage them to take an interest in design and in their environment by involving them when you need to redecorate their room.

Use their hobbies or particular passions of the moment (computer games, pop stars, collecting foreign souvenirs) as starting points for decorative schemes. For fun, paper the walls with posters or charts (one wall or a chimney breast may be enough): the sky at night for budding astronomers; cars for motor fanatics; wild flower identity pictures for naturalists. Add other decorative touches to fit in with the hobby: luminous stars to shine on the ceiling; a racing track painted on to the floor for cars; pictures from pressed flowers. Aviation enthusiasts may want to convert their

In this room, far left, nearly every item repeats the dominant colour theme. The radiator, window, walls, bed-linen, rug, blinds and vinyl floor tiles are all in keeping. Create a farmyard atmosphere, above, with a 'barn' sleeping area, green 'grass' carpet and, of course, a farmyard fence. Clowns are the dominant theme below left. Note how this has been carried through in the stencilling on the chest. For a different effect, top left, a bold scheme of primary colours contrasts starkly with the plain white background.

CHILDREN'S ROOMS

beds to aeroplanes – tongue-and-groove boarding can cheaply convert one end of the bed while plywood cut out and attached to two bedside tables could make the wings.

Older children can have more say in the matter. Even if their ideas are bolder, weirder or more adventurous than you bargained for, let them have their head if you can bear it. Provide some basics like flooring and a bed, and let them do some of the choosing of extra accessories and colours. Never mind if they come up with an all-purple room; they're the ones who have to live with it, not you. Discuss cost with them and point out that they must be able to restore the room to its original condition if necessary (when you move, for example), since their choice may not be to other people's taste.

Today's children are certain to want some very expensive items among their equipment: record players, radios, tvs, computers. Unless you have a lot of money to spare, or have existing but dated equipment which can be relegated from a family living room to make way for more up-to-date versions, it is always sensible to discuss the acquisition of such goods with your children and how these things are to be paid for. If children are aware of the cost of decorations and furnishings they are more likely to treat them with greater respect.

Recreate a traditional but practical nursery atmosphere. The room (left) features an old-fashioned painted brass bed, draped curtains, frilled cushions and lace tablecloth; paint and stencils on furniture (above) echo the colour and design of the smocked curtains.

How practical is nostalgia?

If you feel strongly that an experience you enjoyed as a child or something you remember affectionately would be a good thing to hand on to your children, then why not try to re-create it? You may find, however, that some aspects of the old-fashioned nursery are quite impractical today, while others either still work amazingly well or have been brought up to date without losing their intrinsic charm.

For example, nursery fires and a club fender were fine in the days of vigilant nannies and willing housemaids, but even the substitute gas log or coal fires, while pretty, trouble-free and effective, need just as much guarding when children are around. Not easy for mothers without help.

A good many of the frills and furbelows of lace and muslin that frothed around Victorian cribs are seldom good washing-machine fodder today; they needed to be hand-washed, starched and crisply ironed for maximum effect. On the other hand, there are excellent modern fabrics which look just as pretty and can be tossed into the washing-machine with impunity. Many of these good-looking, easy-care fabrics which have become available only in recent years are quite cap-

able, by virtue of their design, of creating their own nostalgic effect.

Some of the furniture and furnishings one connects with nice old-fashioned nurseries — the capacious stripped pine and painted pieces, the painted and stencilled floor boards, the charming wallpaper — are still often the best and most practical solutions for a real nursery, that is to say, a sleeping/play space for a pre-school-age child. However, the wallpaper might be made that much more practical and immune to fiddling little fingers if it is washable or given a couple of coats of clear polyurethane to protect its surface. And to make it still more impervious you could bring back another sensible old-fashioned idea — the dado. This can easily be done by running a piece of wooden moulding around the room at waist height and painting the wall below white so that any scribbles — and there are bound to be some — won't do much damage. The wallpaper is hung above the dado. It would be even more practical if you covered the area below the dado rail with

An Edwardian pine bed (left) has been made to look authentic with a lace bedcover, flounced tablecloths and matching bed valance – all available in today's easy-care fabrics. Lacy and frilled pillows, arrangements of dried flowers and flowery prints complete the effect.

CHILDREN'S ROOMS

large box kite in bright colours
makes an exciting lamp-shade

dramatic, geometric
design curtains

Built-in storage really is essential if
you are short of space. Here, well-
planned floor to ceiling cupboards
(left and below) offer plenty of space
for toys, clothes and sports
equipment. Note useful wall grid
systems in cupboard interiors.
Equally smart is the brightly
coloured kite picking up the colours
of a tubular director's chair, and the
child-sized wooden folding chairs. A
dark carpet pulls the whole thing
together.

electric racetrack is
neatly built into a
raised unit to keep the
floor space free

open shelves and table
top keep favourite
books and toys on
display

built-in cupboards
with simple, easy-to-use
handles

removable blackboard or black-board paint. There are dark green versions of both that are less oppressive than the conventional but heavy black. This way nostalgia is perfectly workable as long as you are sensible and selective.

Be thoroughly modern

The traditional look, with its old pine or painted furniture and practical prettiness, is one way of treating a child's room; at the other end of the decorating scale is the bang-up-to-date, streamlined modern look. And it isn't at all out of place because by modern I mean using the best of today's surfaces, furniture and equipment with a good deal of sleek but useful built-in furniture that can serve several purposes at once — like the sleep/work/play/ storage units described earlier in the chapter. Thoroughly practical, easy-care, easy-clean from the parent's point of view, they are just as stimulating from the child's.

In the modern room the colours are generally bold or white with bright flashes of accent colour. Or the room can be all wood and cork. Or you could go for the best of both worlds with multi-purpose furniture and the latest in work surfaces with pretty and nostalgic touches in say the window treatments or wallpaper. As in all decoration, it is a question of taste and whatever suits your lifestyle and bank balance.

Pure white with splashes of colour (right) looks very graphic. Walls and floor are easy-wipe to allow children to be artistic and still be practical. Sturdy card furniture is cheap but smart; felt pen scribbles on the walls can be wiped away. This is a fine system if your child realises that the rest of the house is not to be treated in the same way.

Right: A charming nursery, in which contrasting wallpaper designs are cleverly separated by stick-on alphabet, number and clown friezes along the dado, skirting board and ceiling. The matching panelling on the walls is particularly effective.

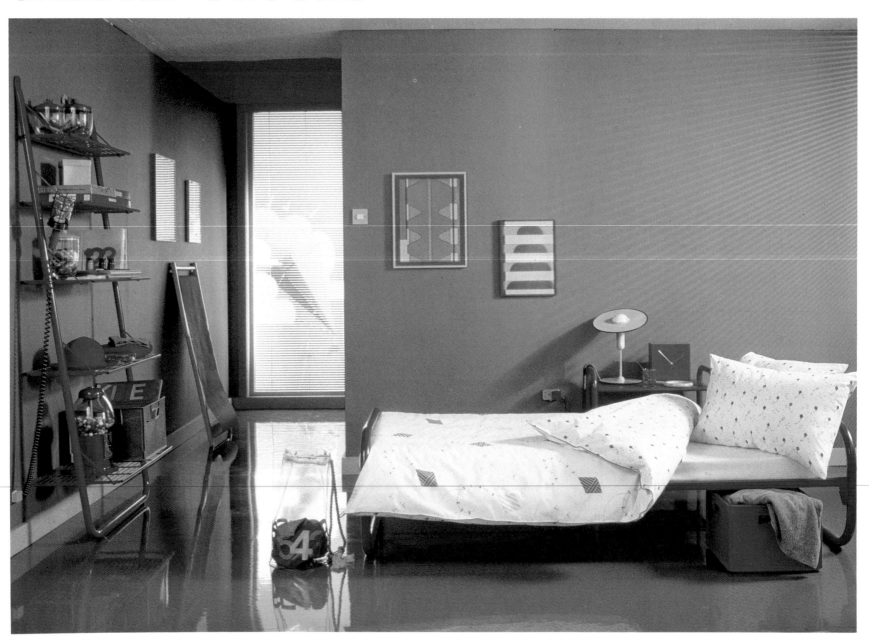

With decorating it makes sense to start with the floor. Once a child is out of the cot, the floor is his natural habitat. Children will happily gravitate there, disregarding all other seating and furniture provided. They lie on it, sit on it, crawl all over it, play on it, draw on it – it's their home. So it's important to make sure that in the early years at least, there's as much uncluttered space as possible and that it's a comfortable place to be. It follows that how you treat it and what covering you choose for it have to be the first and major considerations.

In any child's room the floor needs to be reasonably warm to the touch and free from draughts so that the baby/toddler can crawl about comfortably; it must be very easy to clean and maintain since spills and puddles are everyday occurrences; it should be as non-slip as possible and not too hard so that the inevitable falls and tumbles don't do any damage. At the same time it should be resilient, tough and as sound-proof as possible, especially if the room is not on the ground floor – the patter of tiny feet soon becomes a resounding thump. If the floor is also reasonably flat and smooth it will make a much better surface for children to play on.

Bearing all these requirements in mind you still have to make the basic choice between a hard floor and a soft one, but avoiding extremes in each case.

What are the choices?

Rugs can be very attractive, but they are not so safe for younger children, who may trip or slip on them. A non-slip matting that you place between rug and floor is available – this should make rugs safe to use in older children's rooms (perhaps to cover unsightly spills from earlier days!).

Vinyl-coated cork tiles have a lot to recommend them: they are easy to clean, soft (as hard floors go), reasonably warm to the touch, tough, splinter-free and good-looking. Their natural tones would blend with any colour scheme. They are also economically priced and can be bought in suitably small quantities.

Vinyl tiles or sheet vinyls are easy to wipe clean and hard-wearing but a little on the cold side. They come in a good range of plain colours.

Cushioned vinyl has all the virtues of vinyl plus softness.

For a colder climate, the comfort of carpet might be more appropriate in a child's room (right). Bright paint is an inexpensive way of transforming a room into something special (left). Deep blue for the walls, hard-wearing green gloss with several coats of polyurethane on the floor looks stunning and ideally cool in warm climates.

CHILDREN'S ROOMS

Linoleum is making a come-back and has lots of advantages. It is tremendously hard-wearing, tolerably soft, convenient to clean and can be cut into all sorts of shapes and designs. Its dull drab days are over and it is now being produced and used in very exciting paterns.

Polyurethaned wood looks handsome and can be wiped clean very easily but it must be made splinter-free. An old floor can, of course, be painted with a plain or stencilled finish before being given several coats of polyurethane to make it thoroughly practical. Alternatively, farmyards or race tracks can be painted on the floor for fun. Bear in mind that floorboards, whatever the finish, will be noisier than other surfaces as there is no insulating layer.

Rubber stud flooring is soft and noise-resistant, easy to clean and available in good colours.

On the soft side

Carpet is certainly comfortable and noise-absorbing and can be either colourful in its own right or neutral to go with all the other colours in the room, but it isn't really very practical. It is, however, the best way to prevent sounds travelling to other rooms in the house and is good in apartment buildings. Stained carpet is not easy to clean, so choose one of the new man-made fibres that are more resistant to dirt.

Any carpet should have a smooth

Left: Get the children to help you and create something like this zany paint-spattered and striped room (opposite) where bright colours, a slide and climbing frame and gay furniture instil instant liveliness. Note how stripes across the width of a wall-length Venetian blind have been cleverly extended with paint around one side of the room to end in great sploshes of colour with a matching pattern on the floor.

Above: In this room, brightly coloured vinyl tiles have been used against a bold colour scheme of purple and green. Although the combination might at first seem disastrous, curiously, it works, though this may have something to do with the fact that the pink in the tiles has been picked up in the raised sleeping platform and the chairs.

finish so that toys can be wheeled and pushed without coming to grief; do not use long or shag pile — it is too impractical.

Smooth-finish *carpet tiles* are a good idea because ruined or worn ones can be replaced at comparatively little expense. They are now available in a variety of finishes but all can be picked up individually and cleaned if necessary.

Wool/cord and hair cord and the *man-made fibre mixes* look neat and interesting but they are not very easy to clean; nor is their rather scratchy texture very comfortable for children when crawling or pushing toys.

Practical and fun

The best solution, according to child psychologists and infant school teachers, is to have a mixture of both hard and soft with islands of one or the other in the form of rugs, or different levels of carpeted platforms which can be used for various activities such as sitting, reading and playing. Their great practical and visual advantage is that they define areas and limits without forming any physical barriers. You can add to the island effect and achieve comfort by having lots of floor cushions on any hard floors; they make great playthings for small children and teenagers love lounging about on them too.

If you must have carpet you can always bring in vinyl or rubber mats to cater for any messy activities like working with modelling clay, painting, glueing and so on. Even large ones are quite light and can be easily moved away for cleaning or to another room or to the garden so that the child can play there and still have some temporary territory that he can call his own.

Alternatively, you can have half the room carpeted and the other half covered in vinyl or vinyl-coated cork or polyurethaned wood.

Floors with well defined areas looked at from a child's point of view, that is from a near-horizontal position, will appear like a large sea or lake with safe and accessible islands in it. Far more reassuring than a vast plain expanse.

Insulation

If you can afford it, it is a good idea to insulate floors. The benefits work in two ways. Hi-fi, tv or radio in a downstairs room is less likely to disturb children when they want to work or sleep and their daytime noises are less likely to be a nuisance to you. There are two things to remember about insulation: soft materials are better sound insulators than hard ones and the more layers on the floor, the better insulated it will be. If you are laying carpet, put down insulating board directly over the floorboards, then hardboard. A rubber underlay between the hard-

CHILDREN'S ROOMS

board and the carpet will act as a further insulating layer.

For an unusual but effective finish, lay sheets of chipboard over insulating board for extra insulation and varnish them; the result is similar to cork tiles. When sound waves travel from one room to another, one of the routes they take is through the unplastered portion of the wall under the floorboards. You can improve insulation here by removing the floorboards and rendering any bare bricks or building blocks and filling cracks round joists with ready mixed concrete mortar. Allow to dry out before replacing floorboards.

The decorative floor

As the children grow older you can adapt the floor in various ways depending on what they need to keep them (and you) happy. If they are fairly rumbustious and noisy, the floor should obviously be as indestructible and sound-proof as possible. But it might well be that they would appreciate a rather decorative floor and this can be achieved by painting or stencilling (see page 379). Adding some graphic effects can be a very rewarding exercise and not too difficult. One idea, with practical as well as decorative qualities, is to paint or stencil board-games on to the floor. This could include a giant checkers board or a game of snakes and ladders.

Floors should be hard-wearing and practical as well as looking good: plain boards (above, far left) have been sanded and varnished for a natural finish, while others (left) have been painted pink for a more colourful effect. White vinyl flooring (above) looks dramatic against an all-white background. For older children, a more subdued dark grey (far left) might be more appropriate. Ceramic tiles (opposite) provide flooring for life.

CHILDREN'S ROOMS

The negative view of walls is to look on them as confining and restricting; in children's rooms the opposite should be true. Even when walls act as boundaries to a particular space they should seem to provide a sense of security and, later on, privacy. At the same time they have tremendous potential as areas of great visual interest and as such, a source of constant stimulation. Children start noticing them from the cradle so treat them as blank canvases that can be adapted to all sorts of bright and exciting ideas that change, keep pace and grow up with the child. It is never too early to start decorating the walls of a child's room, even if only with temporary items that you will replace.

Before you start decorating decide whether the wealls need insulating to prevent noisy children (and parents) from disturbing each other. The simplest way to insulate is to put up a second layer of plasterboard over the existing wall finish. For extra insulation, the new plasterboard should be mounted on battens away from the existing wall, and a layer of insulating material (like loft insulation) fixed between the old and new wall. You'll have to remove skirting and electrical fittings before fitting the new plasterboard (see also note on rendering the wall beneath the floorboards, p.230). Even a large noticeboard, made of insulation board and co-vered with felt, will cut down on reverberations in a room and help to insulate it to some extent.

Another alternative is to insulate the walls of a room adjoining a child's room. If your bedroom, for instance, is divided by a partition wall from your child's room, put insulation to work as a decorative finish by lining the walls of your room with polyester wadding, stapled in place, and covering it with stretched, pleated or gathered fabric, fixed to battens round the top and bottom of the wall. Using sound insulation like this will also keep in heat, although this is unlikely to save you much money, since most heat escapes outside.

Decoration

The most practical and economical start for children's walls is to paint them in white gloss which looks clean, can be kept fresh-looking with a quick wipe of a damp cloth, and which makes an excellent and durable background for anything that goes against it. It also gives

Generous use of fabric for walls, windows and drapes (opposite) not only looks good but keeps out the draughts too. Clever painting can transform a plain two-door wardrobe into the semblance of a country cottage (right).

CHILDREN'S ROOMS

you all the scope you need for choosing furniture and decorations that are as colourful as possible.

Gradually add storage units in fashionable pastels or bold primary colours or plain wood, as well as supergraphics, toys, cut-outs, prints, paintings (including the child's own efforts), books, kites, posters, pin-boards, photographs, whatever you, and later *they*, like. They will all look tremendously colourful against the white background. Everything can and will be changed around as the child grows older but all you need do is freshen the walls behind, either with a good wash down or another coat of white paint. It's an easy solution, the maintenance is negligible and everybody will be happy.

One very successful way of getting the best of both worlds is to run a dado or chair rail either all round the room or round one or two walls at waist height or slightly higher. It can be quite easily done by sticking up a length of wood moulding or simply by painting a horizontal stripe of colour. The object is to

Right: Try to consider children's favourite interests and possessions when planning their rooms. A keen reader has been provided with plenty of bookshelf space, plain sand walls for displaying colourful kites and friezes, a dramatic midnight blue ceiling and a smart dado.

give you an upper and a lower wall which can each be given a different decorative treatment. And since children are incorrigible scribblers and chalkers, you'll save yourself a lot of trouble by providing them with an outlet for all their mural activity in the form of a blackboard on the lower part of the wall.

Or make the dado into a frieze of cut-outs of every shape and sort, put together like one of those Victorian scrap-screens and then varnished over. I remember as a child being endlessly fascinated by just such a dado in a friend's house. It was always being changed and added to and I loved it.

To achieve something along the same lines more easily, cover the dado in scenic or pictorial wallpaper. There is a paper on the market which is just right for the job; a jungly-animal design which is only partially coloured. The children are free to do the rest and each roll comes complete with a bundle of coloured crayons. Again, do remind them that the freedom to scrawl on walls does not extend beyond the limitations of their rooms.

Try a mixture of all these ideas to keep the children interested or ring the changes as and when you want to. One easy way of achieving this is to make the whole dado of pinboard or chipboard which can be bought in any timber yard, then painted.

A dado doesn't have to be for ever. When its day is done and its usefulness outlived, the blackboard, the wood moulding and the pinboard can all be taken down to make way for new wall treatments.

A white painted wood-panelled dado (above left) visually straightens an awkwardly-shaped room under the eaves and provides a wipe-down surface for sticky fingers. The area can be safely wallpapered to hide any irregularities in the walls and sloped ceiling. Discourage scribbling on the walls with an area set aside for the purpose at comfortable child level. An area for pictures and doodles (above) can be combined with a blackboard or pinboard and a handy tray for pens, chalks and crayons.

Often your imagination can be triggered by a feature of the room, a poster or favourite toy, and extended quite cheaply using paint, fabric and paper cut-outs to make an exciting colourful setting. A sloped roof (left) has been cleverly transformed into a painted red and white awning. With bright blue walls, matching blind and a border of stencilled flowers, the room has a cheery toy-town atmosphere.

Similarly a giant poster (above) tails off onto the ceiling with large painted stars. The rest of the room is kept a sensible plain white to act as a calming influence.

White is always a good foil for dazzling primaries as well as being easy to clean and touch up. Solid blocks of colour (above right) are sharpened and lifted by white wood-work, ceiling and piano. Right: Dutch partners linked with a line of hearts make a pretty pastel border.

Bright ideas for bold walls

● Huge oversize posters in stunning colours for say, circuses or cars, used like wallpaper on one wall or over cupboards and overlapping on to the ceiling.

● A 'hedge' of green-painted cork stuck on to cut-out plywood panels (in hedge shapes) around the bed area of a room.

● A frieze of toadstools, grasses, flowers, insects, either painted straight on to the walls or cut out of coloured papers and stuck on. Either way they can be removed quite easily when children outgrow them.

● Large cut-out letters of the alphabet or numbers pasted on to the walls.

● Groups of twelve birds or butterflies or animals for easy counting lessons.

● A blown-up map varnished over to cover one whole wall.

● Flowing supergraphics (lines, circles, shapes of all kinds) to help define private or separate areas in a shared room.

● A dark green gloss wall in an otherwise white room for throwing soft balls against.

● A New York or London skyline at skirting board level with cloud-dotted blue skies on the walls, for older children. A night-time version could be achieved with a black silhouette and stars on a deep blue background.

CHILDREN'S ROOMS

Make way for art

You have to be realistic about children. It is absolutely no good expecting them to keep their rooms immaculate or to imagine for one minute that they are going to stay quiet and well-behaved inside a little showcase. What you can try to do is to make them aware that they can do more or less what they like in their own space but not in yours, and then to see that all surfaces in that space are as tough and easily cleanable as possible. There are bound to be marks and scuffs and scribbles and the best way is to face the fact and deal with them on the 'if-you-can't-beat-them-join-them' principle. This is where you can make a virtue out of necessity. Children generally love drawing and all sorts of artistic self-expression, and to them, walls must seem a marvellous natural canvas. So build on that. Bring the two together deliberately by giving them an actual wall or part of a wall to experiment – and daub to their heart's content. This will give them more space and scope than even the blackboard dado but in any case, if you have determined scribblers or Picassos in the making, they would overflow from the blackboard. For the time being you'll just have to close your eyes to conventionality, give them the freedom to express themselves over a large area and take heart from the knowledge that

you can paint or paper it all over later when the scribbling phase is over.

If you cannot bear to see your walls treated like this or you live in rented accommodation, pin up large sheets of paper which can be exchanged for fresh pieces when necessary. Nobody wants to destroy artistic urges but it's better for everybody's sanity to channel them where they can do no harm and to let children understand clearly what is allowed and where. So do stress that this freedom should *not* be extended elsewhere in the home, much less in other people's houses.

Practical or pretty?

If your taste, or that of your child's is for rather prettier decorative effects, one way of achieving this is by using attractive wallpapers. By choosing carefully, it's possible to achieve the prettiness without sacrificing any of the practical advantage of paint.

Look for papers that are washable or wipeable — even scrubbable — tough enough to withstand the onslaught of grubby and fiddly little fingers but still able to act as a good background for accumulated pictures and objects rather than be the main decoration in their own right. Unless of course you can afford the luxury of regular change or a separate bedroom that doesn't have to double as playspace.

Above: With today's wide choice of easy-care co-ordinated ranges, you can choose a scheme that is pretty as well as practical. Cool blue has been used on the walls and mock dado of this nursery and matched with a cot cover and comfy cushion for the nursing chair. The use of wood and blue and yellow accessories adds contrast and a natural warmth.

Right: Blue looks equally good used in conjunction with white and touches of bright red. Pale blue painted trim and chest look fresh and pin neat against a white sprigged paper and dramatic red furniture. Cork tiles on the back of the door make a great space-saving pinboard and there is plenty of room for study, entertaining and sleeping.

If a paper takes your fancy but isn't wipeable or washable you can usually make it stronger and easy to clean by giving it an overcoat or two of matt polyurethane. This has the effect of yellowing most papers a little so you must bear this in mind; also check first that the colours will not run. Do this by applying the polyurethane over just one corner or strip. If you are going to give more than one coat you must let the first coat dry for a full 24 hours before you put on the next, otherwise you will get a rather sticky mess.

Two into one will go

Most children actually prefer quite small spaces: they seem more secure and cosy, they are more manageable and more private. Even an average-sized room must appear vast to a tiny child, so it's quite possible to divide such rooms into two, either to make room for another child or to provide separate sleeping and play areas.

Room dividers can come in a multitude of shapes, forms and materials. You can make them of plywood, wallboard or plaster board; you can have half walls or whole walls and you can cut through them with all sorts of shapes from conventional arches to circles, semi-circles and slits. One good idea is to use a wall of blackboard on castors so it can be moved

CHILDREN'S ROOMS

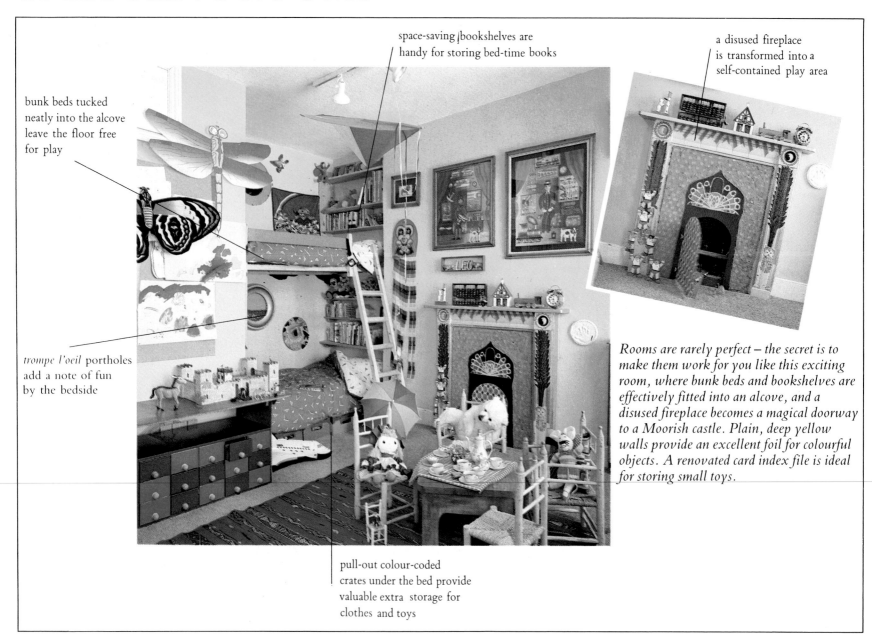

space-saving bookshelves are handy for storing bed-time books

a disused fireplace is transformed into a self-contained play area

bunk beds tucked neatly into the alcove leave the floor free for play

trompe l'oeil portholes add a note of fun by the bedside

pull-out colour-coded crates under the bed provide valuable extra storage for clothes and toys

Rooms are rarely perfect – the secret is to make them work for you like this exciting room, where bunk beds and bookshelves are effectively fitted into an alcove, and a disused fireplace becomes a magical doorway to a Moorish castle. Plain, deep yellow walls provide an excellent foil for colourful objects. A renovated card index file is ideal for storing small toys.

Right: Careful planning means one room can cleverly sleep two teenage girls by partially dividing it with a double desk unit and co-ordinating curtains on an ingenious system of lightweight metal rails. Matching beds incorporate handy drawers for storage and double as sofas during the daytime.

to one side of the room or the other — or away altogether. Or, for fun, how about a divider wall crenellated like a castle, with toys perched in between the crenellations? On one side you could have a cot and play-space for a toddler, on the other, bunk beds and storage for an older child.

Children love tiers and towers and enjoy climbing and clambering up and around them so why not an actual tower structure built from a series of tall plywood panels with curved tops, tall enough to take a couple of bunk beds. One of the panels could take a long curved corner-window complete with a curtain, the other might perhaps have two 'portholes' and a third could support a brightly-painted ladder for reaching the top bunk.

It is essential that such ingenious shapes and devices allow both 'rooms' to benefit from the light from the window and let you look through from one area to the next. In this way even a limited space will never seem cramped.

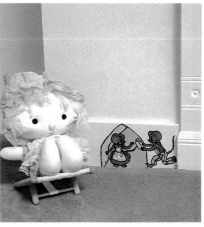

You do not need to be particularly artistic to create fanciful pictures on your walls like these. Use bought stencils and transfers; or trace off your favourite cartoon and nursery rhyme characters, transfer them onto the wall and let your children help you colour them in with quick-drying, wipeable artist's acrylic paints. Even the smallest detail will brighten a corner, like the amusing mousehole (above). This room includes a whole storybook of charming characters cleverly added to the natural features of the building. A sloping ceiling has been transformed into a magical skylight with moon, stars, hey diddle diddle favourites and Rupert Bear dropping in for a visit by balloon. A painted pie on the mantlepiece has released the traditional two dozen blackbirds and Polly Flinders offers a cup of tea by the fire-side.

MURALS AND MOTIFS

Dividers in children's rooms must be securely fixed: they will be 'charged' by toys on wheels and made a target for climbing activities. This should be borne in mind when designing them. Either make them low, solid and easy to clamber over, or upright, secure and sheer – not a temptation for young budding mountaineers.

Ceilings — a chance for fantasy

In a child's room the ceiling can provide an opportunity for indulging in fantasy. You can paint it with clouds or circles like portholes; you can add birds, butterflies, aeroplanes, even footprints. The whole area could be a map, real or imaginary or even, for aspiring astronomers, the sky at night, full of stars and planets. And then, of course, you can create another dimension by hanging things from the ceiling — mobiles, kites, model aircraft, punch balls, flags.

The whole feeling of the space of a room can be subtly altered by painting banks of colour up the walls, over the ceiling and down the other side again, or by sticking paper friezes all round the walls just below the ceiling and edging on to it. Even if you leave the walls plain you can wallpaper the ceiling with a decorative scene or geometric design, confident that it's safe from sticky fingers up there.

Even the door can take on a new dimension when Little Bo Peep decides to drop by (right) complete with Mary's little lamb and Jack and Jill. This combination of trompe l'oeil and bright cartoon characters is remarkably effective in a plain painted room. Remember that children are only a couple of feet tall and place your murals accordingly: here Humpty Dumpty is about to fall off a low wall below an elaborate hickory dickory clock complete with mice. The same room even includes a large, low trompe l'oeil window (above) revealing a fantasy landscape with Little Red Riding Hood and the Owl and the Pussycat. Colourful murals such as these can be made more durable with a quick coat of matt or satin polyurethane varnish which will enable sticky fingerprints to be wiped off at the end of the day.

243

The main consideration about windows in a child's room, apart from seeing that they provide enough daylight and fresh air, is that they should be safe. Even quite young children can be dangerously adventurous and agile climbers.

If windows are set low enough on a wall for a child to be tempted to climb out of them you will certainly need to put up some sort of temporary screen or bars which can be fixed to a frame set into the window. Horizontal bars tend to be an aid and invitation to further climbing, so vertical ones are better; see that they're spaced so that a child cannot get his head stuck between them. If you think they look too prison-like, you can always paint them different colours to cheer them up. A row of turned bannister rails set into a wooden frame make an attractive alternative to plain wood or metal bars.

From the safety aspect, they should be made of – and painted with – safe non-toxic material. And you must leave a gap of not less than 60mm (2½ in) and not more than 85mm (3½ in) between adjacent vertical bars. Moreover, the bars should be easily removable in the event of fire, ideally fitted with childproof locks.

Practical possibilities

It is not usually a good idea to put long curtains in a child's room.

They can too easily be tugged at and pulled down when the child is crawling, or tripped over and generally in the way. If you really want curtains, it is best to keep them short. A double row of café curtains would be both neat and attractive. The area below the window could be used for useful built-in storage – window seats that conceal toy boxes are a good idea.

On the whole, blinds of one sort or another are a more satisfactory solution for various reasons. They're safe, easier to clean than curtains and control the light more efficiently. Black-out shades are practical since they can be pulled right up to let in maximum light and air or pulled down to darken the room totally. With any luck this will delay the start of the day for you when the children are very young by ensuring that they don't wake at the first sign of morning light. Also, if you want them to sleep in the middle of the day it's a great help to have a darkened room, particularly on bright summer days when curtains are rarely adequate.

Blinds are a practical form of window treatment that can come in a wide range of designs and colours. Opposite, they are used as a unifying feature with two contrasting walls. Right, the blind fabric matches the prettily patterned wallpaper, and is dressed with toning plain curtains and pelmet.

CHILDREN'S ROOMS

If you want something that performs the same function but looks more decorative, you can have ordinary roller blinds with black-out backings. Or there are cloth blinds or shades of various designs with silver backings. These are specially useful because they have insulating properties which help prevent heat loss in winter and act as heat reflectors in summer.

Vinyl-coated blinds or shades are practical because they can be wiped clean with a damp cloth or sponge. Venetian blinds are helpful because they allow you to control the light so well — useful for daytime rests and in the summer. They come plain or coloured or in a rainbow of colours and can be ordered in all the shades of one colour, for example from palest pink through to deep rose or burgundy.

Left: In a room such as this, with the child's bed hard up against the window, a blind might not be the best solution as it would be difficult to keep the cords safely out of reach. However, an extremely pretty effect has been created with curtains flanking the bed.

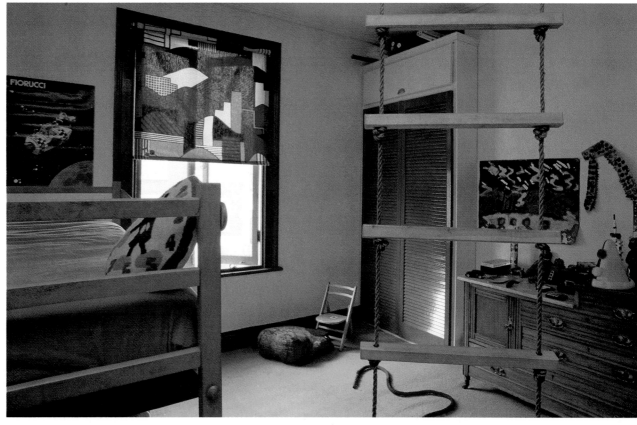

Right: A striking blind can easily provide the focal point for a room and an inspiration for the rest of the design.
Top: The fresh blue, white and yellow colours of this tropical paradise blind have been picked up in the walls and chair.

Slatted wood blinds are handsome, look specially nice in an older child's room and will control the light well. Inexpensive pinoleum or matchstick or bamboo slatted blinds filter the light to a certain extent but won't keep it out altogether.

Vertical blinds look good and neat and they, too, come in white or a wide choice of colours.

If you do decide to put up blinds at the windows, it might also be worth considering using matching ones, instead of more expensive doors, to conceal clothes, shelves and even beds.

A word of caution if you use blinds of any sort. Do make sure that you can keep the cords well out of reach of toddlers and crawlers who like to grab everything in sight. Cords can be a potentially lethal hazard if the child gets entangled in them, quite apart from ruining the blind's mechanism if they are mishandled.

If you buy white or pastel roller blinds they can be used like a canvas to paint designs on. You can also use wooden blinds and pinoleum or matchstick blinds in this way if you spray them white first.

Window frames too, can be used as part of the decoration. Painted in brilliant colours, yellow, blue, red, green, they look marvellous against white walls. And if you hang things from the pelmets, like birdcages, or kites, you get a wonderful decorative effect when the sun shines through them.

The nice thing about windows is that they are virtually as versatile as the walls. You can keep them as plain and functional or as decorative and functional as you like. They can be changed quite easily and at little expense as the child grows older.

Very few children are born tidy. That's worth remembering. However, though a sense of order is not something that comes naturally to them, oddly enough they do enjoy convenience. So organize storage as handily as you can for, in the end, it will benefit you as much as them.

You only have to watch a child rummaging impatiently in a deep drawer for a favourite thing and chucking everything else out in an unruly heap as he tries to find it, to see that stacks of drawers are not necessarily the answer to organization, at least not for toys, and not in the early stages.

The great thing is not to give children an excuse for untidiness. Make it easy to be tidy and make it fun. When they're very small the best way is to store possessions other than clothes in places where they can see and reach them. Low shelves, rows of cubby holes, bins, baskets, trays, low hooks, are all helpful and practical. If you can get children into the habit of *knowing* they will find a particular item in a particular place, they might be persuaded to put it back there for the next time. Pretty labels in easy-to-read script on drawers, cubby holes etc. will encourage children of reading age to find the right homes for their possessions.

Madame Montessori, who started the famous nursery school system, always said that everything that went together should go on some sort of tray; children can then just pull out the right tray and find what they want at once. This way everything is easy to find and easy to put back. The same method can apply even to clothes. Small children's clothes are not bulky and can be folded on to a tray and put away on shelves. Low-sided wicker trays, rather like those flattish baskets used in offices as in-and-out letter trays are good and inexpensive. Rectangular shapes are better than round ones, and you make the best possible use of space if they all fit neatly on to shelves. Whichever type you use, make sure that they can stack together neatly, since some trays will simply topple over, creating chaos, not order.

Clever containers
In fact, you can glean a whole lot of useful ideas by looking at office and even kitchen equipment to see what you can usefully borrow, copy or improvise. Those stacking perspex containers or stacking shallow drawers are ideal for children's

Good storage is essential if you want to keep children's rooms tidy. Whether it is achieved by buying customized units, like the well-planned wood-veneered range, left, or more unconventional furniture, right, is largely a question of budget and taste.

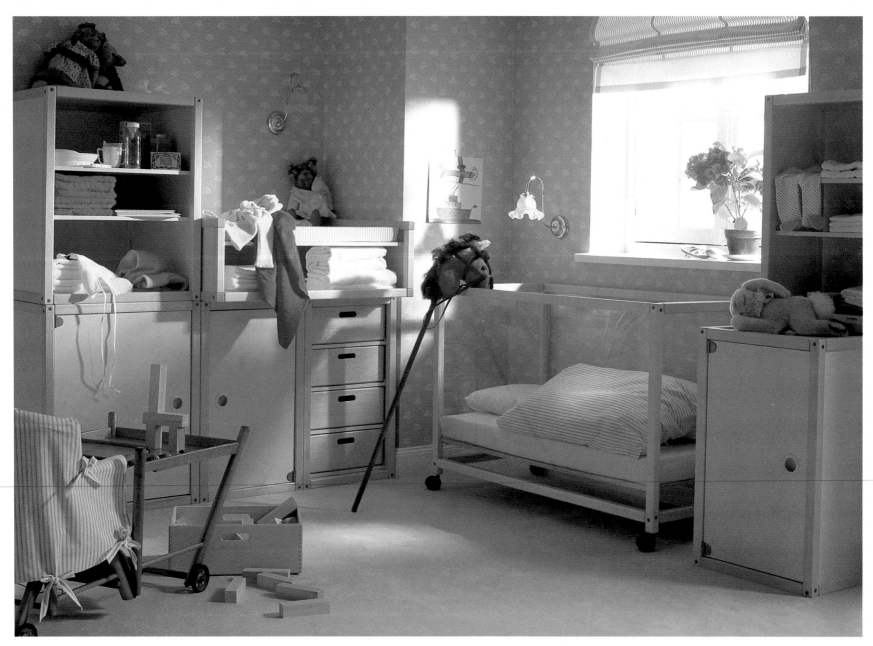

Left: Fitted cupboards and shelving provide ample storage space for clothes and towels in this baby's room.

Above: Design is an integral part of storage in this fun system, where coat hooks are within easy reach of the toddler.

Above right: Recessed shelving in an alcove, and a multi-drawered chest offer stylish but neat storage for a teenager.

Far right: Intriguing paper and raffia containers, decorative as well as practical, are ideal for storing small treasures.

storage: everything is visible and they also come in bright colours. Brand new plastic dustbins can make practical containers for toys.

Again, taking a leaf out of nursery and infant school practice, it is a good idea to make even better use of colour by using it as an essential part of a storage system. If you use large coloured cube containers, all red things can go in a red cube, yellow in a yellow one and so on.

It helps too, to organize things by size. It doesn't do to have, say, crayons, paints, pencils, small toys and so on put side by side with large toys where they get lost or broken. Give small objects their own small containers.

It is an expensive luxury to buy special, small-sized, easy-to-reach storage. Even with several children in mind it'll soon be outgrown and need replacing in no time at all. Better to buy full-size items straight off or improvise until you can afford them. Wooden crates from your local greengrocer, or those tough, round cardboard bins from wallpaper or fabric shops all make sturdy containers, ideal for toy storage. Paint them in vivid colours and fix wheels or castors to them, not just for easy mobility but so that they become playthings in their own right as well. Children are always enthusiastic about anything they can pull around and pretend is something else: a house, a ship, a car, even a horse.

251

CHILDREN'S ROOMS

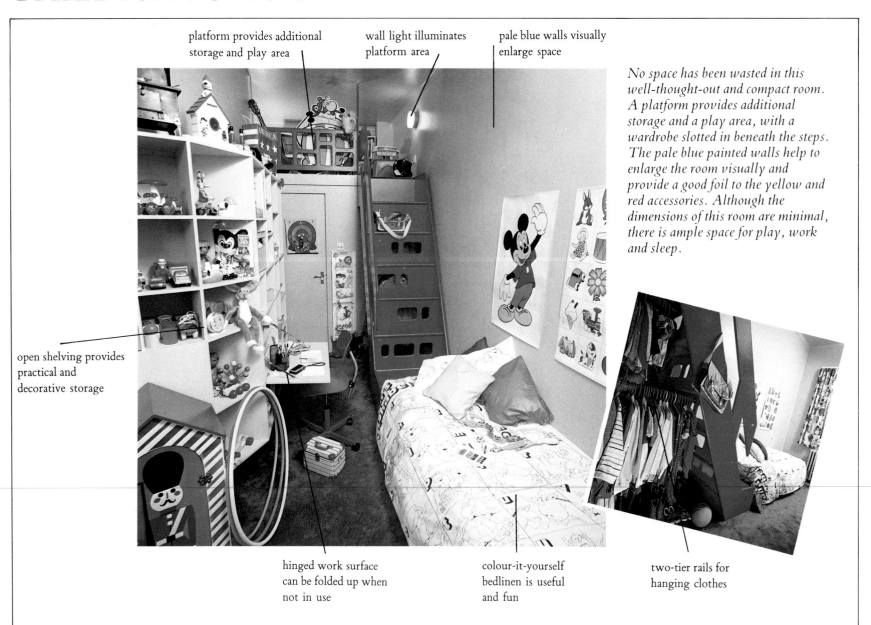

platform provides additional storage and play area

wall light illuminates platform area

pale blue walls visually enlarge space

No space has been wasted in this well-thought-out and compact room. A platform provides additional storage and a play area, with a wardrobe slotted in beneath the steps. The pale blue painted walls help to enlarge the room visually and provide a good foil to the yellow and red accessories. Although the dimensions of this room are minimal, there is ample space for play, work and sleep.

open shelving provides practical and decorative storage

hinged work surface can be folded up when not in use

colour-it-yourself bedlinen is useful and fun

two-tier rails for hanging clothes

Waste paper and rubbish bins, the larger the better, and especially if they are light, plastic and brightly coloured, are great toy containers. So are stacking wire baskets, vegetable racks, laundry baskets, gym lockers or the kinds of lockers used for storing luggage on stations. These will hold everything down to shoes and sports stuff. They don't have to be gloomy grey or khaki. It's an easy matter to paint or spray them any colour you like to match the rest of the room. Later on they make useful wardrobes.

As the child gets older and taller you could also use filing cabinets. It's not such a good idea for small children who could easily pull them over on top of themselves or try to climb up them, but at the homework stage, a row of filing cabinets with a continuous top of wood or Formica and enough kneehole space to sit at, can provide both desk/play surface and storage combined. Buy them, preferably second-hand, with different sized drawers to take both small and large objects and paint them to suit the room.

Right: Well-planned work-cum-playrooms can stop you going up the wall. Flexible shelving units can be adapted to suit the individual needs of each child. These provide a desktop, cork notice-board and storage for books and toys, and look good with the parallel bars set next door.

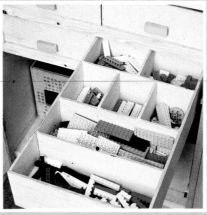

Wood, whether painted or varnished, always looks good. Above right: This unusual form of shelving is not only practical for storing large, rather unwieldy objects, but can also make being tidy seem more like a game. Left and far left: This particular unit has been tailor-made to the requirements of the child concerned, and even the drawers themselves (see detail photograph) have been compartmentized to make finding possessions easier.

From kids' stuff to teenage clobber

It is important to choose storage that can change its role as the children grow older and their possessions change in size and quantity. When they are tiny you will need space to store nappies, clothing (even large amounts of baby clothes don't take up much space), ointments, lotions, and so on; later the same space will take toys and odds and ends, and later still be used for books, models, electronic equipment, clothes and sports gear.

Trolleys or cots on wheels are particularly useful because they can take on a number of different roles, including that of plaything, over the years. Stacking boxes and cubes can be used in all sorts of configurations and their tops made to serve as work/play surfaces. If you decide on a shelving system, make sure the shelves are adjustable and as useful for small children as for teenagers. Units that have horizontal shelves and vertical divisions as well as integral cubes, drawers and even cupboards are marvellously useful because one way and another they will hold everything from books, records and toys to tapes, clothes and pictures. They will still look neat and tidy — even decorative. Since each thing is given its own particular area, it looks well organized — not just a jumble of possessions. If you can get such units on castors

they can also be used as room dividers. There are some kinds you can take apart to break up a large system into small units temporarily, using some, say by a child's bed, others all along a wall at waist level. Later they can all be put together in a floor to ceiling stack for a more sophisticated-looking arrangement.

Industrial shelving, that came into its own with the High-Tech look, has many good points to recommend it. Originally designed for factories, hospitals, restaurants, even greenhouses, it will take almost everything you can think of from folded clothes, shoes, sports equipment to rows of colourful containers for smaller objects.

Storage that's fun

Children's rooms offer the greatest scope for witty, clever, colourful ideas that can even make the serious

When two children share a room you can't afford to waste space. The mattress of each sofa bed rests on a bank of drawers which also serve as low tables at one end. A curtain acts as a room divider for one half of the room while a floor-to-ceiling tower of shelving, to which desks are attached, forms the remainder. The curtain can be drawn during the day to give the room a lighter, airier feeling. The curtains at the end of each bed conceal large closets for storing and hanging clothes.

CHILDREN'S ROOMS

business of being tidy and methodical more like an enjoyable game. Take a perfectly ordinary series of shelves. They may be essential to the room but rather boring. What can you do to liven them up? You could fix cup hooks on to the edges and hang nets or baskets from them for smaller temporary objects like balls, shuttlecocks, draughts, marbles, crayons.

Ordinary whitewood or unpainted wood units are not expensive and can be painted in all sorts of decorative ways: all over, in stripes or different blocks of colour — a different colour for each drawer. Wardrobes can be divided into several levels for a small child and gradually emptied out so they are left for normal clothes use or removed so that hanging space grows with the child. The outside can be painted or covered to look an amusing part of the room. Where every inch of space is at a premium don't forget that the insides of wardrobe doors can be used. Fit them with white or coloured plastic coated grids with shelves and you have a whole new stacking place for odds and ends which otherwise might be all over the floor.

There are endless opportunities to be ingenious and imaginative and the more possibilities you can squeeze into whatever storage you decide on, the happier you and your children will be.

Above: Making a virtue out of necessity – these old fruit and wicker baskets have been painted to give them fresh life as attractive containers for small objects.

Right: Natural wood wardrobe and drawers provide storage in this very traditional-style little girl's room.

Left: Plain white units offer pretty but functional storage in a toddler's room. There is plenty of concealed storage in the cupboards, open shelving units and a hanging area for clothes in the centre.

On the whole, and unless money is no object, special child-sized mini furniture is rarely a good long term investment. It is all too soon outgrown and discarded and generally lacks the solidity and staying power that large and well-used pieces like tables and desks need.

Nevertheless, there are obviously certain pieces that really have to be made especially for infants and pre-school children: cradles, cribs and cots, high chairs and first chairs. The last-named often become some of the most prized of juvenile antiques and are handed down in families. As for the rest, the essential criteria for choosing and buying should be safety, sturdiness and practicality first and then, if possible, an element of fun. With regard to safety, there are government regulations for the flammability of upholstered furniture. You should also look out for items that are difficult to topple over, and make sure that there are no sharp edges. Ease of cleaning is an obvious advantage, and much of today's furniture for children is made of plastic or metal that can be wiped down. Adaptability – items that adjust to grow with your child – is another feature to look for.

Because the choice is often overwhelming for first-time parents, it's best to make things a little simpler by thinking of such furniture in terms of activities and under such

heads as furniture for sleeping, for sitting, for eating, playing, washing and for travelling.

Furniture for sleeping
Newborn babies don't care where they sleep as long as they are warm and well-protected in conditions emulating their mother's womb, particularly when she was walking and moving. What else could account for the popularity of the cradle with its ability to be gently rocked? This and the Moses basket have barely changed in design for centuries.

Of course it can be argued that cradles and cribs are an unnecessary extravagance since they are grown out of so quickly. Their advantages are that for a tiny baby they are snug and can be easily moved and carried around. In any event they can usually be borrowed from some other member of the family or from friends or passed on to others so that they serve their purpose many times over. On the negative side, the British and U.S. Standards Institutions do not encourage the use of items

Contrasting styles: The high-tech room on the left shows the sort of furniture which easily adapts to a growing child. The prettily furnished nursery, right, centres on a crib, which will obviously have to be replaced by a bed later on.

CHILDREN'S ROOMS

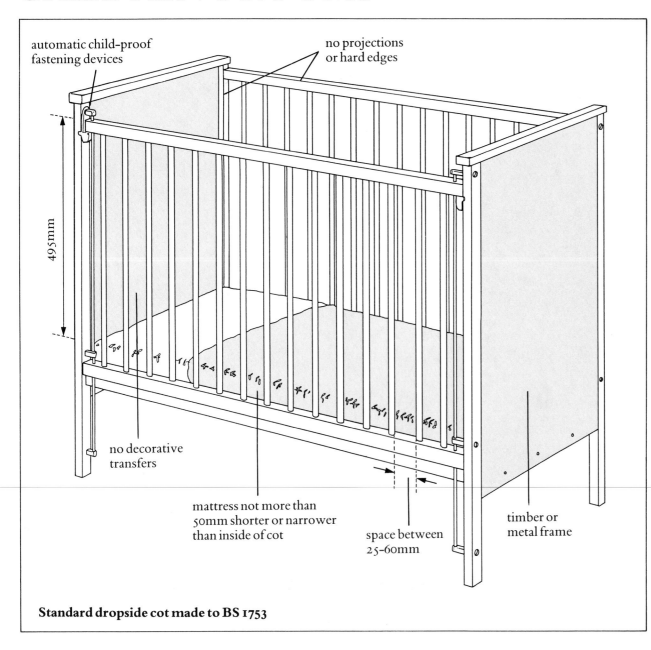

automatic child-proof
fastening devices

no projections
or hard edges

495mm

no decorative
transfers

mattress not more than
50mm shorter or narrower
than inside of cot

space between
25-60mm

timber or
metal frame

Standard dropside cot made to BS 1753

such as cribs, baskets or cradles. There are no standards for them and they are often made to intricate designs with little regard for safety.

Alternatively, you could just as easily use a carry cot for the first few months, or use the pram itself as a cradle, or a rigid Moses basket with a stand or even a converted laundry basket, box or drawer lined and suitably — ie not too softly — mattressed.

Buy a purpose-designed foam mattress – firm with a non-airtight cover. There are generally holes or pockets cut into the foam for extra safety. If you can't find one to fit exactly, buy a longer one and cut it down to size.

Cot

As the child gets older and more active and begins to be more aware of his or her surroundings, you will need to invest in a cot. Apart from minor variations in wood (there are also more costly polished steel versions) and a choice of slatted (preferable) or solid sides, most cots will look alike to the uninitiated. However there are differences and it is important to examine any cot you are thinking of buying with the most stringent safety aspects in mind.

The British and the American Federal Standards Institutes have issued the following directives both on the framework and the bedding.

● The sides and edges of the cot must be high enough to stop a baby climbing out and have no horizontal bars or ledges to aid the act of climbing. They must also have adequate rail heights even when the dropside is lowered.

● The bar or slat spacing must be small enough (60mm/2⅜ in apart) to prevent a baby slipping, feet first, through the bars.

● If there is a dropside guide system, that fastening device should engage automatically so that babies cannot lower the sides on their own.

● Paintwork and materials must not be harmful to babies even if they suck or chew the cot. There should be no transfers on the inside.

● Mattresses should not have any handles (as adult mattresses do to facilitate turning) in which babies can get their arms and legs trapped.

● The cot must be solidly constructed with no projections or exposed sharp edges on which babies could hurt themselves or snag their clothing.

Clever planning right from the start pays off as children's needs alter. Bunk beds make a safe place to rest a crib and will accommodate two children later on.

CHILDREN'S ROOMS

● The fillings should be clean and harmless and only non-poisonous dyes and colours should be used.

● There should be a label telling you which size of cot the mattress should fit.

● Pillows should not be used until after the first birthday and any baby's pillow should carry a warning notice to this effect.

● The pillow and cover should be so designed to ensure that babies can still breathe properly when they are lying on their sides or fronts.

● The pillow should be firm enough to stop a baby's head sinking into it.

● Pillows should always be kept clean and dry. Cotton covers are best since they will allow adequate airflow, but they must fit tightly over the pillow so that there is no possibility of babies sucking any extra loose material into their mouths.

● Always take off and dispose of plastic covers from mattresses and pillows after buying them.

Beds

At an even later stage, the cot can give way to a bed. If you have more than one child, or your child wants friends to stay, and there is limited space, think of investing in a truckle bed (a bed which can be concealed under another bed). Other good space-savers are beds with drawers underneath for clothes, blankets and linen or toys. There are extravagant

The hard-wearing shelving and storage units in these photographs will look just as good in a teenager's pad as in a baby's or toddler's room. The cot arrangement, top left, is built to convert into a bed, and the deep-drawered cabinet, which now provides a surface on which to change the baby and storage will also have a long life. The white cupboards and shelves, above and bottom left, provide a practical work surface, which with the addition of suitable chairs, lamps and mirrors can become desks, bookshelves or even a dressing table as required.

beds — extravagant because they will only be useful for limited periods — in the shape of cars or trains or boats. 'Junior' beds are also available, which are conventional in design but smaller than the standard single. They are equally extravagant in their way, as they are not large enough for adult use and children quickly grow out of them. And finally, there are the best playthings of all, adult-sized bunk beds which are as good for one as for two. These too, come in a variety of shapes and sizes and can be incorporated into elaborate climbing systems, tower structures and various fantasy creations (see page 219). But even the simplest models are good on all kinds of counts quite apart from the exercise, space-saving qualities and the security they provide for the child tucked in on the lower level who feels in a special little world.

The top level can be turned into another private area for reading or playing. Add book racks, lots of cushions, decorate that particular bit of ceiling with a map of the world (good for geography) or the night sky (good for astronomy) or, if the

Beds double as playthings when children can climb up to them and turn them into secret hideaways. Here, a roller blind effectively screens off the sleeping area. A second bed could be added later.

CHILDREN'S ROOMS

ceiling is very high, fix another 'roof', a suspended fabric canopy or a piece of wood on supports above. You can add roller blinds to the sides to give privacy, or more cheaply, pin on sheets which can be pulled aside like curtains.

Some models have drawers or shelves underneath for extra storage and there is a particularly useful kind that comes apart into separate beds for later on. Some even take apart to make good-looking sofas and are thus an excellent investment if you are intent on planning for the long-term.

All bunks should have some sort of guard rails when children are young and it is not a good idea, of course, to put anyone less than five years old on the upper level. Check that the ladder has smooth slats and can be firmly or permanently fixed.

It is possible to buy adult-sized beds which have protective sides to them that can later be removed, or you can improvise your own.

A distinctly nautical feel has been given to this room by covering the walls and ceiling in white-painted wooden slats to create a cabin effect. A blue-and-white folding captain's chair picks out the tiny blue print of the bunk, cushions and Roman blinds. The bed easily becomes a daytime sofa, and model ships, wheel barometer, rope ladder and globe are clever finishing touches.

painted walls are easy to keep clean

The fresh colours and smooth surfaces of this bedroom-cum-playroom are designed to appeal to children while being safe and easy to keep clean. The cheerful curtains, lampshade, bed-linens, flooring and even the wall posters, keep to the same colour scheme. The bunk bed pushed against the wall leaves plenty of space to spread out toys and books, while the alcove inside provides an extra play or living area, with an extra mattress for when a friend comes to stay. A second bed could be added later.

vinyl flooring is hard-wearing, practical and noise-absorbent

decorative screen hides radiator

CHILDREN'S ROOMS

Sensible seating in a child's room is important if the room is to be used to full advantage.

Top left: This sturdy chair and table set, which is ideal for playing, reading and eating on, has no sharp corners on which children could injure themselves. The chair has arms and a built-in footstool for additional safety and it is also comfortably padded.

Bottom left: Practical seating does not have to be expensive. In this light and airy teenager's room, an old 1960s sofa has been pressed into service in its original livery. The colouring of the cushion covers has been repeated throughout the room – in the bedspread, the decorative panel behind, the rug, blind, ornaments and the jazzy geometric bedside table.

Furniture for sitting

Given the way most children prefer to sit on the floor anyway, you would think there was little need for chairs at an early age. In fact there are quite a number of chairs associated with each of a child's growing stages and all of which are very necessary to them.

In the beginning you need a good comfortable chair for nursing and feeding the baby. This should be low with either no arms at all or the sort that will allow the mother plenty of unrestricted movement. An ordinary straight-backed wooden kitchen chair with the legs shortened is ideal, padded out with cushions for comfort. Out of the baby stage you need the sort of relaxed chair that is both good for comfort and comforting and for climbing on: a capacious, overstuffed armchair with lavish arms that will go on to be a favourite chair for a child to curl up in to read. Children love being nursed and cuddled in a rocking chair and the smaller versions are comforting for small children to sit in while they watch a new baby being fed. If there isn't a spare knee to sit on, a rocking chair is a good place to be for watching television or listening to a story.

You will definitely need a strong, stable highchair, preferably one that can be adjusted to a convenient height for feeding the child from the table, or that can come apart to be put on a lower level. Unless you are fortunate enough to have a nursery, this will, of course, be located in the dining room or kitchen. There are low level chairs with trays as well, but a dual-purpose one will save money and space. If the chair is made of metal, there should be no sharp ends or open-ended tubes and when the feeding tray is in position there should be no possibility of the child slipping out from under it. There should also be a safety strap, a seat adjustment device that locks securely and, for maximum stability, the base should always be wider than the seat. You may have to buy the harness separately. Either way, make sure that there is firmly fixed anchorage for it. A proper foot rest adds comfort. As they get older children will need proper chairs so that they can sit at a table to eat, sturdy chairs to climb on to reach things, soft, comforting body-moulding chairs for relaxing in and chairs that give good support for working. They particularly like chairs that move (rockers, chairs on wheels or castors) or chairs that they can sink into, like bean bags or sag-bags. These should have fire-

A raised study area has been cleverly fitted into an awkward corner in this young girl's room. Pale lilac wooden furniture complements the wallpaper and makes the room especially feminine.

Left and above: The sofa bed is an extremely versatile piece of furniture which is capable of turning a bedroom (above) into a teenage bedsit (left) in a matter of minutes, and is particularly useful for children who want to entertain their friends in their own rooms and need privacy. The striped wallpaper and bed linen in the same room are in bright fresh colours to accentuate the non-bedroom feel.

retardant stuffing. Toddlers prefer low seats so that their legs rest on the floor, otherwise they get very tired. Stackable plastic chairs in bright colours are ideal for mealtimes and for working. So are sturdy wooden chairs, especially those with arms which feel safe and are

more restful. Stools, too, are quite good for painting, model-building, drawing; there is an adjustable variety which will grow with the child. If you can get a step-stool you will find it invaluable in the bathroom (for reaching the basin or sink) as well as in their playrooms and/or bedrooms. Look for the kind with suction devices that keep them steady and firm.

Benches, wood-topped or upholstered are useful for accommodating several children, marvellous for games of pretend, especially as they can be turned upside down, good for putting under a window (with bars!) and handy for model-building when things can be spread out along them. From the safety point of view, most *don'ts* about chairs are taken care of by common sense, but here are some points to bear in mind:

● Buy strong sturdy chairs that won't tip over when they are climbed on.

● Don't provide children under eight years old with canvas folding chairs as they could collapse when climbed on.

● Be wary of plastic or wood folding chairs. They might be sturdy enough but the folding mechanism could easily trap and hurt small fingers.

● Make sure wooden chairs are smooth and splinter free.

● Check that paint is non-toxic.

Furniture for playing and working

One of the biggest mistakes parents make when choosing furniture for children's rooms is to forget what it is like to be only a metre (3 feet) tall. Children need chairs and tables and surfaces they can relate to and it is easier for them to be comfortable with their feet on the floor.

If you have the space, a large low table with a wide horizontal surface is ideal for painting and drawing, especially if its legs are adjustable so that very small children can sit around it on the floor. Later it can be used as a desk, and if it is really quite large, for two desks divided down the middle with some sort of wooden or plastic pole or divider. If space is very tight, look for a collapsible table or one that folds down from the wall. It's useful to have this sort of spare table so that children impatient to get on with their own activities don't have to wait till you've cleared the kitchen or dining table.

Try to provide some sort of work surface as soon as the child starts school so he or she will automatically start doing projects and homework on that and not on the floor. If you can find a desk or surface with sides or can nestle it away in some alcove, say between bookshelves or cupboards, so much the better; children like a sense of being enclosed when they are concentrating and

One of the major advantages of this roll-top desk and storage unit is that you can adjust the spacing between the shelves, as well as the height of the work surface. This will suit the needs (and heights) of a growing child for many years. When investing in substantial pieces of furniture it is well worth considering how suitable it will be long-term. Unless you have a bottomless purse or plan a large family, steer clear of designs that are quickly outgrown.

such a space will be different or seem different from the play space around them.

Blackboards, pin or tack boards and easels should all be part of a playroom's furniture, for children need vertical as well as horizontal surfaces. Boards on wheels are ideal

CHILDREN'S ROOMS

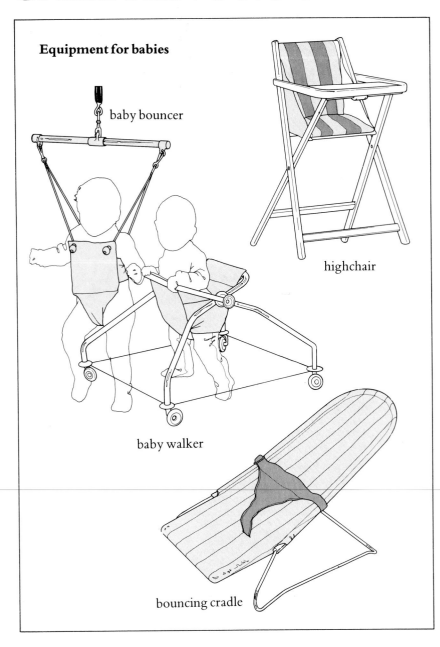

Equipment for babies

baby bouncer

baby walker

highchair

bouncing cradle

because they can also act as space dividers and the bigger the work space you can devote to covering with pin or tack board material like cork, felt-covered masonite or plaster board, the better.

Bulletin boards with brightly-coloured backgrounds are excellent for pinning up drawings, paintings, homework, pieces of first writing and so on. They could also make good headboards for beds.

Baby walkers There are several different types of baby walkers on the market, designed not so much to help or encourage a baby to walk but more to give him or her the chance to enjoy moving around quickly. There's a frustrating stage when they can only sit and crawl and obviously want to be more mobile and a baby walker bridges this gap very nicely.

Baby walkers support the baby in a fabric or plastic seat attached to a metal frame which moves on castors. By sitting on the seat with feet on the floor, a baby can propel herself along. Some models have a bumper all round which helps to prevent the baby from jarring his or herself when he or she bumps into hard or sharp edges and minimizes damage to furniture. Some incorporate a play tray.

There has recently been a certain amount of controversy over the safety of this type of baby walker.

Consumer testers have found that many models are easy to overturn and some collapse much too readily. There is obviously a risk of injuring the child if this happens. If you plan to buy a baby walker, choose one that is sturdy and has no hard metal edges that might injure your child if the walker topples over. And above all, do not let your child play in a baby walker unsupervised – walkers should never be used as a way of keeping a baby occupied while you are busy in another room of the house.

Other models, made of wood or rigid plastic, are more like trolleys which can be pushed along with an upright handle, but these are really a step further along the road. If you buy this more advanced walker or an animal on wheels which can be pushed or ridden on, make sure that it is stable and will not tip over.

Swings and baby bouncers Baby swings and bouncers, like baby walkers, are not purpose-built for travelling (though they can be packed very easily and will certainly keep a child amused at the other end of the journey) but they do help the child himself towards a certain mobility. Just as some babies get quite expert at making a cradle rock by kicking their feet, your baby will probably enjoy the movement of a swing as well. Some high chairs can be transformed into an indoor swing, but you can also buy a purpose-made baby swing that winds up and swings your baby gently for up to 15 minutes. The baby must be strapped in with a separate harness. It's better not to let another child push the baby unless you are there. Never leave a baby alone in such a swing.

From the age of about three months you can put a baby in a bouncer. This is a type of fabric saddle suspended on a rod held by a length of rubber attached to a chain. A clamp fixes the chain to a door frame and you can adjust the length of the chain so that when the baby is in the saddle his or her feet just touch the floor. In this way babies can bounce gently (or not so gently depending on how strong and active they are) and securely in an open doorway. It will keep them amused and at the same time develop good muscles. The doorway must be kept clear by propping the door open. Do not leave a baby alone in the bouncer and always check all the parts of the apparatus regularly for signs of wear.

Baby bouncers are not covered by British or American Standards, so it is especially important to buy one made by a reliable manufacturer.

Highchairs are available in many colours and designs. Painted white, as here, will look pretty in any surroundings.

CHILDREN'S ROOMS

The ability to adapt spaces as well as attitudes is essential when children have to be taken into account, and that applies from babyhood to well into schooldays. You can plan a child's room to perfection to contain all he or she could desire, but however beautiful or fun it is, no child is going to stay cooped up there all the time; the rest of the house belongs to him or her too. So you should be prepared for the fact that certain parts of the house will be regularly used by the children.

Kitchens and Dining Rooms

When you are working in the kitchen (and the average housewife or working couple spends a fair time in the kitchen – even more when there's a baby to feed), you don't want toddlers under your feet and school-age children running in and out to the garden. Try to organise your space so that you have an efficient working kitchen area (preferably *not* a thoroughfare) with an area within it (or an adjacent, open plan room) where children can play, away from the dangers of ovens and pans but where they can see and be seen. You may want to wheel a pram into the kitchen and later you'll need room for a high chair, and possibly a baby walker, so if you're lucky enough to be able to install a new kitchen, think about making room for these things – it may be worth spending a little extra

to get things right at the start. If the kitchen or dining room has doors onto the garden make sure you fit a washable flooring so that the inevitable trails of muddy footprints can be cleaned off easily.

In some households, the dining room doubles as a playroom or a homework room, particularly in winter if children's rooms are cold. In any case, it is worth giving children some storage space in the dining room (or another downstairs room) so that they are encouraged to put things away.

Teenagers have very different needs: you don't need to keep an eye on them as you do with very small children; they are more independent and will probably want to get away on their own or with friends in a different room from you. They'll also have hectic timetables packed with after-school activities and social outings, all of which mean that they'll want to eat on their own at

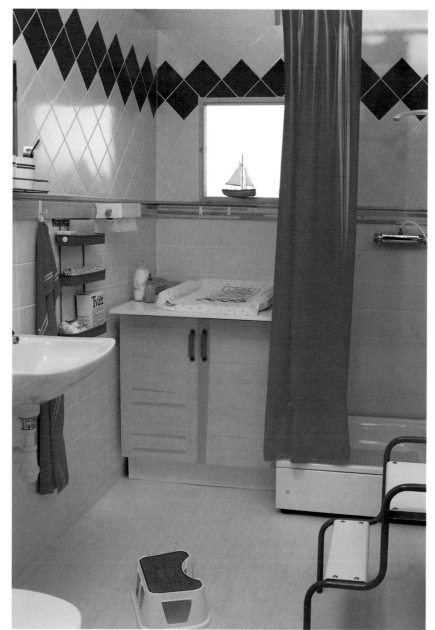

Right: The heights of fittings in the average bathroom are impossible for a young child to cope with. If you do not always want to be in attendance, safe, non-slip steps and platforms provide a good measure of independence for the youngster.
As children make their presence felt throughout the house allowances have to be made for them. The resilient flooring of the modern sitting-room, left, is a good example.

CHILDREN'S ROOMS

If you want to keep the sitting room largely free of children, then you must provide suitable entertainment facilities for them elsewhere in the home – somewhere they will feel warm and comfortable and look forward to being in. The room above is relaxed and informal. The bed obviously does double duty as a lounging area, there is a stereo system – with all-important headphones – and a comfortable place to sit. All in all, not a bad compromise.

different times from the rest of the family; a quiet eating area, a corner or bar arrangement in the kitchen comes in useful here.

Washing arrangements

A growing family puts a great strain on one bathroom, particularly in the mornings during the rush to work or school. It pays dividends in saved tempers if you can plumb a wash-basin into the children's room at an early age. When they are babies it will be useful for changing nappies and washing and by the time they reach school age it will shorten the queue for the bathroom. For the same reason it makes sense to provide a lavatory separate from the bathroom if you do not have one already. Alternatively, if the master bedroom is large, it might be possible to divide it so that there is a bathroom en suite for the use of parents. Even a shower cubicle in a bedroom could make life easier.

Another idea is to build in a shower, washbasin and lavatory (if there's room) under the stairs – great for removing the dirt from a child who has been playing in a sandpit or even for a shower after gardening, and it all helps to lessen the load on the upstairs bathroom.

Living room

There are two ways you can regard the living room. Either it's the warm heart of the house, cheerful,

noisy, cluttered, where everybody congregates – children, parents, friends, visitors, pets, or it's a quiet retreat kept as child-free as possible most of the time and only invaded by the whole family on special occasions. If your house is a very spacious one then there are no problems keeping the living room as a refuge. If it's a small house and you do not want the children to spend all their time in the living room then it is important to make other parts of the house – their bedrooms, the dining room, a big kitchen or breakfast room – as attractive and welcoming to them as possible. Also, early on, learn to make the living room childproof to toddlers by seeing that their belongings don't dominate the scene. Provide some storage with the proviso that it's for special toys, perhaps brought in from time to time from the bedroom cupboard so that you don't have to live with perpetual clutter. A wicker basket is ideal for this purpose; it can be put out of sight quite easily. Later, a shelf or shelves in a cupboard might be better. If children use your stereo system when they are older, provide special separate storage for their records and tapes.

Extensions

If your home seems too small for all this but you don't want to move you might consider various kinds of

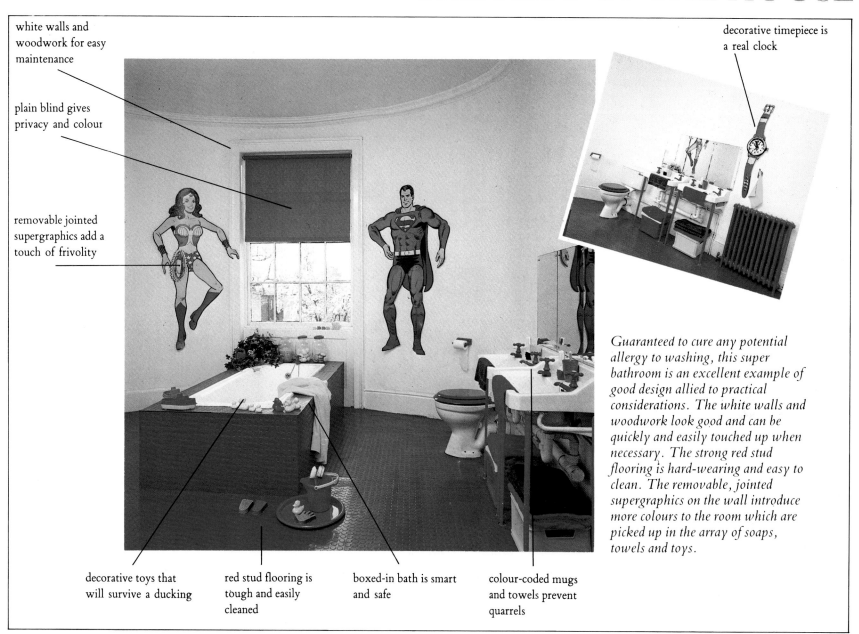

white walls and woodwork for easy maintenance

plain blind gives privacy and colour

removable jointed supergraphics add a touch of frivolity

decorative timepiece is a real clock

decorative toys that will survive a ducking

red stud flooring is tough and easily cleaned

boxed-in bath is smart and safe

colour-coded mugs and towels prevent quarrels

Guaranteed to cure any potential allergy to washing, this super bathroom is an excellent example of good design allied to practical considerations. The white walls and woodwork look good and can be quickly and easily touched up when necessary. The strong red stud flooring is hard-wearing and easy to clean. The removable, jointed supergraphics on the wall introduce more colours to the room which are picked up in the array of soaps, towels and toys.

CHILDREN'S ROOMS

extension. You can build upwards: convert a loft space into an extra bedroom or playroom. You can build outwards, adding a side extension, an extension over a garage or an extra room at the back of the house. And in some older style houses there is a basement or half basement which can be excavated further, waterproofed and turned into a serviceable playroom. Before starting on any building work consult a professional. You may have to get planning permission or satisfy the Borough Surveyor that your plans and building are sound.

If you are building an extra room in any of these ways you can ensure from the word go that they are really soundproof and well insulated against heat loss too. You will also need to make sure that there is adequate ventilation.

Adapting the furnishings
While there are children around it is not a good idea to indulge in pale or delicate upholstery and soft furnishings unless they are easily wash-

An alternative to moving for the expanding family is to find 'room at the top'. Here a converted loft provides plenty of room for sleep and play areas, which are clearly defined by changes in flooring and wall covering. The entire room has been cleverly colour-coordinated in this pleasing and practical space.

able. This doesn't mean you are condemned to have all covers, curtains and carpets in sturdy, serviceable weights and dark, dirt-proof colours but rather that you choose finishes as much for their wearability and cleanability as their aesthetic effect.

Floors in kitchens and dining rooms should be easy to wipe clean. It is not a good idea to have carpet in a dining room where young children are going to be eating regularly. Newspaper or a sheet of plastic under the chair help. Walls, too, are going to take a lot of punishment and will need to withstand repeated cleaning. If you do have non-washable or non-wipeable wallpaper, have it coated with clear polyurethane so that you can sponge it down when necessary.

On the whole, blinds are always better and safer than trailing curtains because there is nothing a small child can trip over or pull down so long as cords are kept well out of reach.

If you have any reasonably big ground floor room in a house or apartment (it is not advisable to consider it on an upper floor in any building), it's worth covering the floor in tough, easy-care vinyl, linoleum, cork or composition tiles of one kind or another. A good tough floor will not show marks, or at least will not retain them, and you will find it a boon on rainy days for

tricyling and even roller skating.

Remember that stairs provide an endless source of fascination and play for children once they get a little older. They will almost inevitably want to slide down banisters, push themselves on their tummies down the stairs or try to walk up the outside of the steps beyond the banisters. You can't do much to prevent this but you can make sure that the stairs and the floor below are well carpeted and hand rails are smooth and splinter free.

Adapting a room

Adapting one room to take a second child is different again. It helps if you start off designing the room with the possibility of more children in mind rather than try to squash later children into a room obviously planned for one. The main thing is to give each child a certain amount of privacy without sacrificing too much of the general play space and there are lots of ways of doing this, depending on the size and shape of the space you have.

Top: An attractive loft conversion with well-lit work surfaces and good storage under the bed make for an ideal boy's room. Hammocks make exciting sleeping alternatives and during the day can be folded away to make extra floor space. Bottom: Delicate colours and light woods create a totally different effect in this young girl's attic room.

Adapting for sharing

There are some situations in which you may need to make a physical barrier in a room where children are sharing – for instance when two teenagers or school-age children of the opposite sex share. Curtains or an old fashioned Victorian screen, re-vamped as a double sided pin board may be enough to divide sleeping areas. Or you can make a more solid barrier with furniture – two wardrobes, backed with posters, put end to end between the sleeping areas, with a door facing each bed, makes a removable room divider. You can make a lower barrier by putting the desks, made up from work tops placed over chests, as described on page 205, between the beds. By fixing a board to the back of each desk you can create more solid dividers, and provide private workspace at the same time. If space is more limited, build double-sided or open bookshelves between the beds as a divider.

If you can't provide physically separated areas, at least define the space, so that each child has his or her own storage area, display area, playspace and so on. For instance, in a room with alcoves on either side of a chimney breast, try to allocate

Tied-back curtains can easily be let down to form a private sleeping area in the shared bedroom.

one alcove to each child. You can build in a desk top with storage below and a noticeboard and shelves above. Choose one colour for each child, and follow the theme through with painted shelves, bedlinen, towels, toy boxes and so on.

Although parents usually take the largest bedroom as theirs, it often makes better sense to use the second bedroom as the main bedroom and give the largest room to the children, so that they have more space for their activities and can spend more time there. It also gives you more scope for dividing the room and giving them some privacy.

Adapting the room, or rooms, as they grow older and develop their own tastes is different again. If you have followed the staged plan suggested at the beginning of the book, the gradual changes won't be nearly as traumatic as a sudden transformation into a whole new room. The basic bones, the main bulk of the furniture, will be there, leaving plenty of space and scope for the teenager to stamp it with his or her own personality.

Even if you hate what your teenagers do to that former pretty or cute little room, try to ignore it; it's more important that each individual learns to express their tastes and they will only grow and improve in this respect by being able to experiment in the first place. If you really can't stand it, just shut the door

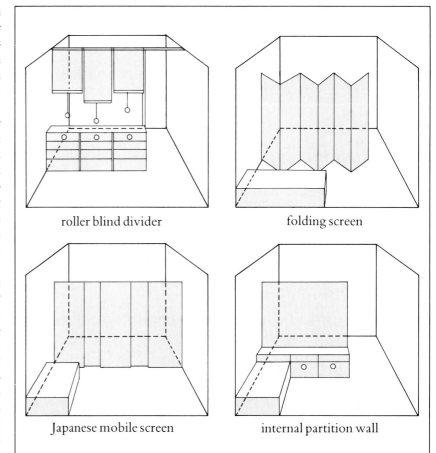

roller blind divider

folding screen

Japanese mobile screen

internal partition wall

Room dividers

All children need a space they can call their own. If you are unable to give each child a room of his or her own, then it's a good idea to provide some sort of barrier which will define territory and afford each child a degree of privacy. Dividers can also be used to split off a work/play area from a sleeping area. Top left: A long chest of drawers is a permanent fixture, while roller blinds can be pulled down to form a screen as required. Top right: A folding screen can be used for posters too. Bottom left: Sliding Japanese rice paper screens cut out less light. Bottom right: An internal partition wall is permanent but gives greater privacy.

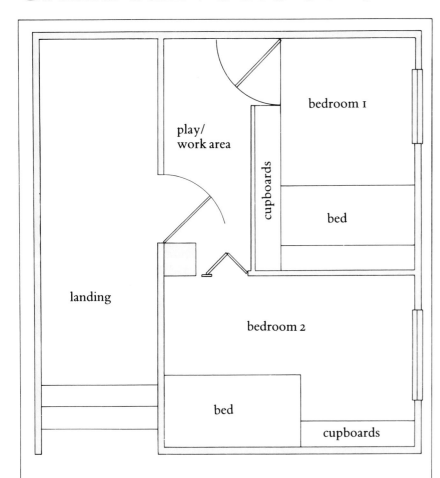

play/
work area

cupboards

landing

bedroom 1

bed

bedroom 2

bed

cupboards

Two into one will go

If you have a sufficiently large bedroom, then one solution to the problems arising from brothers and sisters sharing a room is to divide it up. Here, internal partition walls have been erected in an L-shape so that each child has a small bedroom

with one window, cupboards and the privacy afforded by an individual door. A communal play/work area has also been created which can be used for homework, book-shelves, tv, desk, computer and so on.

firmly and don't go in. Sooner or later it will probably get into such a muddle that even the teenager will want to do something about it. It shouldn't be a constant battle ground. They and you will learn that the hard way but it is worth it in the long run; if you respect their possessions and space they are far more likely to come to respect them too.

Finding the space for one more

No-one needs to be told that in a small house or flat or apartment it is not going to be easy to find space for one more child. But here are some suggestions:

● Make a partition wall three-quarters of the way down the child's bedroom. Furnish one side with two bunkbeds and a desk to give just the right amount of privacy for the older child (or children); the rest can be play and sleeping space for the new arrival. Line the wall with blackboard or pin or bulletin board, or with shelves.

● Build a hardboard room within a room with the outside walls all shelves and a cantilevered panel which lets down to become a table or pushes up to become a bulletin board.

● For another room-within-a-room, build a work/storage sleeping unit with white-laminate plastic surfaces, or in painted wood. This

frees the perimeter of the room to make it look more spacious.

● Build in a wall of storage and work surfaces including a Murphy bed for an older child. This will fold up during the daytime to make more play space.

Safety precautions

It is important to think about safety, especially in areas like the kitchen and living room where children will spend a lot of time with you.

Hall, stairs and corridors

● Make sure that lighting in corridors and on stairs and steps is adequate at all times of day and night.

● Use a non-slip polish if your hall floor is wood or tiled.

● See that stair carpets are well fitting with no loose or worn parts to catch on or trip over.

● Fix a gate to the top and bottom of the stairs *before* your child starts to crawl and explore. Make sure that safety barriers placed in doorways or at the top and bottom of staircases comply with the requirements of BS 4125.

Right: This room can easily accommodate two children. Placing the second bed at right angles to the first, instead of the more usual parallel arrangement, offers extra floor space for play.

CHILDREN'S ROOMS

Kitchens

● Make sure that kettle spouts and saucepan handles are turned inwards on to the stove.

● Keep doors on freezers, refrigerators, washing machines and tumble dryers firmly closed (child safety locks are available) and discourage any climbing on such machinery.

● Don't leave any appliances, particularly chip pans and deep fat pans, unattended.

● Wipe up spills on floors at once.

● Ensure cleaning materials and all dangerous household substances are kept well out of reach of children. Fit childproof locks to under-work surface cupboards if necessary. Make sure you store pills and medicines under lock and key, and purchase them in child-resistant containers.

● Ensure that there are no flexes or cords trailing round the kitchen: sockets should be positioned behind the work surface if at all possible.

Living rooms

● Guard the windows. If you have unbarred windows make sure the bottom part is never open when there are children around. Provide all windows with childproof locks.

● Put fireguards around fires and fireplaces and *never* leave a child alone in a room with a fire.

● Use childproof sockets for electrical fittings and do not have any trailing flexes or wires that could cause accidents.

● Move any arrangements of small objects on low tables to a higher level for the time being.

● Glass doors should be fitted with safety glass or safety film so that if it is banged it will not splinter. Glaziers who are members of the Glass and Glazing Federation will advise on appropriate materials.

Bathrooms

● See that all fittings and switches comply with the relevant special safety regulations.

● Never leave children alone in a bath or in a bathroom.

● Lock up medicines and pills at all times in a cabinet well out of reach. Buy types with childproof lids.

● Never keep any portable electric appliances in the bathroom.

● Provide an adjustable platform or footstool to enable children to reach the sink and lavatory.

● Remove all door locks at child-height to avoid children locking themselves in.

● Put lavatory cleaners, bleaches, detergents in a locked cupboard.

General

● Make sure that cupboards and closets which could be tipped or pulled over are fixed to the wall. Any other potentially dangerous free-standing furniture should be moved out of harm's way.

● Keep flooring firmly fixed down, particularly in doorways.

● Tidy away toys on the floor to prevent people tripping up.

Safety features

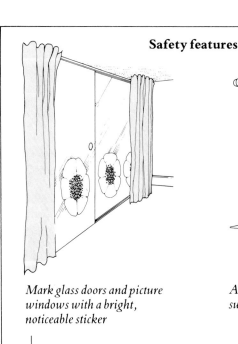

Mark glass doors and picture windows with a bright, noticeable sticker

A moveable steel safety gate suitable for doors and stairways

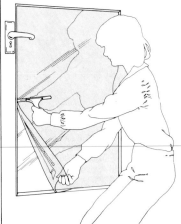

Fit doors and windows with safety film to prevent splintering glass

An adjustable wooden safety gate permanently fixed to the staircase

More than half the accidents that occur in the home involve children under the age of five. A relatively small outlay on some essential pieces of safety equipment could help you avoid such accidents.

Left, top: A strong wall-mounted fireguard is essential for rooms with wall-mounted gas and electric fires. Most models have sides which open for easy access to controls.

Left above: For open fireplaces you need an extending fireguard with an adjustable width. These too fold flat for storage. Fireguards are also available for cabinet heaters which are fitted with castors. Neither fireguards nor heater guards should be used to air clothes or bedding.

Centre, top: Buy a hob guard with telescopic front and side panels to give a secure fit on most hob-type cookers. Always ensure that pan handles are pointed inwards to avoid scalding.

Centre, above: An electronic baby alarm with a sensitive listening device that is activated by the slightest murmur, enabling you to hear baby's cry no matter where you are in the house.

Right, top: Electric shock can kill or burn. To prevent a child poking objects or fingers into electric points, switch off and cover unused points with a safety cover. Put away all electrical appliances after use.

Right, above: A childproof lock will prevent nimble little fingers from opening a window. Keep the key nearby, in case of fire.

BEDROOMS & BATHROOMS

INTRODUCTION

Bedrooms and bathrooms are the rooms in which we are supposed to relax our bodies, restore our energies, and take comfort. In short, they need not be just for sleeping, for storing clothes, dressing, bathing, washing and shaving.

So there is no reason – especially given the general shortage of space – why bedrooms should not be on 24-hour duty, used for working in as well as sleeping – and for watching television, listening to music, and even for eating; a small table for leisurely breakfasts and comfortable little suppers could be a great luxury.

Bathrooms too – given the square footage – can be multi-functional. Some people deliberately turn a large bedroom into a comfortable bathroom/dressing/exercise room, keeping a smaller room for actual sleeping. But even a very small room could probably be made considerably more luxurious and comforting than it is at present.

The first priority in any bedroom or bathroom, whatever its use, should be comfort. In the case of bedrooms this is not just a comfortable bed and bedclothes, although they are essential since we spend one-third of our lives in bed – but also really good lighting. And that means good to make-up by, good to read in bed and work by, good for general dressing and easy on the eye. You will want comfort underfoot too. If ever there was a place for carpet, or at least generous rugs, the bedroom is that place. Heating too, should be well regulated so that the temperature can be as good for sitting in as it is for sleeping. Quiet is an essential. If you live in a busy area or over a much-used street, you will certainly need to consider fabric-covered walls as well as carpet and multi-layered window treatments, if not double glazing, all of which will help to deaden outdoor sounds.

Bathrooms too, need good lighting and heating and warm, non-slip floors. Some kind of ventilation, e.g. an extractor fan, may be necessary to combat condensation. Handgrips on baths might seem a small detail but it is an important one if you have children, elderly people or invalids to consider.

Whether you do it all at once or aim for a series of staged improvements will depend on your budget and your circumstances. If you are planning bedrooms and bathrooms from scratch you are lucky, because with a very limited budget you can decide your priorities and plan sensibly to achieve them as and when you have the cash. If you are hoping to improve existing rooms but cannot do it all at once you will find that even the slightest change can uplift the spirits . . . cushions on a bed, a new bedcover, tie-backs on curtains, pictures, new towels, an added plant.

The aim of this section is to define the functions of both rooms and show you how to make the best use of your available space; how to achieve an appropriate style; and how to plan storage, lighting and furnishings.

Most importantly, it aims to show you how to fit your rooms to the way you live; how to make them really work for you. After all, bedrooms and bathrooms are, or should be, the foundations of your personal comfort. They deserve to be well-planned.

Bedroom and bathroom are very nearly combined by an adjoining door. There is barely a glimpse of the en-suite bathroom, but just enough to see that both rooms have been designed with the same stencilling around the wall, in the same shades of cream and grey. A totally unifying effect.

Most people would like, and indeed need, to think of their bedrooms as more than just a place for sleep, storing clothes, dressing and making up. In today's world the bedroom often has to be office, study and second living room as well. The ideal would be to have a desk as well as a bed, an armchair or two and a couch, generous bedside tables and storage cupboards for clothes, bookshelves, television, stereo, as well as space to stash away a sewing machine and an exercise machine so that they do not spoil the elegant harmony of the whole. There should also be space for storing impedimenta like files, records, tapes and sewing stuff. Space in fact, to ensure that the bedroom really is a room for quiet and rest, a room away from the family for pursuing your own interests and work, and above all a room for comfort.

Alas, the reality is that most bedrooms are far too small for most people's ideals and need to be meticulously planned if they are to hold more than the minimum of a bed, a couple of bedside tables, clothes storage and a chair. Almost everywhere, except in roomy country or suburban houses and old-fashioned mansion apartments, bedrooms are sacrificed for the greater good of the general living space. Cottage bedrooms, small flat bedrooms, new house bedrooms, conversions and bedsitting rooms all suffer from lack

of the square footage that is desperately needed for real comfort. And if so-called master bedrooms are small, rooms meant for children are often no more than cells fit for a couple of bunk beds.

Luckily, a number of furniture designers are now producing modular furniture that can be shaped and re-shaped to suit awkward spaces and differing needs. These units are available in expensive, middle-of-the-road and budget ranges to suit most purses. If you can afford it, fine; if not, you can still do a great deal with decoration and ingenuity.

Space, one cannot stress too often, is as much a matter of *feeling* spacious as of actual room measurement. If you can foster the illusion by clever and imaginative use of mirror, lighting, colour and pattern (stick to one shade or pattern for walls, floors, curtains and bedspread) and multi-purpose furniture (beds that have storage underneath, chests of drawers that are also

A smaller-than-normal double bed, a tiny bedside table on the far side where the angled wall is difficult to utilize and a chair doubling as another bedside table all help to give the cottage bedroom on the left a more spacious feel.

The small room on the right gets its fresh look from the blue and white scheme, deep window and plants.

BEDROOMS

Top left: Light colours and a wall of mirror effectively double the size of the tailored guest room. Bottom left: A mirrored headboard gives an illusion of even more space and light in this already soft and light bedroom decorated in delicate hues of apricot and cream.

work surfaces; cupboards and closets that hold files and equipment as well as clothes) you are well on the way to manipulating every inch to its best advantage – and every inch well used in a bedroom really does make an enormous difference.

From singles to doubles

Adapting bachelor accommodation – whether male or female – to take a partner can be very testing. I am not talking here about the merits or demerits of feminine or masculine decoration, but rather of making room for one more person's effects. It can come as a great shock, once the all-embracing, all-forgiving 'honeymoon' period is over, to wake up to somebody else's clothes and clutter. So every possible inch of storage has to be utilized to cope with the changed circumstances and, if possible, to disguise the overflow of possessions. And all in such a way as to give each a fair share of the space, leaving no room for complaint or irritation.

Doors, and this includes wardrobe or closet doors, are often an under-used ingredient of the room ripe for conversion. Racks, hooks, the sort of spring clips used for holding brooms and cleaning apparatus can all be used to provide extra storage. Is there room for a window seat? If there is, make it one with a lift-up lid so that belongings can be stored inside.

The old-fashioned ottoman or a similar sort of chest is another good solution. Either can be put at the foot of a bed, in a corner, or under a window to provide extra seating as well as storage. If there is a dressing table think too about a hollow upholstered stool with a lift-up lid. Make as many things as possible do two jobs rather than one.

If there isn't room to add a dressing table and/or desk, think of buying three or four whitewood chests of drawers, or chests plus a cupboard and arranging them against a wall so that there is some knee hole space. Cover the lot with a long counter top, perhaps covered in plastic laminate, paint the chests in with the room and you have a desk, dressing table, work surface and clothes storage all in one.

Right: A large drop-leafed table set behind this bed acts as bedhead as well as drawing/work surface. Floor-to-ceiling open bookshelves effectively divide off sleeping from sitting/breakfast/casual eating area. The rose and cream colour scheme freshened by touches of white in light shades and chair cushions makes this multi-functional space seem light and welcoming. Long swing-armed work lamps provide powerful light when needed but can easily be pushed up and away; so can the rise-and-fall fixture over the pedestal table in the seating area of the room.

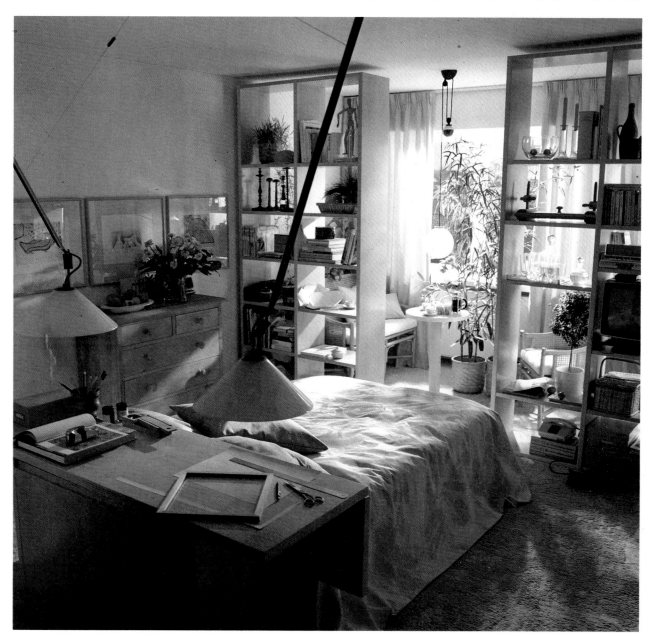

BEDROOMS

Above: Bookshelves tucked under a window sill and permanently drawn-back curtains make a handsome bedhead as well as solving an awkward space problem in this small room. Adjustable wall lights provide the answer to where to put lamps when there is no room for bedside tables. A blind ensures privacy.

Left: Recessed as it is, with shelves above and round it, this bed has almost become a storage unit in itself. Folding shutters serve to close off the sleeping area when the bed is not in use.

Making room for guests

Today's tight spaces rarely allow for a spare room and rooms used exclusively for guests are practically non-existent in most current homes. More often than not the guest room is where the sofa bed or convertible happens to be, and it could be anywhere – in the living room, study, den, dining room or a convenient alcove in the hall. Happily, good hospitality is more a matter of *how* you accommodate your guests than *where*.

However, with a little careful planning and foresight you can make space for a guest almost anywhere in the home. If, for example, you have a sofa bed in the living room you could arrange to have a cupboard or closet in the hall which can be cleared enough to take visitor's clothes. If you can make a bed in the hall the same storage would naturally apply. If there is a sofa bed in a study, den or dining room you could try to fit a built-in closet in that room which would in any case be useful for other storage.

Most living rooms will already have a floor or table lamp and a small table which can be moved close to the sofa bed. All you need do is add books, a carafe of water or bottle of mineral water, a glass, generous towels and clean, tidy bathroom space and you are well on the way to making a guest feel just as much at home as in a self-contained bedroom.

Tricks for stretching space

When you are planning – or re-planning – a room remember the following well-tried space stretchers and see if you can apply any of them to your own particular situation and needs:

Mirror used at right angles to a window and, if possible, all along one wall, will make a room look twice as big and twice as light. A huge old mirror used as a bedhead will appear to double the space, particularly if the mirror reflects a window.

Flooring with a diagonal design will make the space seem larger, so will most geometric designs.

Using the same print on everything – walls, windows, bedspread, upholstery – will deceive the eye about the real size of the room and, by making you forget about limits, edges and boundaries of walls, seem to enlarge the space.

Disappearing wardrobes will appear to increase the wall space. Make them vanish by decorating them the same as the walls so that they don't stand out. Better still if you can merge the wardrobe frame with the walls *and* cover the front with mirror.

Screens can hide a multitude of unsightly but necessary equipment (like filing cabinets, if you use the room for working in) and at the same time give the illusion of space because of their angles.

Light colours make surfaces retreat. Use them on ceiling and floor and choose light backgrounds to fabric designs.

A platform will virtually give you two rooms for the price of one, so if you are able to plan a room from scratch and need to expand a comparatively small area, it's useful to know that you can do this.

The use of mirror always increases the feeling of space and light. It is particularly effective used at right-angles to a window to give the maximum reflection of light.

Shelving at the top and bottom of the bed can make an enormous difference. A low shelf at the foot can hold tv, stereo, books, magazines and could provide extra seating as well. High shelving at the top can act as bedhead as well as being used for books and general display purposes. If you build out such a storage and display wall a short distance from the wall proper, you could use the space behind as a study/work area.

Putting the bed in a corner or even in the middle of the room rather than against a wall, often makes the whole space more generous.

Uplights set in one or two corners of the room will make the space seem much bigger at night because it will bounce light up and soften the hard edges.

Small chests of drawers either side of the bed instead of bedside tables will make better use of the space.

A highish bed will free the space underneath for storage.

Cupboards and closets that go right to ceiling height will press into service all that otherwise wasted space, and cope with things that aren't used a lot and need to be out of sight most of the time.

The window used as sort of bedhead and curtains combined will save space in a very small room. Or if you have two windows, use the space in between for the bed.

An unused or unusable fireplace can provide extra storage: fit some shelves across the space and, if possible, a door in front.

Storage built around the bed will free the rest of the room and make it look much more open.

Use mirror panels at right-angles to a window to create an illusion of increased space and light

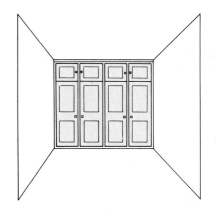

Build cupboards that go right up to the ceiling to make walls look longer and provide more storage

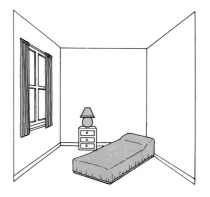

Position the bed at an angle to the corner of a room rather than flat against a wall

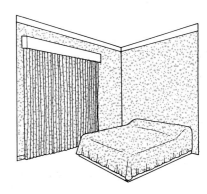

Use the same small print on a light background for walls, curtains and bedspread

BEDROOMS

border gives definition to unruly angles

dark blue velvet ribbon gives distinction

panels and bed head edged with blue

transparent perspex table and glass lamp take up no visual space

pale matting adds textural interest

skirted table gives softness and width to space

Attention is drawn away from the awkward angles of the room to the left by the pretty cornflower and white colouring, against which the pale furniture and matting, soft festoon blind and skirted, lace-covered table all take the eye. While above, another blue-white room is given definition by plain blue edging on door panels, the cushioned bedhead slotted onto a blue-painted pole and the blue china jardinière.

Of course, you are not limited to sofa beds. You might include a fold-up bed as part of a storage wall in the living room or study. (When shut up it is an innocent-looking cabinet – when down a bed pulls out.) Or there are deep armchairs that become single or double beds, stacking pillows or cushions or covered blocks of foam that pull together for night duty, as well as folding beds that can be hidden behind a screen or stored in a cupboard.

If you do have the luxury of a spare or guest room try to make it the sort of bedroom you yourself would enjoy staying in. Make sure it is pretty, cheerful and clean, with comfortable beds, good lighting, plenty of dressing table space, and if at all possible, a desk or writing table of some sort together with a comfortable chair. If there is a fireplace you could hardly do better than light it for guests; or have a gas flame fire.

Most important of all, try out a guest room from time to time yourself to make sure everything works and is in good order.

Right: A sleeping alcove lined and curtained with washable cheesecloth, and a matching archway, make brilliant use of space in the hallway to accommodate guests. The rather austere grey of the carpet and bed base is softened by the pastel patchwork quilt and heaped cushions.

Bedrooms are obviously very personal. They are not on show to outsiders like the living room and can, therefore, be as idiosyncratic, or as fanciful as you like providing that they are quiet to be in and, I repeat, comfortable. If you have a good mattress, a window and some space to play with there is practically no limit to the way you can decorate a bedroom.

Most people, once grown up, have some sort of idea of how they would like their ideal bedroom. If you had a room all to yourself through childhood, or at least from adolescence on, it was the place where you spent hours reading, did your homework, thought great thoughts, make plans, practised an instrument, played music, experimented with make-up, hair and clothes styles, entertained your friends and was, in general, a real refuge. You may have been lucky enough to have had a free hand with its decoration, or you may have had to put up with the same old wallpaper and hand-me-down furnishings, but either way you would have evolved a deep gut feeling for the sort of room you would like to have, given an absolutely free rein.

When it comes to the crunch of course, and you do have your own place, the bedroom is often the last place to be decorated, or at least decorated in the way you have imagined. But this is almost invariably from lack of funds rather than lack of ideas. People might be short on plans for living rooms but everyone can give a ready opinion on a bedroom.

What's your style?

There are clearly both very feminine and very masculine bedrooms at either end of the scale with compromises for couples made in between. But there are no rules and, interestingly, you often find in the most otherwise modern of households that the main bedroom has been decorated in a traditional way. The reason is that the bedroom is a private, secluded area of the house. Unlike the kitchen or living room it is not automatically seen by guests or casual callers, so it does not necessarily have to reflect the style of the rest of the house. So as long as you feel comfortable, the bedroom can be the room in which anything goes. You could create a minimal look with the only furniture a futon unrolled at night. Or for traditional cosiness fill up the room with antique furniture and buy either an old brass, painted iron or mellow pine bedstead. Now too, the

English rose bedspread, curtains and pillows with natural woods, add up to a clean, cheerful country bedroom, left, in sharp contrast with the rather opulent and exotic, fantasy-style sleeping area, right.

BEDROOMS

four-poster bed has become popular again, whether it is the real thing, a modern version of the same, or an approximation devised with fabric. Half-testers – beds with a canopy which only overshadows the pillow area; filmy drapes attached to a corona; back hangings – all these are currently much in vogue.

All the same, there are certain general styles which are firm favourites and can form a framework, if you like, within which you can incorporate your own personal touches and ideas.

Cottage-in-the-country style rooms with brass or pine beds or pretty fabric bedheads, pine chests and wash-stands; lace or broderie Anglaise or both combined with fresh mini-prints, co-ordinating plains; and stripped floors either covered with rugs or stencilled.

Prosperous Victorian style bedrooms with mahogany or brass beds or fabric-draped four-posters with either a couch or chest at their feet; pelmeted and tied-back curtains; handsome carpets and equally handsome furniture.

Edwardian style bedrooms with brass beds, possibly with muslin or lace hangings or drapes, dressing tables with muslin skirts and a wealth, as they say, of silver or ivory-backed brushes, combs, mirrors and boxes; probably prettily flower-printed

walls, and again lush curtains or festoon or Austrian or just white holland blinds; a period fireplace and an overmantel.

Real English style would be a mixture of both the above with flowery glazed chintz, probably with leaves and roses, or leaves and birds, deep carpet, deep, maybe well-worn armchairs, nice mahogany or paintd furniture, an imposing bed, lots of cushions, books, prints, pictures and memorabilia. There would be a desk complete with writing paper at the ready and, of course, pretty little posies of sweet-smelling garden flowers everywhere.

Thirties style with perhaps a limed-oak bed or polished walnut, or a sumptuous Hollywood-style upholstered bedframe; perhaps Jazz Moderne rugs on a carpet, a whole bedroom suite to match the bed and all kinds of 30s details – almps, cushions, vases, bedspreads – probably collectors items.

French country style might be soft whitewash or small flowered patterns on walls and ceilings, matching fabric on bed, windows and chair covers. This can look splendid in a tiny room with pine, cherry-wood or painted furniture, and fruit or flower prints framed in bird's-eye maple or fruitwood.

Fantasy style could be done entirely in fabric with a fabric tented ceiling,

Top left: A truly English traditional look, with faded floral print on bedspread and curtains, matching wallpaper and dark woods.

Bottom left: True Edwardiana with drooping lace, lots of wicker and elaborate silver frames.

Bottom near left: French sophistication captured in a Louis V-style bed with embroidered headboard and footboard. Tapestry chairs and cushions complete the effect, which is still one of overall elegance, despite the plain walls and rustic tiled floor.

Right: Difficult to define in style, this bedroom could be called prosperous but updated Victorian, or just prettified Mid-Atlantic. The half-tester with its mellow lining matching the eiderdown has two different scales of pattern in the same subtle colouring. The shawl on the upholstered stool blends gently with the cool greys of the dhurrie rug, and the frilly, lacy cushions are matched by the beautiful lace tablecloths. All nicely set off by the soft wicker chair and squashy basket.

BEDROOMS

Left: American Country, and how, with its display of rosettes strung along the mantelpiece, primitive paintings and its Colonial post bed complete with obligatory quilt. The window is always given interesting treatment, here elaborately pelmeted curtains. Upholstered chairs complete this mellow roomful of comfort.

Above: Tailored style with a hint of Japanese, visible in the screen above the bed and the collection of porcelain on the shelves. Colours are muted and disciplined. Furniture lines verge on the severe.

or a fabric four-poster with elaborately shirred top, padded fabric walls, padded bedhead, generously gathered flounce or bedskirt and masses of pretty, feminine cushions, frilled or trimmed with lace, round tables with luxurious skirts and over clothes; or all in Indian mirrored-fabric or lace, with bamboo or mirrored furniture.

American Country style could have a nice Colonial post bed with an old quilt – perhaps in one of the traditional American patchwork designs – polished floors with rag rugs, filmy lace curtains and interesting window treatments, comfortable chairs, good reading lights, naive portraits and masses of cushions. Or it might have a fabric four-poster lined with, perhaps, a check cotton with matching curtains and blinds, ribbon rugs on stripped floors.

Tailored style would be quite the antithesis of all these. Walls might be covered in suede wallcovering or felt or just dark paint or hessian, perhaps given a neat border of brass or contrast fabric of some sort. If there is wallpaper instead it might be dark and geometric. The bed would be neatly tucked with a tailored piped bolster. The window might have Roman blinds; furniture and possibly doors would be mahogany, wardrobe doors would be very well-appointed with interior lighting and mahogany linings.

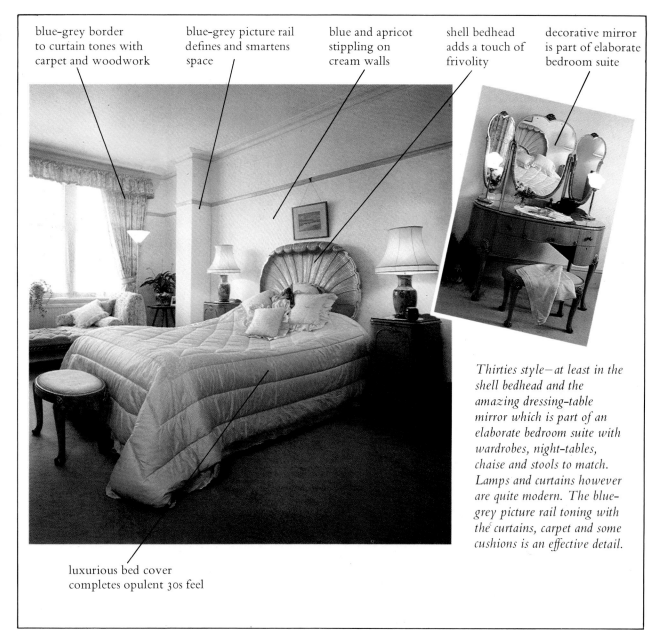

blue-grey border to curtain tones with carpet and woodwork

blue-grey picture rail defines and smartens space

blue and apricot stippling on cream walls

shell bedhead adds a touch of frivolity

decorative mirror is part of elaborate bedroom suite

luxurious bed cover completes opulent 30s feel

Thirties style – at least in the shell bedhead and the amazing dressing-table mirror which is part of an elaborate bedroom suite with wardrobes, night-tables, chaise and stools to match. Lamps and curtains however are quite modern. The blue-grey picture rail toning with the curtains, carpet and some cushions is an effective detail.

BEDROOMS

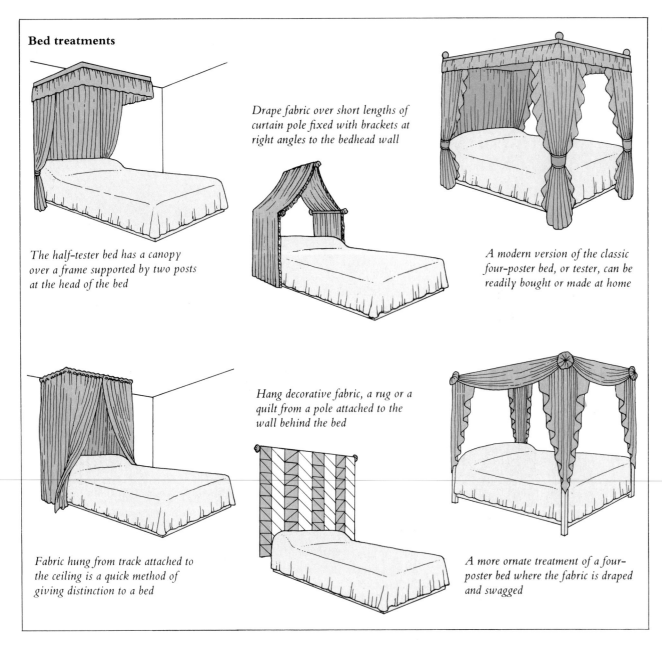

Bed treatments

The half-tester bed has a canopy over a frame supported by two posts at the head of the bed

Drape fabric over short lengths of curtain pole fixed with brackets at right angles to the bedhead wall

A modern version of the classic four-poster bed, or tester, can be readily bought or made at home

Fabric hung from track attached to the ceiling is a quick method of giving distinction to a bed

Hang decorative fabric, a rug or a quilt from a pole attached to the wall behind the bed

A more ornate treatment of a four-poster bed where the fabric is draped and swagged

Japanese style bedrooms are styled around the futon bed. Paper and wood screens, low-level lacquered or stained tables and tatami matting on the floor complete the look. Colours are contrasting combinations like white and black or red and grey.

Putting style into the basic bedroom

All the above vignettes are the ideals of course. Unless you are particularly fortunate, you are far more likely to have to try and inject some sort of style into an otherwise fairly basic room. Given that you have just about afforded to paint or paper the room, buy a good bed and carpet or rugs for the floor, what can you do to give it a quick shot of personality?

Start by scouring jumble sales, secondhand shops and antique markets. It is surprising what you will be able to find and recycle. Examine objects in the light of their potential, rather than their current appearance – bear in mind what you can do with a coat of paint.

It is quite easy to make a significant difference with very few and often fairly inexpensive importations. You can add a heap of cushions on a bed, or cover pillows with pillow shams and leave them propped on top of a matching or co-ordinating bedspread. You might find a chair in a junk shop which you could paint or re-cover the seat; or you could find an old shawl to drape across the foot of a bed or a chair. If there is room, you could get a round wooden table made up and cover it with a fabric skirt and an overskirt in a co-ordinating material. Add a lamp, some odds and ends, a framed photograph or two, a small plant perhaps, and the room will immediately look more inviting.

Then too, you could add a tall plant in a big cane basket, a whole lot of prints, a screen which you could either find and re-cover, or one that you've made yourself. Given the basic screen frame you could stain it mahogany and fill it in with voile or muslin shirred onto stretch wire like the Edwardians used to do. Or make your own version of a Victorian scrap screen either with traditional scrap pictures, which you can still buy, or with your own cut-outs.

Cane or bamboo chairs are cheap, light and attractive, and there will almost always be room, even in the smallest bedroom, for something of this sort. Add a pretty cushion and again you will make a difference. Attractive old bedside lights; a new mirror; an upholstered stool; tie-backs or a contrast border added to curtains, or a blind underneath; a paper border stuck all round the walls; such comfortable touches, and they are really no more than these, can make an amazing change to an undistinguished bedroom.

Left: Futon, low-level tables with plants, 'tatami' floor matting and contrasting black and white colours all go to create a Japanese-style bedroom. The total effect is enhanced by paper and wood 'shoji' screens, which also act as interesting room dividers.

Above: A gallery overlooks the sleeping area in this large loft converted into a bedroom.

301

BEDROOMS

Designing from scratch

If you do have the chance to design a bedroom from scratch you are really very lucky, although couples might not think so after they have spent hours quarrelling about who should give in to whom about ideas! A sybarite might never have realized that he or she had linked up with a Spartan until the subject of decoration came up. The important thing, of course, is to learn how to compromise in a way that is comfortable and agreeable to both partners.

Discuss the subject thoroughly, pool your ideas, look around, see what you can afford and what you must discard and don't be afraid to take your time. If the bedroom is to be the restorative room it should be, then it is worth spending a long while to get it right. If you need to buy a bed, buy a good one, and a rug, and hang your clothes from hooks until you have worked out the best furnishings and methods of storage to suit you both.

If you do not have to consider a partner you are in luck again, and if you do not have to worry too much about a budget you are luckier still, although it actually helps to have the supporting framework of a limited budget. It immediately cuts down on the available choice and actually encourages you to compromise, to be ingenious, to think up new solutions which make for a much more

personal room in the end.

If you have no very set ideas on what you like, then the best thing to do, as always, is to buy what books and magazines you can, and go conscientiously through the pages marking the rooms that appeal. Or it may be that you like one idea here, another there. Note them all, see what you can afford, and go from there. There really has never been such a choice in co-ordinated wall-coverings and fabrics, bedheads, lamps, carpets, blinds, china, rugs and bedlinen. And don't forget that sheets can make splendid curtains, bedhangings and table-cloths.

Style with comfort

As I have said before, comfort should be the overriding theme of any bedroom. Of course, standards of comfort vary. What is comfortable for one, is suffocating for another. Some people are only comfortable with soft opulence; others thrive on simplicity and firm lines. The important thing to remember is that whatever style of room you choose, make sure that everything in it functions in the best possible way. Mattresses should be the best you can afford; storage should be really functional; lights should be the correct height and intensity for reading, bed linen should be comforting and beds should be easy to make.

Real comfort and style depend as much as anything else on the small

touches. The little details that count are things like inconspicuous but capacious waste paper baskets; containers of tissues and cotton wool always to hand; carafes and glasses for water, or bottles of mineral water; nicely lined drawers and cupboards complete with sweet-smelling sachets; curtains and blinds that pull easily and fit well. Some people like to wake up with a chink of light, others most decidedly do not, so try to determine this in the beginning. If you are having curtains

specially made for you, ask for them to be made light-proof, and be sure to stipulate this right at the beginning. If you possess curtains that are not sufficiently light-proof, consider putting up black-out blinds behind them, or ordinary roller blinds lined with black-out fabric. People often forget in the first rush of enthusiasm for romantic, filmy curtains, that the same fabric is not nearly so romantic during a cold night in winter, or first thing in the morning after a particularly late night.

CHANGING THE IMAGE

Left: Mirrored alcoves and an all white room look luxurious, though the treatment is simple and fairly inexpensive.

Above: A skirted table to match the curtains, blue and white china and a blue painted wicker chair make this room instantly more romantic.

Right: A neutral scheme is given immediate impact by converting the standard double divan into a handsome draped four-poster.

Starting over again

If you are sick and tired of your old bedroom but cannot afford to start over again, don't despair. Go into action with one or two or more of the instant improvement suggestions mentioned earlier. A new wallpaper alone might do wonders. If that's too expensive, add one of the new borders around the room, or superimpose a fabric border, stuck with an appropriate adhesive.

A crisp, pretty new bedspread or valance wouldn't break the bank and there has never been a wider or more exciting choice around than there is now. If you hate throwing things away that still have life in them you could always cut up your old spread to make cushion covers or move it to another room.

A stunning and dramatic way to change the look of the whole room is simply to give the bed an entirely different treatment by making a fabric four-poster or half-tester or interesting back hangings.

Even changing your old bedside tables for two skirted round tables introduces a softer, more romantic look. If you have not got a tv in the room try bringing one in for your own private viewing away from the family; or add some bookshelves and more pictures, or a comfortable chair, stool or desk if you can afford it and have the space. The bedroom really is the easiest room to alter with the minimum of effort and expense.

Any problem is easier to solve if you can break it down into various components. It is the same with the decoration of a room. If you think – in the case of a bedroom – of walls, floor, ceiling, windows, bed, furniture, fabrics, and – last but not least – lighting, and then take each of them in turn, deciding what you can and cannot do, the whole exercise becomes very much more simple. It helps too, to commit it all to paper in the form of a check list which you can refer to and revise as you go.

Although most people would obviously think of the bed as the most important ingredient of a bedroom, it is still necessary, as in any room, to get the actual framework (walls, ceiling, floor and windows) planned out in detail even if it can't be done all at once. If you cannot afford to complete the whole room right away, at least knowing what you hope to do will help you avoid the sort of mistakes and compromises which could spoil the final look.

Walls and ceilings

Bedroom walls can either be painted, papered, or covered with fabric (or wood, or carpet, or some other covering if you are daring). Three things will guide and affect your choice: the position, condition, proportion and shape of the room, your existing furnishings and your budget. Although ceilings are very often neglected, the same applies to them, and they can make an enormous difference to the look of a room.

Paint

Paint is generally the cheapest way to cover a wall as long as the wall is in good condition to start with. If it is not, you should make it good and at the same time find out the cause of any stains on walls or ceiling and have them dealt with. If walls are merely uneven and the house is old and in the country, you might actually like to keep a slightly bumpy look. Or you might prefer to disguise the defects with an alternative wallcovering such as paper or fabric, which will cover a multitude of sins. Country-style furniture and fabrics combined with a simple white, slightly uneven wall, can create a charming effect.

Left: With just a little emphasis on detail, the dullest bedroom can be converted into the most charming of places. A radical transformation has been achieved here by the use of pretty coordinated fabrics and wallpaper – even the lampshade matches. In contrast, a room with interesting features, like the simple bedroom, right, can be quite bare of pattern and furnishings. Here, blue paint is used to highlight the attractive arched windows, and wooden floor, furniture and walls are quite plain.

BEDROOMS

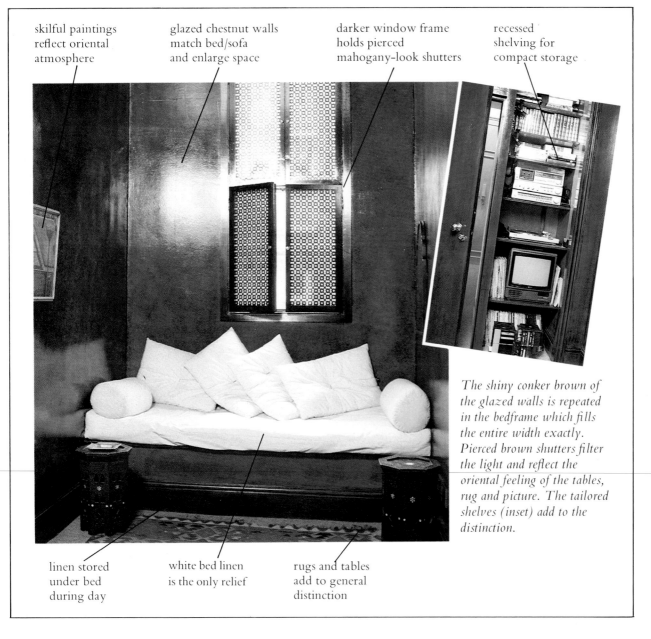

skilful paintings reflect oriental atmosphere

glazed chestnut walls match bed/sofa and enlarge space

darker window frame holds pierced mahogany-look shutters

recessed shelving for compact storage

linen stored under bed during day

white bed linen is the only relief

rugs and tables add to general distinction

The shiny conker brown of the glazed walls is repeated in the bedframe which fills the entire width exactly. Pierced brown shutters filter the light and reflect the oriental feeling of the tables, rug and picture. The tailored shelves (inset) add to the distinction.

Colour counts If you do decide to paint, the next thing to consider is colour. If you want to put the focus on the furnishings and have a laid-back, relaxed scheme, choose neutral tones: soft white, soft cream; pearl grey, sand, camel or blush pink. Woodwork and ceiling could be white, or you could paint them the same shade as the walls if you want the space to seem as large as possible.

If the room receives little or no light, choose a warm colour, unless you are prepared to keep white walls very white all the time which means frequent re-painting. Make sure there is plenty of clear colour in the room as well: pinks, greens, apricots or yellows, with a lot of mirror and sparkle. One of the most spectacular bedrooms I have seen was mostly white, but the white curtains were lined with rose, there were white and rose cushions on the bed, great pots of marguerites in baskets, and above all the flicker of flames from a gas flame fire – the fireplace, of course, being a splendid extra bonus. All white-on-white rooms, pristine and beautiful as they can be, are really only good in a hot and sunny climate or in a well-staffed household. Dark walls can be restful in a bedroom. I once had a dark room with an off-white carpet, ceiling and wood-work, and the room always seemed to trap the light within itself in some mysterious way, mostly because the

brown was sandwiched between very light colours. Darkish tones can also make a room seem much better furnished than it is: dark green, dark rose, chestnut, dark blue, are all sophisticated and will give incidental colours used with them much more of a glow in contrast.

Finishing touches Painted walls can be pepped up in a variety of ways. You could add one of the many new paper borders just under the cornice or cove if there is one, or just under the ceiling if there is not. Or you could run a contrast fabric or

webbing border (to match curtains say, or carpet) under the ceilings, around doors and windows and over the top of skirtings or base boards.

You could make your own panelled effect with lengths of beading or picture framing stuck on the walls in rectangles or squares or both. Framers will often sell it by the foot if you ask, and it comes in natural wood (paint it to suit your scheme), gilt and silver. If you can first work out the panels to scale on a plan of the room, so much the better. If not, at least draw it out on the walls carefully with a long ruler, chalk or pencil, and use a level. When this has been completed the 'panels' can be painted in a contrast of a darker or lighter tone to the main body of the wall.

Another idea is to make a dado, again with picture framing or

Above: Delightful and unusual results can be achieved on walls with stencilling.

Above left: This heavily beamed room was transformed by the simple application of all-white paint.

BEDROOMS

moulding or even something like a double border of grosgrain ribbon. All you have to do is run whatever frame you have chosen around the room at dado height (about 90 cm [3 ft]) and fill the space below with contrast paint, or paper.

Alternatively, you can try out one of the many decorative finishes like rag-rolling, stippling, dragging, colourwashing, marbling or sten-cilling which have now become fashionable again. Clear instructions for all these techniques can be found in the *Paint Finishes* chapter, on pages 368–79. And there is also a variety of excellent manuals to choose from, full of ideas to spark you off.

Wallpaper

Quite apart from softening the look of the room, wallpaper is also an excellent disguiser of awkward angles, architectural imperfections and wardrobes or closets which might otherwise break up the har-mony of a space. It is also, of course, a splendid unifier for rooms that seem all doors and windows since the paper design will link the unbroken areas togeher, especially if woodwork is painted in one of the colours of the paper.

There is such an enormous choice of wallpapers now in every sort of scale, colour, design and price, many of them with their own co-ordinated borders, 'partner' papers (for alcoves, behind bookcases etc.)

Painted tendrils of flowers wind their way round walls, window frame and cotton blind in an otherwise all-white room, top left. Swags of painted stencilled flowers on doors, bed curtains and border, below, are echoed by stencilled garlands on walls and bed linen. A combination of techniques (below left): Delicately dragged walls are complemented by woodgrained bedside cupboards with spattered tops.

Left: Green and white mini-print wallpaper and a matching border make the most of a tiny space which is dominated by a decorated pine bed and knitted patch quilt. The useful storage hampers under the bed are repeated in larger scale by the wicker laundry basket. Notice the build-up of colour in rug, towels, plants and cushions.

Top right: A pretty pink wallpaper serves to unify a room with awkward angles and corners. The border separating light and dark tones creates a particularly interesting effect.

BEDROOMS

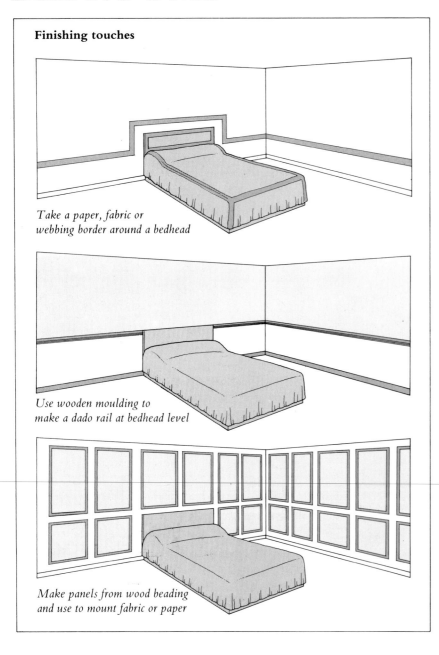

Finishing touches

Take a paper, fabric or webbing border around a bedhead

Use wooden moulding to make a dado rail at bedhead level

Make panels from wood beading and use to mount fabric or paper

and fabrics for an effortlessly unified look, that the problem is rather eliminating the unsuitables than finding the right ones.

Small rooms can be made very much more interesting by using co-ordinated or matching wallpapers and fabrics for walls, ceilings, windows, soft furnishings and the bed. The repetition of a single pattern, the use of the positive and negative of a design, or different scales of the same pattern, will add immediate distinction to a space and an all-over flower design for example, will add instant summery freshness to an otherwise dingy area.

How to cheat with wallpaper

What happens if the particular paper you've set your heart on is hopelessly expensive? Don't abandon the idea. The answer is to cheat a little. You could have it, or at least the effect of it, by painting your walls the background colour of the paper with matt paint, and then using the paper itself in panels. By doing this you can get away with the minimum number of rolls – maybe only one if your room is not very big. Or you could use a small amount of paper up to dado height in much the same way as I suggested with paint earlier on.

At the other end of the scale, cheaper wallpaper can be made to look much better and will last much longer if it is given a coat or two of matt or eggshell polyurethane –

allowing the first coat to dry thoroughly before adding a second. The polyurethane will yellow the paper a little, but this often has the happy effect of making it look more mellow, and certainly more practical since it can then be wiped clean with a sponge or damp cloth.

Preparing the walls If there was a previous wallcovering it may need to be stripped off before you start with the new. Old wallpaper can only be left if it was well put up in the first place, that is to say butt-edged with no lumps, bumps or wrinkles. If you are putting up a vinyl covering, any old paper will have to come off first. Likewise any old vinyl wallcovering must always be removed before putting up new paper. Any previously painted walls must be free from grease and dirt otherwise the adhesive will not work. So wash the walls down with water mixed with detergent or household ammonia, and for a really professional job, line walls with good quality lining paper before applying your wallpaper.

Fabric wallcoverings

Fabric walls are particularly appropriate in the bedroom for their look of softness and luxury and for their sound and heat insulating properties. There are a good many specially treated fabrics, some of them paper-backed and flame-proofed, sold especially for the purpose, the most common being felt, hessian or burlap, suede fabric, wool, silk, moiré, grasscloth, linen, cotton and denim, all of which should be spot cleanable.

But it is quite possible to put up just about any fabric, fixing it in position by one of the following methods:

Sticking Firmly woven fabric, which will deter any adhesive from seeping through the weave, may be stuck to the wall like wallpaper. The adhesive must be applied to the wall, not the fabric.

Stapling Use a proper electric staple-gun and choose materials with the sort of design which will help to conceal seams. If you can line the walls with a layer of padding so much the better: the effect will be very like the soft, upholstered look of battening but achieved with far less trouble. Seam the fabric first before you start applying it. Any frayed edges can be covered with a matching, contrasting or co-ordinated braid, or lengths of picture

Cool greeny-grey cotton is here gathered on rods fixed just below the cornice and just above the skirting. The top of the lace-edged Austrian blind is gathered to match, and the general softness is repeated in the generous fall of the flowered cloth.

BEDROOMS

Fabric techniques

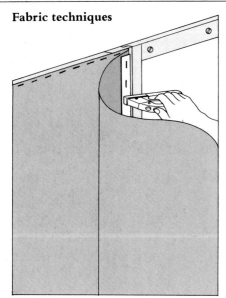

Fabric stapled over battens

*Fabric may be staple-gunned either
directly to the wall or stretched over
wood battens which have been
previously screwed into the wall*

*A wall-track system is an almost
foolproof way of fixing fabric to
walls and requires neither glue,
nor battens nor staples.*

*Fabric hung loosely from poles
provides instant drama and is easy
to put up and take down*

*Gathered fabric stretched between
curtain tracks, fixed immediately
below the ceiling and above the
skirting board, looks luxurious*

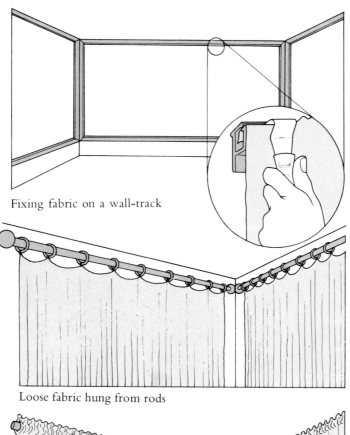

Fixing fabric on a wall-track

Loose fabric hung from rods

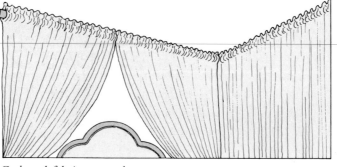

Gathered fabric on tracks

framing, or strips of brass, chrome or
wood beading, depending on your
taste and pocket.

The wall-track system This consists
of lengths of track which you can
fix all round the wall just below
the ceiling and above the skirting or
base boards. The seamed fabric is
clipped into the track at the top and
stretched down to be clipped into the
bottom track. It is practical because
fabric can be taken down for cleaning, moving or just changing.

Walling or battening Upholstering a
wall, or 'walling' or 'battening' as it
is called in the trade, means stretching pre-seamed fabric over strips of
thin wood or battens which have
been lined with strips of synthetic fibre padding. It is quite
complicated, but well justified by
the final result. It looks professional
and luxurious and, in addition, its
double layer helps to muffle sound
and preserve heat.

   Probably the best way to do it is to
staple the battens horizontally, just
below the ceiling or mouldings and
just above the skirting. Take vertical
strips of wood cut to the size
required (i.e. the height from skirting board to ceiling) and fix them at
metre (three foot) intervals all round
the walls. If you plan to have paintings or prints on the wall, work out
where their positions are likely to be
and fix your battens in these places.
Remember to make provision for

wall-fixed lighting, sockets, and switches at the same time. When the fabric is up the battens can easily be felt through it and hooks or nails hammered through in seconds.

Thumb tack lengths of padding between the strips, then stretch the fabric and tack it to the battens. Cover the tack marks with lengths of braid which should also be used round the top and bottom of the fabric and around doors and windows to hide frayed edges.

Hanging Hung fabric looks especially soft and appealing when draped on the walls like curtains and is a useful method when money or time – or both – is short. It's good for temporary accommodation since the fabric can be taken down and moved. It can also be cleaned very easily since it can be removed from its fixings and put in the washing machine or sent to the cleaners.

There are several ways of hanging it. Very light (and inexpensive) fabrics like cheesecloth, muslin, or cotton can be shirred onto stretch wire or long thin poles attached just below the ceiling and just above the skirtings or baseboards in much the same way as fabric is fixed onto those nice old-fashioned fabric screens. Heavier fabrics can be suspended from more substantial poles, either shirred, or from rings, and left hanging loose and just touching the floor. Catch fabric back over win-

dows (use blinds underneath) and doors, fireplaces and wardrobes or closets and either cover any bits of wall thus exposed with matching wallpaper if it exists, or have extra short bits of fabric in those areas.

Be different, be daring
Although paint, wallpaper and fabric are the most popular wall-coverings for bedrooms there is nothing to stop you using unusual alternatives. Quilts or bedspreads for instance, can look very exotic – Indian cotton bedspreads make marvellously inexpensive wall-coverings if you can get matching, or nearly matching ones – or what about rolls of bamboo or oriental matchstick like the kind used for blinds – or even a series of blinds themselves let loose and hung side by side if the ceiling is fairly low and the blinds are long, or if you have a picture rail.

One of the simplest ideas is to use double sheets which are in any case the cheapest way of buying a lot of seamless fabric. Or you can buy sheeting by the metre (yard) in a wide range of beautiful colours and patterns. Even carpet, or fake fur if your tastes run to it. I once saw a bedroom entirely lined with sheepskin on ceiling, floor and walls and the effect was like a woolly igloo. All these alternatives can be coverings stapled or stuck according to the weight of the material.

Plain and patterned Indian cottons have been used to line this sleeping alcove, along with bordered Indian bedspreads. Ceiling and wall fabric have been stapled onto battens and stretched. Bedspreads used as curtains are pulled across a bamboo pole for privacy at night. By day the alcove becomes transformed into a comfortable, stylish sitting area.

BEDROOMS

Floors

On the whole, I think, bedroom floors should be soft, or at least have rugs by the bed, as much for comfort and warmth underfoot as for reducing noise.

If your choice is carpet, be sure to choose the right grade, usually described as bedroom grade; it does not need to be of the same hard-wearing quality, and therefore high price, as carpet for the living room, hall and staircase. In a guest room, you can get away with an even less hard-wearing carpet unless you have a perpetual stream of guests. If you feel you cannot afford carpet for the moment you can always compromise temporarily with extra thick felt topped with rugs to distribute the wear and tear. Or it might be worth while considering carpet tiles which are comparatively inexpensive, and can be taken up if you move.

If you have a wood floor in good condition, it can be stripped, sanded and polished, or bleached to a much paler colour and then adorned with rugs. Wood in not particularly good condition could be painted or painted and stencilled and again given rugs where necessary. Pick up a colour in the curtains or walls, or paint the floor a neutral colour, like white or cream or bluey grey or – very popular in America – Indian red or terracotta.

As long as you coat the paint with a couple of coats of eggshell polyurethane (left to dry a good twelve hours in between each coat) you do not need to use expensive gloss or enamels. Give the boards a couple of layers of undercoat tinted with the final colour and you can get away with just one coat of flat or eggshell oil or alkyd (oil-based) paint. Alternatively you could use yacht or deck paint for a denser effect.

If you feel like stencilling painted floors it should be done before the final coats of polyurethane. Stencil kits, complete with a charming choice of designs and detailed instructions, are sold in specialist stationers and art and craft shops. You could also cover old boards with vinyl tiles or sheeting or linoleum, especially if you livened it up with inset borders or a patterned inset of your own design.

Right: Bare oak-stained floorboards add to the simplicity and charm of this bedroom, though a few rugs would not come amiss.

Far right: Deep-piled, dusty-blue carpet provides a luxurious and sophisticated touch. It contrasts well with the warm wood units and furniture. A fitted carpet serves to create an effect of luxuriant softness, particularly in winter. Select a colour that tones with soft furnishings (or soft furnishings that pick up the carpet colour) for a co-ordinated scheme.

BEDROOMS

Windows

Few of us have beautiful, elegant bedroom windows; sometimes they are downright ordinary but quite often they are just unusual enough to present problems when it comes to decorating. Whether you have bows, bays, casements, dormers, skylights, sloping or otherwise oddly shaped or proportioned windows, explore all the possibilities of curtains, sheers, blinds and shutters before deciding on the treatment. There are all sorts of decorative tricks you can resort to to overcome awkward or ugly windows and which will actually transform a negative feature into a very positive asset.

Windows worth looking at

Bedroom windows can be treated to look as romantic, as spare or as chaste as your taste, circumstances and the actual shape of the window – and its view – dictate. If a window is unusually beautiful or just plain unusual, it might be better to show it off rather than hide it with curtains. But you will almost certainly want some sort of covering for it in a bedroom, for even if you are not overlooked you might well want to block out the light occasionally. In this case it would be better to have a blind or café curtain which would still show off the frame and shape by day. Alternatively, translucent (but

not see-through) screening could be used if you only want occasional privacy.

Blinds and shades

Blinds might be the plain roller variety, or the more tailored Roman blinds which fold up on each other in flat horizontal pleats, or the softer festoon, or Austrian blinds or pull-up curtains or balloon blinds. All

these last five categories have vertical tapes through which pull cords are drawn to raise and lower the blind or shade. Or again, there are Venetian, bamboo, matchstick, pinoleum or vertical louvred varieties. In fact, whatever your style or requirements, there's a blind to match them. If there is nothing particularly extraordinary about the window or windows, and, let's face it, there very

A rich floral print on co-ordinated Austrian blinds and bedlinen. Walls and woodwork pick up colours from the print.

Top right: Shiny olive green painted shutters add just the right subtlety of colour in this Mediterranean-style room. Note the nice change of textures introduced by the creamy crocheted cushions and plant.

often is not, but you have a radiator under the sill which you do not want to cover, or a piece of furniture there like a desk or dressing table or even the bed itself, you could still use a blind rather than short curtains. Or if you want to be really lavish and like the look of it you can use blinds with dress curtains, or curtains proper which can be elegantly arranged and tied back either side. This sort of treatment will make any window look soft and graceful and will help to cut out any unwelcome morning light which could otherwise intrude around the edges of the blind.

Incidentally, if morning light is a problem, or if you work at night and have to sleep during the day make sure that the fabric of your blinds is backed with a black-out material or thermal lining. And if somebody else is making the blinds for you, inform them right at the start that you want black-out backings. It is pretty well impossible to laminate black-out material onto already-made roller blinds and cumbersome to do it on all other finished varieties. In any event, festoon or Austrian or pull-up curtains only really look good in light filmy fabrics, so if you want that effect have them in conjunction with properly lined and interlined curtains that can be drawn across on top of them. Or have them with concealed black-out-backed roller blinds that can be pulled down underneath beforehand.

Blind identikit

Blinds are a useful adjunct to window decoration, whether used on their own or in conjunction with curtains. They come in all kinds of textures, sizes and prices ranging from the relatively inexpensive pinoleum or matchstick and bamboo, through Venetian and vertical louvres to the more expensive custom-made fabric varieties.

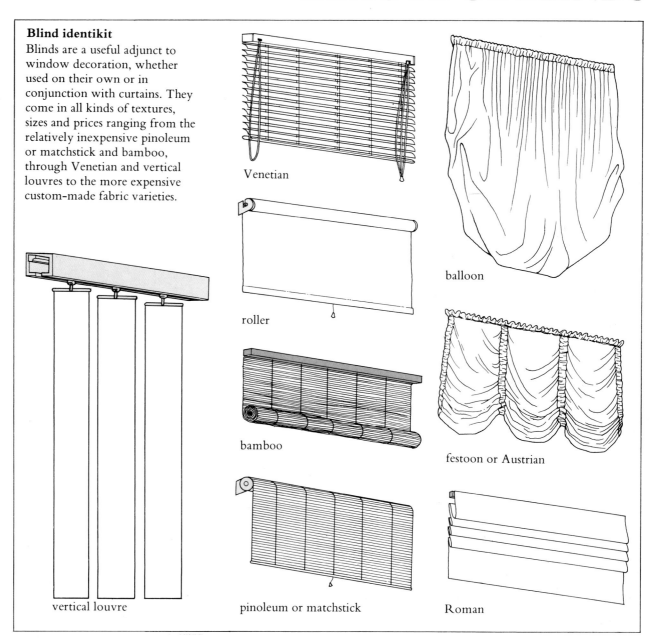

Venetian

balloon

roller

bamboo

festoon or Austrian

vertical louvre

pinoleum or matchstick

Roman

BEDROOMS

Create an illusion

It is quite easy to change the look and apparent proportion of windows by the sort of window treatment you give them. These are some of the tricks you can use to deceive – and please – the eye.

To make a window look taller Fix the curtain track or rod 15–20 cm (6–8 in) above the top of the frame. This is most effective at night when the curtains are down over the track. If you have a deep pelmet fixed about 20 cm (8 in) above the frame, the windows will always look taller during the day as well.

To make a narrow window look wider Choose a wider track or rod than the window frame so that curtains hang either side of the frame instead of overlapping any part of the window. This will also let in more light.

To make an over-tall window look shorter This is not often necessary, but if it is, put up a deep shaped pelmet or gathered valance, which will distract the eye from the expanse of glass.

To make a wide window look narrower Let curtains meet in the middle and loop them back at the sides with tie-backs or cords or deep ribbon.

To make a small high window look larger You could raise the height of the floor below by making a platform. If this is too complicated, hang café curtains on a pole which is wider than the frame.

To make the most of an arched frame Try to fix a curved track, pelmet or valance to follow the contours of the window. If this is not possible, put up a pole or track high enough and wide enough to allow curtains to clear the frame during the day.

To do without net curtains If a window faces on the street so that you need privacy but don't like the look of net curtains think of using a roller blind which pulls up from the bottom, rather than down from the top. This way you will get both light and privacy.

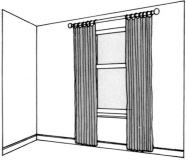

To make a narrow window wider hang curtains well to either side

To make a window look taller fix track well above the frame

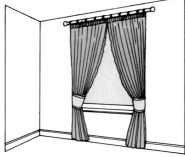

Make a wide window narrower by making curtains meet

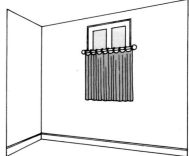

Café curtains make a small window bigger

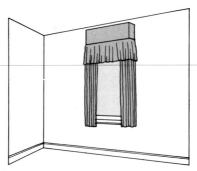

Deep pelmets shorten a too-tall window

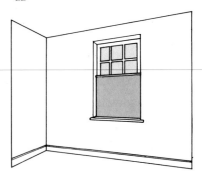

Up-pulling roller blinds are a good alternative to net curtaining

Choosing curtains

To get the best value and effect from your curtains it's important to bear certain points in mind: be generous with the amount of material – it's fatal to skimp; line them and if possible interline – they'll hang better and keep out unwanted light and draughts; get the length right – they should either reach the floor or the sill, nothing in between. (Short curtains are best kept for tiny cottage or attic windows.) Then go for the sort of curtain treatment that will be in keeping with the general style you are aiming for in the room.

The romantic, country look For this you might want rather heavy formal tied-back curtains in lace, muslin or net. Or you might decide on billowing floating lace curtains, or fresh broderie Anglaise over a more substantial holland roller blind.

Pelmets of all sorts seem to be making a come-back; deep gently-gathered fabric pelmets or valances, which might be edged or bordered, over tied-back curtains in a flowery print can look charming. A real pelmet is usually fabric-covered board or buckram, or a smooth stretch of fabric; soft, gathered tops are known as valances.

Creamy-white gathered curtains are here tied back over plain white roller blinds in a monochromatic room where the emphasis is on texture.

BEDROOMS

Top: White Austrian blinds under white curtains frame a sea view.

Above: Short chintz curtains look right in a cottage room.

Right: An attractive window seat.

The cottage look Sill-length curtains have an immediate cottage feel. They could be frilled along the leading (inner) edges and tied back with ribbons perhaps, or used in conjunction with either a gathered café curtain, or a café curtain on a pole for slightly more importance. If windows are very tiny, and the rooms rather dark, as happens frequently in old cottages, it might be better to hang a blind just above the architrave so that no light is shut out or wasted during the day. Alternatively, you could do away with any sort of curtain or blind and use the window like a picture frame to encapsulate the view. With equal simplicity you could just have a vase of flowers, a plant, a single stem in a glass, or some sort of pretty object on the sill and leave it at that.

The tailored look If you use curtains in spare, tailored, rather masculine rooms they could be in tweed or corduroy or woven wool hanging from a wooden or brass pole. But these sort of rooms might look best with roller or Roman blinds which could be edged or given a double or inset border. Crisp vertical blinds would also be in keeping, or wooden or Venetian blinds in an aluminium finish for real slickness.

Saving money – saving time
Custom-made curtains and blinds can be expensive because you are paying for labour, expertise and fabric. Ready-made on the other hand, are about half the price, come in a huge choice of colours, designs and styles, unlined, lined and sometimes thermal-lined and can be bought, taken home and hung up within a day. The only problem is that they come in standard sizes and while this is not a problem with the width it does often affect the length. This can sometimes be overcome by adding a deep border in a contrast or co-ordinating fabric and making it look intended by adding tie-backs in the same material.

Obviously, you get what you want and save money by making curtains and blinds yourself and there are now numerous books to tell you how to do it, but you can save time by improvising as well. Bedspreads, particularly Indian bedspreads and sheets can make excellent window coverings. All you have to do is turn over the tops to make a pocket for a rod or track, possibly add tie-backs – and hey-presto – you have instant curtains. Use the same material or bedspread on the bed for an instantly co-ordinated effect.

You do not even have to turn over the top come to that. Rods with clip-on café rings, like shower curtains, could do away with all sewing and give extra length – useful if the spreads are not quite long enough to reach the skirting board.

Shutters and screens

You are not, of course, limited to curtains, blinds or shades; there are other alternatives. Shutters and screens can make excellent window coverings and give an interesting architectural look to a room. Shutter panels can be bought louvred, in solid or open framework panels, and louvres, vertical and vaned shutters can be adjustable or stationary as you like. Open framework panels are also useful because you can insert shirred fabric, decorative glass or grill work of some kind into them. Solid panel shutters can be covered in fabric or wallpaper, painted or stencilled. If a room is rather small and otherwise broken up, solid shutters covered in the same finish as the walls will give much more unity to the space.

The Japanese Shoji screen with its black lacquered framework and translucent panels is another decorative way of letting in light without sacrificing your privacy. They are fairly widely available and can be made up by a good carpenter or handyman using, say, cheesecloth or lightweight sheets as the infill, and are especially useful for windows with a dreary outlook.

Hinged reversible screens which can be covered in different fabrics or finishes and reversed according to season or mood (try one side mirror, another side a colour to go with either soft furnishings, carpet or

walls) will make even an undistinguished short window look long, graceful and a decorative feature in its own right. Use them like shutters with a couple of panels on each side of the window which will meet in the middle when shut.

Shoji screens form a bed alcove as well as partitioning off the room in general in a Japanese designed room. An interesting contrast of textures and scale is made by the much coarser vertical lines of the bamboo window covering. The room seems calm and serene and when you look carefully at the various features in it you will notice that every surface has a different texture, and that, far from conflicting with each other, they, like the subdued colours, all blend into one mellow, harmonious whole.

The importance of lighting

As in all but the most functional rooms, bedroom lighting should be as good to look at as it is to see by. And in bedrooms it is particularly important that both general background lighting and specific lights for working or making-up are as warm and welcoming and restful as possible.

There are three main areas in which light should be concentrated: the head of the bed, the dressing area, and the dressing-table. It is also useful to have ancillary areas of light in wardrobes, on any side tables, beside any armchairs, and perhaps concealed behind plants or in corners in the form of uplights.

Remember that some of the activities carried out in the bedroom (such as reading and making up) need very good light. So mix bright lamps with softer, more atmospheric ones.

Plan ahead

Whether you are planning a room from scratch or just trying to improve it, try to have outlets or points positioned where the bed is to go, near the dressing-table, and the main room light in such a position that anyone dressing could have a clear undistorted vision in the looking glass. If you are planning on having wall-mounted lights over the bed, get them wired in before the walls are decorated. It is a good idea to

Different shades of opinion: Period lamps like the art nouveau lamp, top left, and the converted brass oil lamp, top centre, are as important for the atmosphere they provide as they are functional. The third table lamp, top right, is modern but, like the other two, is decorative as well as useful. Each has been used as the focal point of a charming still life carefully echoing the surrounding objects as well as illuminating them. On the right, background lighting is provided by two table lamps on the dressing table at the far end. The lit candle by the four-poster bed, while not over-practical, adds a charming touch of period authenticity.

BEDROOMS

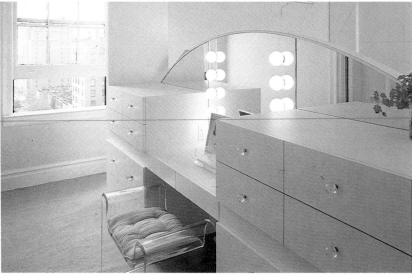

install dual operating controls at the same time; that is, one switch by the bed and a second one by door. It is always useful to get points put into corners of a room because it allows flexibility with uplights, floor lamps, and any other appliance that you might wish to use, like hair dryers, vacuum cleaners, a fan or extra heater.

Light for reading

Bedside table lamps should be high enough to shine on a book, but not so high as to disturb anyone else. Swing arm wall lamps placed just above the bedhead and slightly to the side are good, especially if they have dimmer switches to allow one partner to read without disturbing the other. Incidentally, in this respect there are now tiny extra lamps to keep on a bedside table which are adequate for reading or making notes in the middle of the night. Adjustable spots (again on a dimmer) or small angled lights are another solution. Table lamps should have the sort of shades that cast light downwards, rather than up.

If there are any armchairs or chaises in the room where you can relax and read, the best solution is to have either a table lamp on a small side table, or a floor standing lamp of some sort, like a brass pharmacy light, which you can move around to suit your particular needs and which does not look out of place.

Light for dressing

Light for dressing is usually the general or ambient light in a room. If the ceiling can take recessed down-lights so much the better. They will give better and softer overall illumination. If you cannot do this and have to use a ceiling point try using a Japanese paper shade, or a pretty pendant which will diffuse the light rather than emit an over bright glare. If there is no ceiling point, or you prefer not to have a central light you can either use table lamps switched from the door, or wall-mounted uplights which will bounce light off the ceiling and give a soft overall light – especially beautiful and flattering if the ceiling is white or a pale cream or pinkish blush.

In general, fluorescent bulbs of any sort are to be avoided in bedrooms, although they get better and better all the time; incandescent light is still better for clothes and make-up. However, if a room is very dark it does not hurt to conceal fluorescent tubes under valances or pelmets just over the window to give extra concealed light from the point where you would most expect it. You can have light thrown up to the ceiling and you can have light falling down onto curtains or blinds.

Light for make-up

If you have a dressing-table in the bedroom it is very important to have the sort of light fittings that will throw light onto your face. If you can have both top and side light so much the better. Strip lights on top of a mirror are not nearly so good as a down light fixed just above the dressing table area boosted by lights either side. The sort of strip that people have on top of a mirror is not really very effective, but of course it is perfectly possible to get a domestic version of the theatrical mirrors with lights all round that actresses have in their dressing rooms. Although not particularly beautiful, they could hardly give you a clearer picture of yourself. If you can, use them in conjunction with a dimmer switch, unless your face can stand up to the sort of brutal frankness that they provide when turned full beam.

Top left: The lamp on the dressing table in this bedroom acts as an effective downlight on the face for, say, applying make-up, while at the same time being positioned sufficiently downwards to prevent a distorted reflection.

Bottom left: Theatrical make-up bulbs are set into the sides of the mirror at this dramatic dressing table. Note how the expanse of mirror ties in beautifully with the glass knobs and the transparent perspex stool.

Right: The lights next to the bed provide a perfect light for close reading, and might well serve as the main light source in this bright room.

Since we are always being told that we spend a third of our lives asleep, or at least in bed, it is extraordinary how neglectful we are about actually choosing and buying a bed. People spend days fussing about what make of car to buy, its performance, potential and looks, whilst a bed, in which they are probably going to pass many more hours, rarely gets more than a perfunctory look and prod. Not that a bed is a life investment, for even the best mattress won't last for ever, but given a good choice, you should at least get a decade or so of comfortable use from it and with care, several more years after that.

If you have had the same bed for yeas you should definitely take a good hard look at the mattress. Is the surface lumpy? Are the edges sagging? Are there any ridges and hollows? Can you feel the springs when you press it with your hands? If the answer is yes to even one of these questions, you should start looking for a new mattress forthwith.

The mattress matters

There are five different kinds of mattresses to choose from: foam, interior sprung or inner spring, water-filled, air-filled and futon-style.

The foam variety is made from latex rubber or polyurethane which is manufactured in large slabs and cut to size. Latex rubber ones are the most expensive, but because of their high cost are scarce. High-resilience polyurethane mattresses, or mattresses with embedded thermoplastic beads give good support and last well and are usually dense and quite heavy. A lightweight foam mattress, therefore, is not usually of good quality and will not last long.

Interior sprung or inner spring mattresses are made of coiled springs sandwiched between insulating materials and usually come in two varieties: those with pocketed springs and those with open springs. Pocketed springs are individual units, coiled, compressed and sewn into calico pockets, unaffected by the compression of neighbouring springs and so particularly good for double beds with two partners of widely differing weights.

Open springs are cheaper and consist of a network of hour glass springs. The more springs there are in both types of mattress the better, the thicker the wire the better, the greater the number of coil convolutions the better. The best mattresses generally have coils made of low-

Dramatic effects can be easily achieved with fabrics. This canopy-like drape (right) transforms an ordinary bed, while rustic charm (left) is set off by lace-trimmed linen.

BEDROOMS

Choosing a bed

The sort of bed you choose depends on several factors: whether you sleep alone or with a partner, your size – and your partner's size, the style and size of your bedroom.

Bed sizes Basically, single or twin beds are 90 cm (3 ft) wide by 195 cm (6 ft 3 in) to 230 cm (6 ft 8 in) long, although they can be bought in a narrower size for very small rooms. A small double measures 135 cm (4 ft 6 in) wide by 195 cm (6 ft 3 in) long, and a standard double 153 cm (5 ft) wide by 200 cm (6 ft 6 in) long. A lot of people like to buy bedlinen in the States so it's useful to know American sizes include Queen size which is 168 cm (5 ft 6 in) wide by 230 cm (6 ft 8 in) long; and King size which is 198 cm (6 ft 4 in) wide by 230 cm (6 ft 8 in) long. There is also in America a longer single bed measuring 230 cm (6 ft 8 in) and a Californian King size which is 183 cm (6 ft) by 213 cm (7 ft). You might see some English beds described as King or Queen size but these sizes are not standard over here. Remember that the length of a bed is just as important as the width; it should always be 15 cm (6 in) longer than the person sleeping in it.

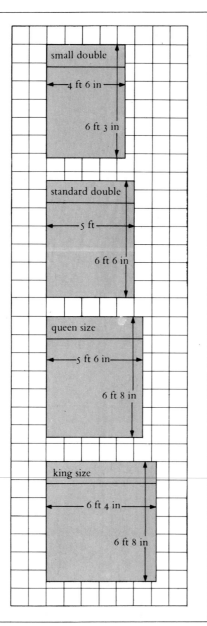

gauge wire with six turns – lesser qualities have thinner wire and fewer turns. The springs should be covered with an insulator – to prevent the mattress cushioning from working down into the coils – and this is generally made from tough fibre padding, wire, or netting, or a combination of the three. The cushioning is usually made from polyurethane foam combined with cotton felt and other fibres, and the thicker this cushioning the higher the quality.

When you buy a mattress you should buy a partnering box spring base at the same time, it will reinforce the mattress' support and cost approximately the same amount of money. They, too, have coil counts, or they may have metal grids bent in a squared zig-zag shape, or, the least expensive, be a combination of wool and foam. The foam should be at least 5 cm (2 in) thick to give any sort of adequate support.

Water-filled mattresses come in two different kinds: a sort of bladder filled with water, or a hybrid 'flotation' system which sounds, and is, more complicated. The first type is designed to be inserted into heavy-duty framing resting on a pedestal base. The second or hybrid has a water-filled bladder which is surrounded by a foam shell, covered with conventional heavy duty ticking to look just like a normal sprung

or inner spring mattress. The matching foundation is specially designed to support the water's weight. In fact, this second variety is lighter than the first because it uses less water and is shallower than the ordinary bladder type. It is also 'waveless', that is to say, special baffles reduce side to side and up and down movements of the water, and in some makes an added chemical partially solidifies the water to reduce motion.

If you are seduced into choosing a water bed, do make absolutely sure that it has a vinyl liner to contain all the water in case, dreaded thought, the mattress gets punctured. You can also get special water bed heaters which not only make the whole thing more luxurious but prevent condensation.

Air-filled mattresses are the latest thing. These are based on the same principle as the collapsible mattresses used for swimming pools, beaches and camping. The centre of the mattress is another heavy duty vinyl sack or bladder, which is enclosed in a foam shell with a cushioned zip-on cover like the hybrid water bed described above. Some of these air beds can be filled by means of a vacuum cleaner or even a hair dryer while others are available with a compressor unit and electric controls. Some larger mattresses have dual air chambers with

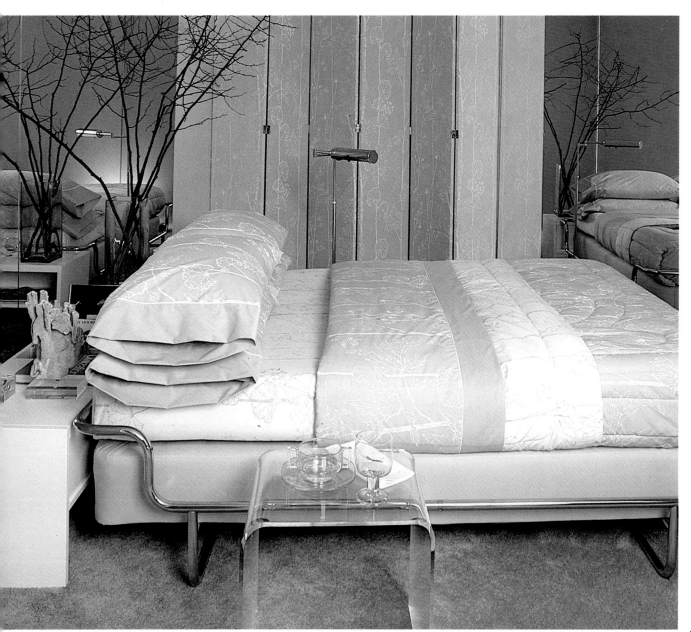

dual controls to allow for differing tastes in firmness.

Futons are a Japanese mattress made from layers of cotton, or occasionally wool, fibre. Originally laid on the floor at night and rolled up by day, they can be used on low-level slatted wood bed or sofa bed bases.

Does it pass the test?

The only way to tell if a mattress is right for your particular shape and weight is to try it out. Take off your shoes and lie down on it for at least ten minutes. Almost any mattress is going to feel comfortable at first but give it time and don't mind the sales people. They have got to make a sale, you have got to be satisfied. Stretch, turn over, make the sort of movements you would make in bed. A good mattress should feel firm and resilient, give support to your shoulders and hips and make your back feel thoroughly relaxed.

When you are satisfied that it feels comfortable, check the sides. They should be reinforced to prevent sagging when you sit on the edge of the bed. Sit on it and see. It should

This chrome-framed bed with its leaf design comforter/quilt and bed linen looks coolly elegant in a mirrored setting. The curved perspex table and chrome floor lamps are exactly right for this sophisticated modern room.

BEDROOMS

give a little, then spring back to shape when you get up. See if there is a cut away model on display which will show the insides. You have every right to ask to see one and the salesman should be able to explain it to you. Check the manufacturer's label which should give you complete details of construction and care. The most expensive mattresses are like the iron fist in a velvet glove, with a firm, heavy-coiled sprung core under a deeply soft top, thus providing both firm support and luxurious softness. If you and your partner prefer different degrees of firmness you can always buy different mattresses and get them linked with a zipper. Check too, about guarantees or warranties. Good quality mattresses will generally be guaranteed against defects of workmanship for some 15 years, lesser qualities for less. Good water beds, however, generally have a six to ten year limit and the heaters for three to five.

And so to the bed
Quite apart from the importance of the mattress and base there is the question of the look of the bed itself. Today you can choose from a huge range of styles from antique and reproductions of antique four-posters to specially-constructed frames with electronic controls to raise the foot and head of the bed to the occupier's fancy, or beds with

integral tv, stereo, clock, bookshelves, massage unit, lighting controls, the whole works.

If you are short of space you can get beds that fold right up into a wall of neat-looking storage units, or that are part of a series of slick modular units, or beds with lift-up divan bases and drawers inserted either at the side or at the end. Or there are the more straightforward sofa beds.

If you are nostalgically-minded there are shops full of originals and copies of Victorian, Edwardian and Colonial beds in mahogany, oak, brass or painted iron depending on the type you prefer. If you like a romantic look there are all sorts of elaborations that can be produced with fabric.

Bedheads
If comfort is of paramount importance to you, this will obviously affect the kind of bedhead you choose. Padded and upholstered bedheads should be attached to the bed frame and covered in some sort of easily sponged and cleaned fabric, or at least a cover that can be removed for cleaning, and it should either match or co-ordinate with the bedcovers or curtains. You could also cover a couple of squares or rectangles of foam and attach them to a wooden or brass pole behind the bed. Zip-on covers can be quickly zipped off again for ease of cleaning.

If aesthetics and looks are more important to you than comfort there is almost no limit to what you can use at the head of a bed. Bookshelves, screens, old gates, rugs, tapestries, huge posters, pin boards, windows, storage boxes, old mirrors can all be used to great effect. Use upended pillows and masses of cushions on the bed itself and you can get your comfort as well.

Dressing up the bed
There could hardly be a better choice of bed linen than there is now. Manufacturers are offering every conceivable permutation of colours,

Above: Milky-white crocheted bedspread and lacy cushions look good against the severe cane bedhead.

Top right: This brass knobbed, black painted Edwardian bed with side wings demands and gets romantic-looking lace curtains and valance.

Bottom right: Mini-flower printed duvet, pillows and curtains are teamed with co-ordinating paper and calm grey-blues and apricots in this peaceful little room.

Far right: Broderie Anglaise on a charming late Victorian bedstead.

BEDROOMS

Sheets as show-offs

Since sheets are both highly
decorative and the cheapest way to
get a large amount of fabric
together for comparatively little, it
stands to reason that they can come
into their own in more ways than
one in a bedroom. Sheeting is also
more convenient to use than
unfinished furnishing fabric – ideal
for the non-sewer.

Use sheets –

Instead of conventional material for
a four-poster or half-tester.

To make festoon blinds or balloon
shades or pull-up curtains and
match them up with the bed
treatment (on the bed itself,
swagged across the top of a four-
poster . . .)

For graceful tablecloths on round
tables beside the bed, topping them
with a contrast sheet or lace or
broderie Anglaise.

To cover armchairs and/or a sofa
or chaise longue in the bedroom.

To cover a dressing table.

To make pillow or cushion covers.

As wallcoverings, hanging them
direct from a rod running all
around the room.

*Hang sheets at the bed's corner from
curtain track on the ceiling*

*Use contrasting sheeting to cover
bedside tables*

*Tie a sheet around an armchair for
instant re-upholstery*

designs, co-ordinating sets of sheets,
valances, bed skirts or ruffles, pillow
cases, bedspreads, duvet covers,
comforter and blanket covers and
pillow shams. These last three are
innovations from America which
has long been the instigator of every
sort of bed fashion and comfort.
Pillow shams go on top of pillow
cases so that the pillows can be
propped on top of the matching
comforter (an elegant slimmed-
down eiderdown-like version of the
duvet) or blanket cover (like a thin
sheet-weight bedspread). And pillows come in every shape and size to
be piled in luxurious confusion or
profusion at the head of the bed.

Duvets, comforters or blankets?

The look of your bed will depend a
lot on whether you have a duvet,
comforter or blankets and bedspread. Points in favour of duvets –
they're warm, light, about a quarter
the weight of blankets, and they do
away with bedmaking. Duvet covers are changeable, washable, highly
decorative and can be matched with
pillows, valances and curtains.
Comforters are thinner and neater
than duvets, often come with their
own matching valances and pillow
cases. On the other hand, many
people like to feel the weight of
blankets and to be warmly tucked
in. It's also easier to throw an extra
blanket on or off, whereas you're
stuck with a duvet, which can be

too hot in summer. Comforters are
more useful for year round use
although duvets are now available
for summer use, designed on the
same principle but lighter. Duvet
and comforter fillings can either be
natural or man-made. Down gives
warmth with minimum weight and
in order of quality and cost you can
choose from eiderdown (very expensive), goosedown and duck
down, down and feather (51 per
cent down) and feather and down.
The more feathers the heavier and
cheaper the quilt. These natural fillings should be sent to a specialist
cleaner. Duvets and comforters filled with synthetic fibre or mixtures
like polyester with feathers and
down are more moderately priced
and usually machine washable – so
good for children – though not as
warm as a natural quilt. The categories of warmth of duvets are
known as tog ratings (tog is a
measurement of heat insulation).
Low is 7.5 tog, high is 10.5. The
one you choose will depend on how
warm your bedroom is and how
much you feel the cold. Electric
duvets are also available; they work
on the same principle as electric
blankets.

Marvellous uses for fabric

Since there's no ignoring the bed, go
to the other extreme and make it the
most spectacular object in the room.
And you can do this with fabric,

achieving the most extravagant, elaborate and beautiful effects with hangings, drapes, bed curtains and canopies. If it's illusions of grandeur you're after, fabric, imaginatively used, will get you there.

● A modern four-poster in wood, brass or steel can have billowing side curtains in a light flimsy fabric like cheesecloth, voile, batiste or gingham, or be neat and tailored with straight folds of heavier fabric – tweed, corduroy or flannel.

● Attach a ply canopy or tester to the ceiling over the bed or have it cantilevered from the wall behind and cover it with fabric. Use it as a support for four sets of tied-back curtains. Alternatively, fix ceiling-mounted track around the top of the bed and hang with curtains and a valance. Curtains can be hung from small pieces of track mounted on the ceiling above all four bed corners.

● A half-tester or canopy can be attached to the ceiling just above the pillow area or cantilevered from the back wall about 1.80 m (6 ft) or so up, covered with fabric and hung with back and side curtains.

● A straight panel of fabric can be hung behind the bed, or a length of fabric can be looped over a central dowel or bracket fixed, say, 150–cm (5 ft) above the bed and then over a pair of brackets.

Using fabric to effect. In the room top left, wooden curtain rods are attached to the ceiling and hung with a valance and curtains of ribbon-edged voile to form a full tester. A very original treatment, top centre; multi-coloured ribbons are suspended in front of a panel of striped cotton hung from a brass pole. Thin blue, red and yellow lines on the bedspread repeat the ribbon colours. Crisp pink cotton is used to edge, line, and cover this white and brass four-poster, top right. The ends of the bed in the blue room, bottom left, have been upholstered in the curtain and quilt fabric, while left, voile curtains billow round bed and window.

Bedroom storage has to take care of most if not all of our personal possessions so it must be an essential and well planned part of any bedroom design. Somehow there has to be found space for all or some of the following: clothes for each season, shoes, underclothes, hats, make-up, jewellery, personal papers, books, files, shoe-cleaning equipment, sporting equipment, bags, briefcases, luggage, accessories of every description, hobbies and the extraordinary amount of other impedimenta that inevitably ends up in the bedroom.

In an ideal world there would be a whole wall of storage behind not too conspicuous cupboard or closet doors where there would be carefully designed slots for most of these things. They would all have their allotted place and therefore they would all remain tidy. In addition, there would be space in the room for a large but elegant pedestal or bureau desk to take all papers, and plenty of shelves to take all books and other paraphernalia.

Alas, it is not an ideal world and there is seldom ideal space in a room to plan out the kind and amount of storage you would like. All the same, if you really set your mind to it and consider all the possibilities you can usually work small miracles. And even if it is impossible to give any sort of blueprint on storage that will suit everyone, there are

certain common sense methods of organizing whatever space you do have at your disposal.

How to fit it in

First and foremost, whether storage is to be custom-built, bought ready-made or somehow improvised, it must be fitted into the room as neatly as possible. Otherwise the most elegant of furnishings can be spoilt by the undisciplined welter of belongings. If you are planning a room from scratch you should take a long, detached view of storage possibilities right from the start. Take particular note of your room's proportions and architectural details. In an old building, bedrooms with high ceilings and nice mouldings might be best served with a free-standing cupboard or wardrobe. Large old pieces can often

Left: Storage space has been used to maximum effect in this fitted bedroom. Tall cupboards and wardrobes hold clothes and large unsightly objects, while open shelving in the corner displays more attractive possessions. Even the corner of the room has been cleverly used, providing both shelf and cupboard space.

Space-enhancing mirrored doors are used to conceal a wall of wardrobe, right, in a well-planned bedroom. Note useful two-tiered rods.

BEDROOMS

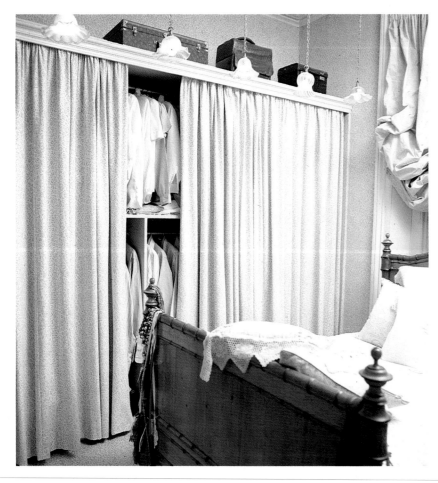

be bought gratifyingly cheaply, and can often be re-organized inside to take an extraordinary number of possessions.

If you definitely decide on built-in storage (or built-in *looking* storage because most storage units are modular and can be made to look custom fitted) and you have convenient recesses or a spare wall or corner, try to ensure that the cupboards reach ceiling height and that any mouldings or base boards or skirtings that are covered are re-introduced and matched along the fronts. Few things spoil the proportion of a room so much as an unsightly gap between the top of a wardrobe and the ceiling quite apart from the fact that it is an unnecessary waste of space and a dust trap. If the cupboard is then very high you can put away your least used objects up there and reach them when necessary with a small pair of steps.

To be really unobtrusive any sort of cupboard fronts should be made to seem part of the walls and brought in with the same decorative treatment whether painted, wallpapered or covered. Wallpaper or covering should either be wrapped around the doors or brought to the edge and covered with thin beading to prevent frayed or torn or worn edging. If you give the wallpaper a coat or two of matt or eggshell polyurethane this will make it much tougher. Alternatively, wardrobe

doors can be mirrored. This can be an excellent solution especially in a small or darkish room where it will serve to expand both space and light.

If you want cupboards to look like objects in their own right they should still, if possible, incorporate some detail or feeling from the rest of the room whether it is in colour or trim or general proportion. If you decide on louvred doors, try to buy half rather than full louvres to prevent too much dust entering the slits. Panelled doors can be painted to match the room door or doors, or inset with a colour or paper or fabric that matches the walls.

How to conjure up space

Sometimes you can look at a room and feel that there is simply no place at all to put a cupboard. But look again. A wall that has one or two doors in it, for example, could have cupboards built *around* the door or doors so that you seem to walk through deep closets to the room, landing or corridor beyond. This is often a very effective way of getting good storage space without seeming to encroach on valuable room space. The same thing could be done around a window or windows, especially if you can incorporate a dressing-table and drawers as well.

Occasionally in a smallish room you can build cupboards around the bedspace with the top cupboards continuing over the bed to form a

In a small room where any sort of conventional wardrobe space could look obtrusive, soft storage might well be the answer—that is to say, clothes covered or concealed by curtains rather than more rigid doors. In the room above, well-planned storage is arranged behind curtains which match the wallpaper. They are suspended

behind a piece of moulding which repeats the cornice above. The top gap—which could have been unsightly—is filled with handsome old luggage while a series of old milky glass light shades suspended from brass chains hanging in front form a kind of unusual and decorative visual screen, an imaginative solution.

All about storage

Skinny painted gym lockers make good cheap storage.

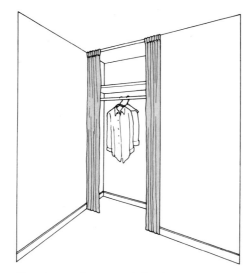

Curtains can disguise rods fixed into recesses.

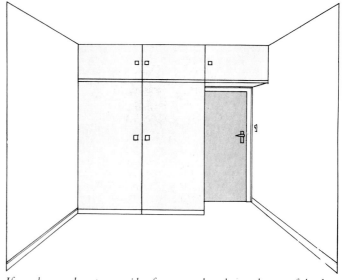

If you have a door to one side of a run of wardrobes build in another *cupboard over the top of the door frame to form a neat lobby.*

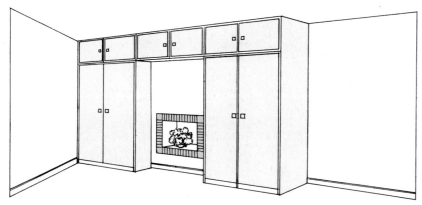

Fit wardrobes and cupboards either side of a chimney breast and run a *bridge of cupboards over the top to neaten the look of the two units.*

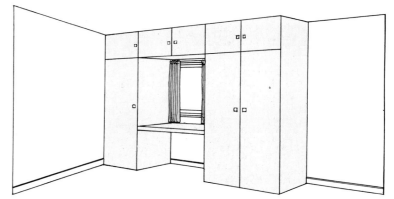

Build wardrobes and a run of high cupboards all around a window and *fit a shelf across at sill level to make a useful desk-dressing table.*

BEDROOMS

sort of recess. Sometimes it is even possible to fit small shelves into the sides of the cupboards to hold books, and other bedside clutter. Lights can be fitted across the underside of the top cupboards or on the side walls so that everything looks and is beautifully and neatly integrated.

If there are two windows, the space between the windows might be used either for a cupboard or shelves, or the space might just be big enough to take the bed, leaving the rest of the wall space clear for storage.

Again, you might put a bed up against the window (as long as it is well draught-proofed) which will put more room space at your disposal for storage purposes.

In a very small room, it might be best to put up cupboards in the corridor outside rather than curtail sleeping and dressing space still further.

Or a bed can be set up on a neat platform of carpeted drawers, or right up on top of low cupboards. In any event, if there is space under a bed for extra storage drawers so much the better.

Other space-saving tricks are folding doors on top and bottom sliding tracks which will take up the minimum of space when they are opened; cupboards with curtained fronts rather than doors; cloakroom racks concealed by curtains or screens as a temporary measure.

Organization and method

Whether you are building new storage or trying to re-organize the storage you have or that already exists in a new room there are certain helpful pointers to using the space to its – and your – best advantage.

For example, clothes racks are often fitted unnecessarily high so that the space below is not properly utilised. A reasonable height is 1.5 m (5 ft) from the bottom of the cupboard leaving the top part free for generous shelving space. Alternatively, you can have two banks of rods for short clothes like shirts, jackets and skirts in one wardrobe, or part of a wardrobe, and longer hanging space in another. If there are few drawers in a room but many shelves, wire or cane baskets are a good idea for keeping underclothes, shirts, sweaters, tights, socks and similar items tidy. Tie racks can be fixed to the insides of doors, so can racks or hooks for belts. Stacking plastic drawers can be inserted into any suitable space for shirts and sweaters and are especially good in clear plastic so that you can see contents at a glance. It's a good idea to store shoes on shelves one above the other rather than in a heap at the bottom of a wardrobe. Or shoes can be stashed away in one of those hanging wardrobe bags or shoe tidies for extra efficiency.

If you're lucky enough to have a whole wall of storage or a walk-in

Top far left: Industrial shelving and wire baskets hold an amazing amount of clobber from luggage to linen, clothes and general paraphernalia. A desk top has been fitted in too.

Bottom far left: A glimpse inside this fitted wardrobe shows just how much can be achieved with careful planning. With hanging rails, shelves of different sizes and drawers, there is easily room for everything.

Left and above: The sloping walls and unusual angles in this room have helped its owner to discover imaginative storage space. The bed has been cleverly partitioned off by shelves and a storage unit, and the shelves have been given an attractive sloping cover.

BEDROOMS

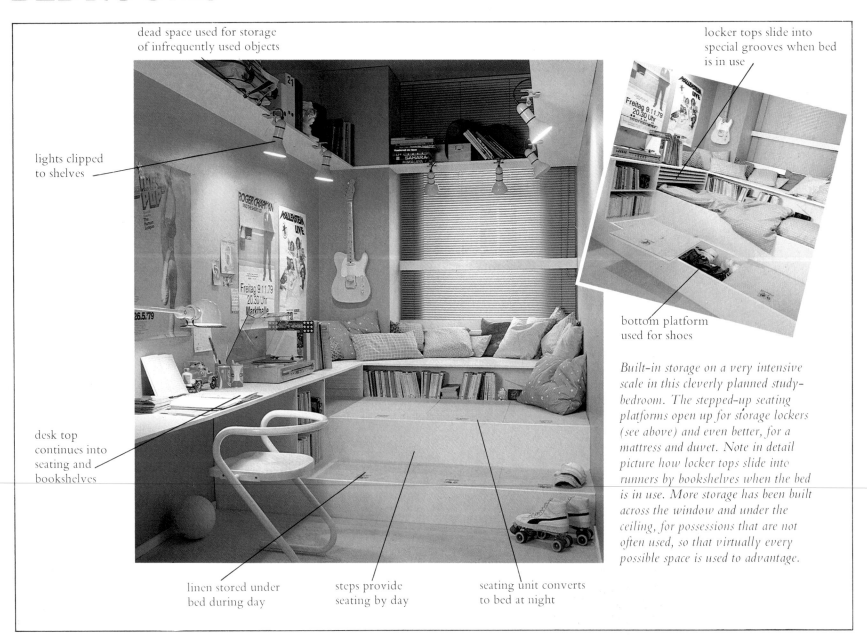

dead space used for storage of infrequently used objects

locker tops slide into special grooves when bed is in use

lights clipped to shelves

desk top continues into seating and bookshelves

linen stored under bed during day

steps provide seating by day

seating unit converts to bed at night

bottom platform used for shoes

Built-in storage on a very intensive scale in this cleverly planned study-bedroom. The stepped-up seating platforms open up for storage lockers (see above) and even better, for a mattress and duvet. Note in detail picture how locker tops slide into runners by bookshelves when the bed is in use. More storage has been built across the window and under the ceiling, for possessions that are not often used, so that virtually every possible space is used to advantage.

cupboard, drawer or shelf space will be part of this. Otherwise you might have room for a chest or chests of drawers or a dresser. If a dressing-table is not included in a storage wall (or in the bathroom) a separate one could be used as a desk/dressing-table with drawers for papers as well as cosmetics. Another space-saving idea is to leave sufficient knee-hole space between two or three chests of drawers or 70 cm (28 in) high filing cabinets, and run a separate top over them; this gives you a writing and dressing-table surface as well.

And don't forget that most valuable area of storage space – under the bed. Drawers here can take lots of spare bedding or clothes.

Building-in the basin

If you have room for a wash basin in the bedroom, this will certainly relieve pressure on a family bathroom, and if you can incorporate it into a cupboard which can then act as a dressing-table area as well, you will have solved several problems very neatly indeed. Build the basin into a small vanity unit with a vinyl or tiled top and try to include a drawer unit, a towel rail, some hooks, electric points for razor, toothbrush and hair dryer, and, of course, a well lit mirror (one with lights all round, like a theatrical mirror would be ideal). If there isn't room for such a cupboard, a screen would make an admirable substitute.

How to improvise

If you're short of space or money or both, there are various ways to improvise quite adequate storage. A piece of wood with hooks to take hangers will serve very well as a temporary measure. Always add hooks to the backs of doors too, to take coats, dressing gowns and the odd overflow of clothes.

Cloakroom racks can be bought comparatively cheaply and can look quite decorative if they're tidily hung with clothes and left like that, or concealed by a screen or curtains. Old gym lockers can be painted and used for shirts and underclothes. Recesses either side of a chimney can be used very effectively for temporary storage by mounting dowelling or broom handles across them from which to hang clothes.

Old lace curtains hung from a brass rod repeat the feeling of the bedspread as well as concealing rather more utilitarian storage. Wood shelves can be varied to hold everything from luggage to linen. Wire filing baskets are slotted in for smaller items and the same system is stretched to form full length hanging space as well. The whole concept is as effective as it is simple.

BATHROOMS

THE BATHROOM IS A ROOM TOO

I was going to say the bathroom has come a long way from the uncomfortble cold space it often was. But in fact Egyptian bathrooms, Roman bathrooms, ancient Greek bathrooms were immensely sumptuous affairs with good plumbing and a great deal of luxury. That there was a gap of so many centuries before we really began again to treat the bathroom as the healing, cleansing, refreshing place it should be is almost incomprehensible, but there it is. Once again we are taking enormous interest in the room as a room to enjoy and not just a place to house those indispensable items, the bath, washbasin, shower and WC.

Bathrooms need some deep thought of course, especially if you have the opportunity of planning one from scratch. Young childless couples, elderly couples, families with babies or teenage children, those with spare, Spartan inclinations and those who love comfort and glamour all have their differing needs. But basically the problem can always be defined and isolated by your answer to the following three questions: How much money have you to spend? How much space have you got to play with? Do you want a luxurious bathroom or a practical, hygienic splashing place?

Practical bathrooms that come in from the cold

If you live in a modern house or block you will generally have efficient new plumbing even if the actual bathroom or rooms are given very little space, and nondescript space at that. If your bathroom is one of these and has a shower over the bath you might think of tiling it all over. Although it will be more expensive initially than painting or wall-papering you won't need any more maintenance for years to come.

You can create different effects with coloured grouting cement between the tiles and there is an infinite range of patterns that you can make with tiles of various colours and designs. In fact there is so much opportunity for variety that the best advice is probably to be restrained and not to try patterns that are too contrived.

Forget about tiles being cold and clinical; these days the repertoire of beautiful colours and patterns is enormous and you can always soften any hard lines with large fluffy towels in luxurious shades, with interesting fabric window treatments and a stunning (rubber-backed) carpet. However, if you do want to save yourself some money

Boldly striped cotton is used to form a decorative canopy over the bath area in an interesting bath-exercise room, left. The same fabric is neatly pinned back by the shower. Stripes again, right, are used to good effect to give character to a wood-lined room.

BATHROOMS

by using mostly white or cream tiles you can insert a border of patterned tiles to run underneath the ceiling, down corners and around the bath. This will inject colour, relieve the monotony and take away any arctic feeling.

If you live in an older house or block you might trade elderly fittings and antiquated plumbing for more space. Although changing the plumbing around is a major expense – if indeed it is possible at all, you can at least change the fixtures for contemporary versions which will work a whole lot better.

For example, you might think of looking for water-saving WCs or showers which will conserve your hot water supply. If changing the fixtures seems impossibly expensive (and don't forget – you can often find second-hand baths, basins and WCs in good condition for half the price because they have been thrown out in favour of later models or different colours) think of changing the taps and shower fittings: this comparatively minor change will instantly give a more stylish look.

New baths for old

If the plumbing works well but the fixtures are jaded, chipped and stained do not automatically think of throwing them out. Baths, basins and even WCs can be renovated and resurfaced by professional firms (listed in trade directory). Or

Far left: Border tiles are used to create a panelled effect in this elegant, restrained bathroom. The polished wood bath panel looks good against the mole grey carpet.

Above: A tiled partition wall divides lavatory and shower stalls in a neat blue and white room. Floor tiles have been used to form a defining border below the ceiling.

Left: A bath has been cleverly inserted here into what might have seemed an impossible space. Mirrored walls and cleverly designed storage make the most of the remaining area.

Styles for tiles

Plain white tiles are usually the least expensive type to buy. Make them look more distinguished by laying them on the diagonal, colouring the grouting with added pigment, adding border tiles to the leading edges or just below the top run, or making a checker board effect.

Use border tiles, or ordinary decorative tiles, for a decorative edge

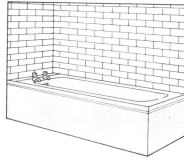

Rectangular tiles look interesting if you lay them like stepped bricks

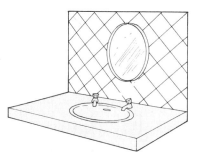

Lay square tiles diagonally and they will make the area seem much bigger

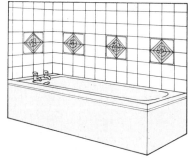

Cheer up an expanse of plain tiles by dropping in the odd decorative block

BATHROOMS

Far left: A completely mirrored wall gives a light and airy feeling to the bathroom of this tree-surrounded country house. The polished wood cabinet for the basin and the arched mirror superimposed on the larger slab of mirror look especially effective with the stripped and polished floors, the beamed ceiling and the abundance of plants which serve to link inside with outdoors.

Top: Tawny faux marble cornices, skirting boards and splashback blend well with the fabric used for the elaborate festoon blinds. They also provide an effective counterpoint to the art- and photograph-covered walls.

Bottom centre: The border on the graceful long white curtains is carefully matched to the tiled bath surround in another elegant and personal room. An old painted chair, wood framed prints and nice old hanging shelves are handsome additions.

Bottom left: Modern lozenge-shaped floor tiles look good with the classic twin basins on their sturdy porcelain pedestals, the long curtains, the fireplace with its flowers and mirrored overmantel and the painted, towel rail and chair. Although mostly white the room looks very far from clinical.

you can resurface them yourself with epoxy paint if you are handy and, above all, patient. You must first take the time to prime the original surface to ensure a really smooth slick finish when you spray or roll on the epoxy, and you must wait the requisite time (usually a day or two) before you can safely use the fixtures again.

Outsides of old baths can also be painted with a design, or stencilled to look especially interesting. It's often a good idea to have the sides built-out a little and panelled with wood so that they look both generous and contained, especially if the sides are deep enough to sit on or to put things on. Old basins too, with their sad underpinnings of twisted pipes, can also be enclosed with wood to gain respectability and provide storage space at the same time.

Plants in the bathroom

An instant facelift for an existing bathroom can be achieved by the addition of plants. Their vivid colours, plant pots and often sculptural leaf shapes can all be used to great effect for little outlay in either time or money. Moreover, the warm humid conditions are often particularly suited to certain varieties of houseplant. But remember that they need good light as well as bright direct, though not necessarily hot, sunshine. Few plants thrive in deep shade or gloomy places. Air con-

ditioning will de-hydrate them and if your bathroom has fan ventilation this will cause draughts which plants dislike. Some require constant humidity and should be stood in plastic trays on a layer of constantly moist gravel or pebbles. If your bathroom is kept at a low temperature – around 5°C (40°F) – your choice of plants will be more limited, but *aspidistra, hedera canariensis, rhoicissus rhomboidea, sansevieria* and *ficus pumila* are sturdy enough and should be satisfactory. Bowls of mixed plants are a good choice for a small bathroom; they take up little room but give a variety of colours and textures. Don't overwater these and remember that containers without drainage holes should have a thin layer of gravel in the bottom. Some plants, like ferns, hate drying out and some, like aspidistras, dislike dust and need to be sponged occasionally. All plants should be turned to let the light get at all sides. To avoid disappointment, only buy plants that come with good instruction labels telling you how to care for them and what sort of temperatures and conditions they prefer.

Not only but also

If your room is big enough there's no reason why it shouldn't serve not one but two useful purposes. You could consider making a bathroom–dressing room, a bathroom–exercise room, or you might add a bathroom

end to a bedroom, simply screening it off. If there is room for clothes storage, either in the room, or in a lobby just outside, you can add a hanging cupboard or closet, bring in a chest of drawers, install a long mirror or a mirrored wall, insert a comfortable chair, maybe a rocking chair or an old wicker chair, put down a carpet and you will have an interesting dressing-room – especially if there is space to add a dressing-table and chair or stool as well.

Keep-fit enthusiasts might find the bathroom a good place for an exercise bicycle, a rowing or jogging machine or whatever. If all this gym equipment doesn't look particularly beautiful it could be masked off with a screen, a hardboard partition or tall plants. But if your bathroom is a gleaming modern design, you should have no difficulties fitting this sort of equipment into your decorative scheme – it can even provide a focal point.

The bathroom–gym

Combine beauty care with health and fitness for the latest in bathroom schemes. Whatever your room size, you can fit a bath with foldaway sunbed/massage deck or built-in water spa effect. If you have a spacious room you could incorporate multi-gym equipment, an exercise bike, sauna, hot-tub or jacuzzi in your plan.

BATHROOMS

Everything has a highly nautical air in this blue, white and red bathroom. Well, perhaps not everything. There are two amusing exceptions: the Shakespearean bust to the side of the basin, and the baskets more pretty than shipshape. For the rest, the room is very spruce with its blue outlined trim, red door, pipes, lavatory cistern and radiator, nautical towels and its porthole-like wall lamps. The bath is set interestingly at an angle and divided from the red-edged deckchair end of the room by the radiator. Note the life-belt.

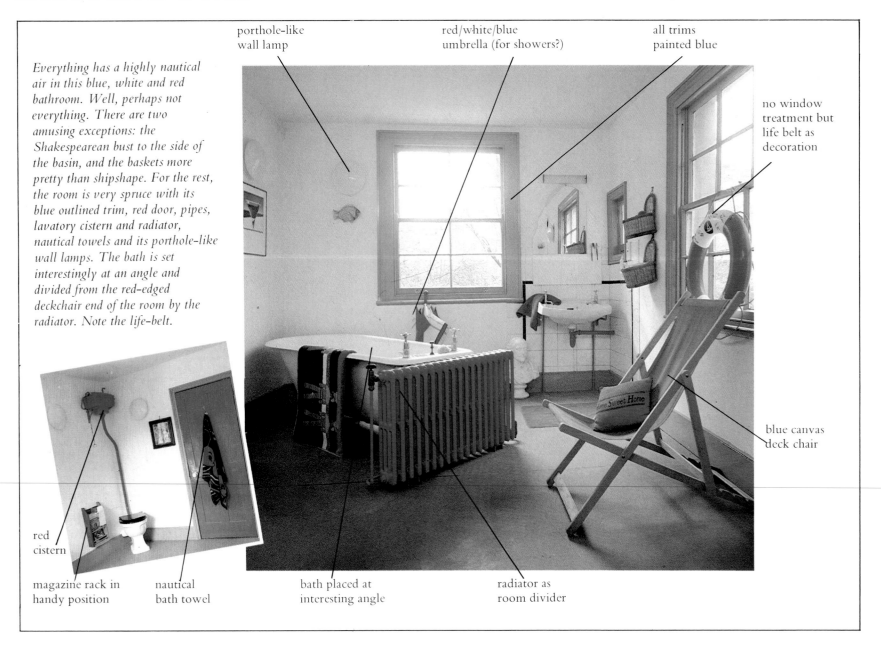

porthole-like
wall lamp

red/white/blue
umbrella (for showers?)

all trims
painted blue

no window
treatment but
life belt as
decoration

blue canvas
deck chair

red
cistern

magazine rack in
handy position

nautical
bath towel

bath placed at
interesting angle

radiator as
room divider

Incidentally, the new cordless telephones are perfect for calls in the bath and if this is where you have your inspirations, a battery operated recorder could be at hand.

Comfort on a shoe-string

My own feeling is that bathrooms should be comfortable, civilized, rather decorative, and certainly personal rooms – an ambition one can achieve more cheaply in this area than in any other part of the house bar the cloakroom or powder room. For with care, one can usually manage to achieve an air of luxury for a comparatively small sum, using expensive fabrics, tiles, and wall coverings that can be afforded here because they are only needed in small quantities. Conversely, you can of course spend a fortune, and still end up with an unsatisfactory and uninteresting space, since bathroom personality depends much more on colour, mood and accessories than on actual equipment.

Problem areas

If you inherit an existing, boring little space with fixtures that cannot be moved or changed it isn't the end of the world but it does call for positive action. There are literally dozens of cosmetic changes you can put into effect without spending a fortune. Here are some instant face-lifts that will give any jaded bathroom a new lease of life.

● *Large expanse of tiles in a colour you hate* Paint over them with eggshell yacht paint followed by a coat of gloss paint for a lustre finish, or with epoxy paint. Give the walls a good clean first to get rid of all lingering traces of dirt and grease and then apply a coat of primer. Alternatively you can tile over the top, either with new tiles or with sheets of ceramic tiles or mosaic with flexible grouting already in place.

● *Shabby walls* Put up plastic-laminated surfaces which can go over almost anything. Or panel the walls with wood, or cover them with tongue-and-groove wood coated with polyurethane.

● *Unexciting walls* Cover them with a wallpaper which might be far too expensive to use in a larger space; or with fabric or felt above a run of tiles, or at least a run of transparent perspex or plexiglass or glass around bath or basin.

● *Uninteresting room* Paint the walls a dark rich colour and use them as a background for prints, drawings,

Right: Stencilling can work wonders when re-vamping a bathroom – especially, when, as here, it is, literally, given a new twist. These free-flowing tulips make a delightful break from the tradition of using straight borders and create an attractive feature of the handsome period window.

BATHROOMS

Left This small bathroom was made to look extremely pretty at very low cost by painting every surface white, curtaining off the bath with white lace-curtains and adding plenty of plants.

Above: Fabric curtains are used to conceal the storage area below the set-in basin in this graceful bathroom.

Right: A grand look is given to a tiny bathroom, by an elegant water-lily stencil on the central wall, and stencilled wooden doors. Plaster busts complete the rather classical effect.

photographs, collections of this and that, memorabilia, whatever you fancy, in order to add lots of interest and impact.

● *Dull dark room* Paint everything white from top to bottom, white tile or sheet vinyl the floor (white carpet would get dirty too quickly but you could put down easily washable cotton rug) and mass every available space, including the window embrasure with plants. This will make even the dreariest little room look fresh and airy.

● *Cramped space* Don't forget the power of mirror. Panels will open the most confined space even if you only mirror the back of a door.

● *Ugly windows* Pretty them up by covering horrible obscured glass with a permanent blind in flimsy fabric or put up café curtains – in two tiers if necessary, one for privacy, the other to let in the light.

● *Tired old towels* Jazz up old white towels you cannot afford to change by adding a border of contrasting colour, say pink, or green, or use both colours, all round the edges. This will also restore the chic to towels with frayed and dog-eared edges from too much washing.

● *Unsightly plumbing* Hide unsightly pipes below washbasins with a cupboard or closet which will also be useful for extra storage. If you cannot build such a cupboard, shirr

fabric on a rod, gathering tape, or stretch wire and fix it around the basin. Hide other pipes by boxing them in if you can. The resulting ledge can be used to stand things on. Alternatively you can make a feature of them with bright paint.

● *Bath that's seen better days* Cover bath panels with carpet to match the one on the floor. Or tile them. Or paste them with vinyl paper or wallpaper protected with at least two coats of polyurethane (test the paper first to make sure that it does not run. If it does, you could try covering it with a protective film of clear plastic). If there is not a bath panel to cover, you can always make one by boxing in the bath with plywood, leaving a deep shelf all around which can either be tiled or covered in plastic laminate and used to hold objects, bottles and jars. This will also give the effect of having a luxurious built-in bath.

● An extension of the above idea is to frame both bath and basin with mahogany panelling to give a semblance of Edwardian opulence. Get a carpenter to fit neatly panelled wood sides (or do it yourself, fixing the real thing if you can afford it or staining the wood mahogany and polishing and lacquering it if you cannot).

● *No atmosphere* Create it. Add a small set of shelves for books (best covered in clear plastic in case of splashes) or objects, or collectables,

BATHROOMS

Left: Mahogany-stained wood was used to make the vanity unit and panelled doors and bath panel as well as to frame the mirror. Doors are filled in with alternate panes of mirror and obscured glass for reflection, extra light and privacy. Rose and cream mini-print wallpaper was given a coat of clear eggshell varnish for extra toughness and goes well with the blue and off-white Brussels Weave Carpet.

Above: You can, of course, recess basins into almost any sort of unit, including a pine chest of drawers as here. The drawers provide instant storage facilities.

or small plants or an interesting mixture. Bring in a cane table and a cane or wicker chair and spray them white or leave them natural, and cover a cushion or two with towelling to match the towels you are using. Have a small table drawn up near the WC with piles of magazines. Keep a bottle of mineral water near the bath together with a glass.

- *Lacks luxury* Pile a glass dish or brandy balloon with pretty soaps in an appropriate colour. Decant bath salts and oils into beautiful glass jars or carafes. Let it *smell* expensive – perfume, oil, talc. Even if you just manage to buy some really luxurious deep-pile towels in a beautiful colour or a few china or brightly coloured plastic accessories, you'll be amazed at the difference such small touches make.

Family bathrooms can still look good

With the best will in the world it is almost impossible to keep a family bathroom looking tidy and elegant. All too often, towels are dropped in a soggy heap, bath toys are left lying around or stranded like sea flotsam in dry baths. Shelves are filled with a litter of ancient toothbrushes and half-finished tubes of toothpaste. Shower curtains have gone mouldy at the bottom and bath edges are thick with mostly-finished bottles, jars and tubes. It is a sorry sight. What can you do about it?

How to foresee – and forestall – eyesores

Abandon all thoughts of using wallpaper or wallcovering in a room used by a multi-generational family; it will get splashed and start to look forlorn in no time. Much better to tile all over or use plastic laminate or even paint such an area.

Fit in as much storage as possible; children and teenagers are invariably untidy. See that there are places where bath toys can be stashed away when not in use, where cleaning things can be within easy reach but out of sight and where unsightly clobber can be hidden away.

Fit a glass partition rather than a shower curtain which can get shabby or at least disarranged all too quickly.

Have separate and distinctive tooth mugs, face flannels and towels in co-ordinated colours for each member of the family – they won't look a mess, or get muddled.

Try to double the amount of heated towel rail space or have a long radiator with a rod going all the length of one wall. This way towels will at least dry quickly.

Put up hooks everywhere: on the back of the door; by the bath (for face cloths); by the basin or basins for hand towels.

Try to have double medicine cabinets, or a whole wall of cabinets like a kitchen. In fact, kitchen cabinets might be a very good idea if you have the wall space. Some manufacturers make cabinets that will go in any room.

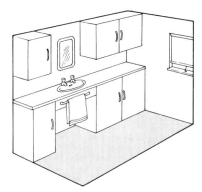

Kitchen units maximise storage space

Perspex screens are tidier than curtains and don't rot

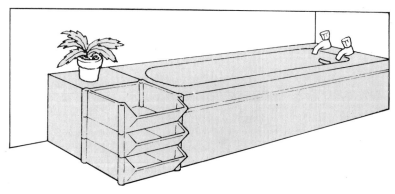

Fit storage units at end of bath

Whether you are re-modelling a bathroom or starting one from scratch there is a huge range of equipment available from the most luxurious to the purely functional.

Don't just go out and buy a bath without arming yourself first with as much information as possible. These days there are oval baths, octagonal baths, corner baths, curved baths, copies of old baths on claw feet . . . you name it . . . the choice is tremendous, not to say bewildering. So do your home-work, research the market and shop around to see what's available. Re-member too, that for those who are able to afford the money and the space there are now steam baths, whirlpool massage baths, shower massagers, hot tubs, jacuzzis and baths big enough for two, any of which will add to the sybaritic pos-sibilities of your bathroom.

Basically, the more conventional baths are 1700 mm (5 ft 6 in) long by 700 mm (2 ft 3 in) wide but you can buy many other shapes includ-ing lengths from 1475 mm (4ft 11 in) to 1800 mm (5 ft 11 in–6 ft) in widths from 700 mm (2 ft 3 in) to 800 mm (2 ft 7½ in). If space is very tight you can find corner baths or sitting rather than lying baths which measure about 1375 mm (4 ft 7 in) by 710 mm (2ft 4 in) or 120 mm (4 ft) square; or extra deep baths or shower trays which can be used for both shower-

ing and bathing. It's important to take note of these measurements when planning a space where every inch may count. Before ordering decide exactly where you want your fixtures placed; this will determine the size of the space you have to play with and the type of bath you can fit in and still have room to man-oeuvre.

When you are planning where to put the bath, remember the plumb-ing. If the drains and supply pipes will not go where you want them, you will have to think again. More often than not, baths are fitted against a wall, tight up to a corner, but if both your space and your plumbing runs and waste pipes can stand it, you could plan for one to be centred along a wall or even in the middle of the floor. If you centre a bath in the middle of a long wall you can build a floor to ceiling partition at either end which will make it look built-in. This will allow both a WC and a bidet to be placed one side and

In this ultra-modern ensuite bathroom, left, delicate, apricot-coloured walls and pale floorboards are offset by a dramatic black and white chequerboard panel, which serves as a divider from the adjoining bedroom.

In the room on the right walls covered with mirror panels make all the difference to this cramped space.

BATHROOMS

basin on the other. Add shower curtains from a track inset into the ceiling or fixed tight up to the ceiling, tie them back on either side and you immediately get a gracious look. You can achieve much the same look of a curtained-off aperture if the bath is fitted tight into one end of a small room.

Whatever the size and colour of the bath you choose, do try to get one with handles either side. You might be limber enough now but a bath is a long-term investment and you have to reckon on growing older and stiffer with the years. Also, handles are essential for small children and elderly people or people with back problems.

Baths: which material?

Acrylics The cheapest and most common material for baths is acrylic, which can be moulded easily to incorporate seats, soap dishes, bath-rests and so on. Water stays hotter in acrylic than metal baths and they are fairly resistant to knocks and chips although they can get scratches. The best way to cope with these when they happen is to make sure the surface is quite dry and to rub the scratch down with metal polish and rinse off thoroughly.

Acrylics burn easily, so avoid cigarettes in the bathroom. They can also be damaged by nail varnish, varnish remover and some dry cleaning liquids.

It is important to install them exactly to manufacturer's instructions or they may not remain rigid.

Glass fibre These baths are made of layers of glass fibre bonded together with polyester resin. They are much stronger and more rigid than the acrylic variety and come in a range of colours, including metallic and pearlized finishes.

Pressed steel These are fairly light and rigid baths with a smooth vitreous enamel coating and good wearing properties.

Cast iron This is the traditional and the classic, but expensive material for baths and still holds its own mainly because it has an excellent, fairly stain-proof and easy-to-clean finish or porcelain enamel fused onto the metal at very high temperature.

Bath surrounds

Unless your bath is in the centre of the room you absolutely must have a splash-resistant surround which is usually of tiles or plastic laminate. Some people choose to fix a sheet of clear or milky perspex, plexiglass or lucite over paint or wallpaper, but I have found that water can all too easily seep down the back. Whatever the material, the surround should be at least 500 mm (1 ft 8 in) high and come up to the ceiling if your bath

The green and white bathroom above has been made to look much more interesting with its centrally-placed bath flanked by bamboo chests, useful and decorative. The bath itself has also been made to look more substantial with its green tiled surround, which is quite wide enough to make a convenient seating ledge. Slim Venetian blinds at the window add to the neat architectural look as well as giving a pleasant filtered light.

Planning your space

When planning a new bathroom from scratch, you will have to consider whether to include the WC in the main area or install it separately elsewhere. There are points in favour of each arrangement and you should decide which is best suited to your needs.

Bear in mind that each fitting must have enough surrounding space for it to be used comfortably and easily. Allow 1100 × 700 mm (43 × 28 in)

alongside baths and 2200 mm (86 in) headroom. Wash-basins should have 200 mm (8 in) on either side and 700 mm (28 in) in front. WCs and bidets need 200 mm (8 in) either side and 600 mm (24 in) in front. For showers enclosed on three sides allow 900 × 700 mm (35 × 28 in) alongside and for enclosed showers 900 × 400 mm (35 × 16 in).

It may seem as if you need an enormous amount of space to accommodate these appliances. But as only one or two of them are likely to be used at the same time, the activity areas can easily overlap.

These layouts for different-shaped bathrooms indicate the *optimum* space around fittings

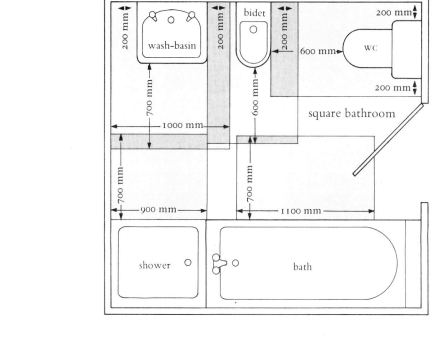

square bathroom

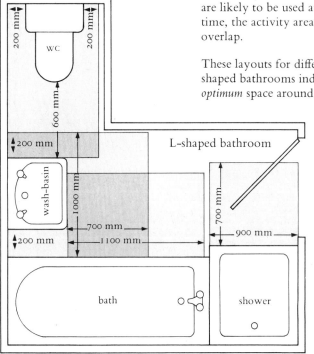

L-shaped bathroom

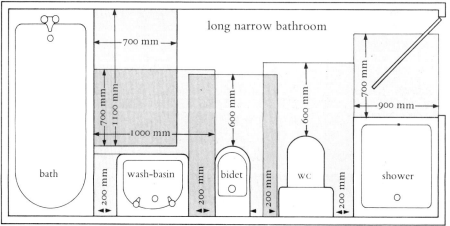

long narrow bathroom

BATHROOMS

includes a shower. The gap between bath and wall – and there will always be a slight one – should be well sealed with a ceramic tile trim, a sealing strip or a non-hardening mastic, otherwise water can trickle down and cause rot.

If you want to square off the bath you can either box it in yourself, using boarding, which you can stain, tile, carpet or laminate. If you are not handy, get a carpenter to do it, or buy ready-made front and back panels. Remember to have one removable panel so that pipes and waste can be inspected and repaired.

Save with a shower

Quite apart from being refreshing and invigorating, showers save water because they use about one-fifth of the amount needed for a bath. And they save energy, especially if you connect them to an instantaneous electric water heater which heats only the water actually used. Another advantage to a shower is that since it only takes up about one square metre (1 sq yd) of floor space it can be installed in all sorts of odd corners providing that there is a water supply and drainage near to hand and the sort of instantaneous electric heater which takes water from the mains. Otherwise the water cistern should be at least a metre (3 ft) higher than the shower head or there will not be enough pressure for the shower to work.

If you have a shower built in you will need a mixer valve and spray attachment with a thermostatic valve and a ceramic, steel or acrylic shower tray. Install them in a corner or an alcove, cover the walls with tiles and fit a glass door, glass screens or curtains according to what is appropriate to the position and your pocket. It is also very easy to put in a shower above a bath tub, again screening it off with a glass panel if that is possible with your bath design, or shower curtains. Or you can buy special shower cubicles which range tremendously in price.

Basins

You can buy free-standing pedestal wash basins, wall hung basins, basins partially supported by front legs, or basins that can be sunk into counter tops or vanity units. Like baths, they are available in porcelain enamel over cast iron, acrylic, glass fibre or in the popular vitreous china. They can be oval, round, square, rectangular, corner-shaped or shell-shaped and range in size from the small 300 mm (1 ft) widths to around 750 mm (2 ft 6 in) or more. They come in the same range of colours as baths or they can be decorated in some way. It is often sensible in a family bathroom to have two basins set side by side in a counter or vanity unit which can be made from plywood or other wood, then either stained, polished and

lacquered or covered with tiles or with plastic laminate. More lavish counters can be made from marble or slate or stone.

Choose your taps and hardware at the same time as you order your bath. Again, there is an enormous choice to suit all tastes and pockets. The cheapest place to have taps installed is at the end of the bath and above the waste. You can choose between a pop-up waste (controlled by a lever or handle of some sort) or a plug and chain. But you can, of course, buy baths without tap holes to use with wall-mounted taps, or with separate function taps – the spout at one place, the controls in another.

WCs

WCs are generally wall-hung or the pedestal variety and can come as low as 230 mm (9 in) from the ground or considerably higher and in a variety of widths. Wooden seats are popular again, or you can buy seats to match the lavatory colour.

Bidets

If there is room, bidets should definitely be included in bathroom fixtures. They should be as near the WC as possible and, generally take up about 350 mm (1 ft 2 in). Again, you can buy them in the same colours as baths and WCs or in white. If possible, choose one with a built-in douche spray.

Above: A mini-bathroom is given a Victorian feel with a traditional style pedestal basin and etched glass doors on the shower enclosure.

Right: No expense has been spared in this elegant, traditional bathroom, which is almost large enough to entertain in. The black and white floor tiles have an Edwardian feel, as do the mahogany panelled bath and the 'his and her' basins, each with their own overhead light and mahogany-framed mirror and shelf. Period style paintings add a finishing touch.

BATHROOMS

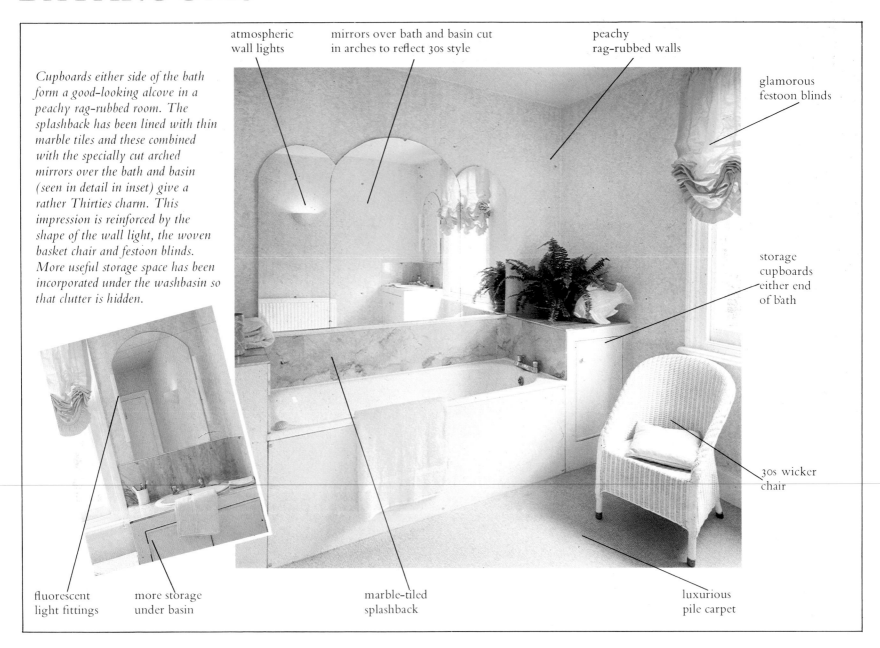

Cupboards either side of the bath form a good-looking alcove in a peachy rag-rubbed room. The splashback has been lined with thin marble tiles and these combined with the specially cut arched mirrors over the bath and basin (seen in detail in inset) give a rather Thirties charm. This impression is reinforced by the shape of the wall light, the woven basket chair and festoon blinds. More useful storage space has been incorporated under the washbasin so that clutter is hidden.

atmospheric
wall lights

mirrors over bath and basin cut
in arches to reflect 30s style

peachy
rag-rubbed walls

glamorous
festoon blinds

storage
cupboards
either end
of bath

30s wicker
chair

fluorescent
light fittings

more storage
under basin

marble-tiled
splashback

luxurious
pile carpet

Neat and tidy storage

Bathroom storage is generally a real headache – especially storage in a family bathroom. Medicines and medicaments, powders, soaps, toothpastes and toothbrushes, razors, personal electric equipment, shampoos, bath oils and salts, tissues, cotton wool, cleaning accessories, bath toys, toilet paper, towels and wash cloths all have to be accommodated somewhere, somehow, since they cannot all crowd the counter top and bath surrounds. The conventional medicine cabinet is hardly big enough and yet there seems no other space in the standard box-shaped bathroom. Where do you go from here? For a start, if you have not already got a built-in basin or vanity unit what about that area? It's a good space for a cupboard which will also cover any previously exposed pipes. You can always curtain-off a basin and hide a multitude of stuff behind the fabric; it isn't very difficult to fix a skirt to the basin itself. You should allow double the measurement of the basin in material. Turn over the fabric at the top and run a gathering string through it. Cut some 'gripper tape' to length and glue it to the bottom of the basin. Sew exactly the same amount of tape onto the gathered skirt and clamp it to the tape on the basin. Or buy some stretch wire, run it through the top hem of the fabric and attach it to the wall either side of the basin.

Tiny bathrooms

When space is at a premium such desperate situations call for desperate measures. See if there's room for shelves or cupboards in all sorts of unexpected places. What about above the window or door or toilet or at the end of the bath? You only need narrow shelves on the whole so the smallest alcove could be used up and given a door too, if you like. If space is very tight think about fixing shelves on the backs of cupboard doors.

Corners are always possible either for an old corner cupboard, for floor-standing étagères in wood or cane, or for narrow cabinets set at right angles. Always fix a couple of hooks to the back of doors and have plenty of towel hanging space: at least one heated towel rail if there is room or a long pole over a radiator as well as hooks or rods near the basin for hand towels.

Right: Eighteen inches or so of wall depth have been stolen here to turn into a handsome mirror-lined alcove surrounded by a whole range of top and bottom storage cupboards. The other side of the room (reflected in the mirror) has been similarly treated with open shelves for towels as well as a full length linen cupboard. The neutral print wallpaper on walls, doors and ceiling harmonizes with the cream-painted dado and bath panel and is offset by the towels.

BATHROOMS

An elegant period country style. The delicate stencil on the roll-top bath was adapted and enlarged from the pattern of the wallpaper. Tongue-and-groove panelling to dado height is stained green to co-ordinate. Plants and antique green glass bottles complete the fresh look.

Right: Grey and lemon sponging on the tongue-and-groove panelling echoes the grey and yellow stripe in the wallpaper.

Floor and wall treatments

Obviously in a bathroom you have to think first and foremost about surfaces that are resistant to steam and water. Ceramic tiles are clearly very practical for both surfaces: with a high glaze for walls and a skid-proof surface for floors. But you could also use quarry tiles, earthenware tiles like Mexican and Portuguese, and glass bricks or mosaic. I once saw a small bathroom entirely covered – ceiling as well – with mirrored mosaic tiles and the effect was stupendous.

Cheapest of course, is paint which is best in an eggshell or high gloss finish. Wallpaper looks good, but must be applied above a good run of tiles around bath and basin, or else covered in clear perspex or plexiglass or glass around the damp prone areas. Vinyl and vinyl-coated papers are practical. Another good idea is to paint over any bathroom wallpaper with a clear eggshell glaze like polyurethane. This will preserve the paper for a far longer time.

You can apply laminated panels of hardboard with a baked-on plastic coating in a large range of colours and finishes including a realistic marble. A wide choice of panels is available which can be applied straight to the walls as well as to counter tops, and then there is the real McCoy – marble itself – which now comes in 12 mm ($\frac{1}{2}$ in) thick veneers for floors, walls and other surfaces. If you don't mind the occasional steaming-up, mirror-lined walls look very glamorous and will also expand the space. Wood panelling or tongue-and-groove boarding with a coating of polyurethane looks warm and interesting, as do nice wood floors.

Vinyl-coated cork is a popular choice for floors and so are vinyl tiles, resilient sheet flooring and the new fibre carpets and carpet tiles which are more practical than wool in a wettish environment. Cotton tumble twist comes in a large range of colours and lifts up easily to shake, clean or put in the washing machine. If areas around bath and basin are very well protected and occupants are reasonably docile in the bath and shower, wallcoverings like felt or wool, cotton, hessian or burlap can look warm and smart. So too could lengths of towelling stapled to the wall with the cut edges covered in a braid or beading.

Right: Their waterproof and hardwearing properties make ceramic tiles one of the most popular and practical of wall and floor treatments for the bathroom. Here, an otherwise clinical effect has been softened by the use of pretty towels in co-ordinating colours, and attractive objects displayed on glass shelves in the alcove. A co-ordinated thick cotton rug warms the floor, while a toning radiator warms the towels.

BATHROOMS

Window dressing

Bathroom windows are generally small so can lend themselves to quite lavish treatments that might not be affordable on larger windows. If you are not overlooked you can use tied-back curtains or festoon or Austrian blinds in muslins, laces, light cottons or broderie Anglaise for a particularly pretty look. If you want to disguise ugly bobbly bathroom glass which you cannot replace, try using café curtains, or translucent net, or white holland blinds. Matchstick or bamboo blinds can look good, so can Venetian and wooden louvred blinds. Shutters, especially the adjustable variety look very fresh and rural. Again, if you are not overlooked, you could try leaving the windows bare and just standing plants or a row of glasses on the window sill. Another idea is to fill the window frame with narrow glass shelves on which you can mass

Left: Sweeping lace curtains frame both bath and window in a nicely unusual country bathroom with its old-fashioned claw-foot bath and china jardinière. Bountiful plants provide almost as much green inside as can be seen through the window. The romantic window treatment has the added effect of literally framing the thoroughly pleasing view outside. The gentle feel is helped by the Edwardian light shade and warm cork floor tiles which blend with the wood.

plants or coloured glasses or blue and white jugs or what you will.

If you do have a big or biggish window, treat it like a living room or bedroom and use a blind with tied-back dress curtains. And if you do have an otherwise slickly-tiled bathroom, the way you dress the window will make all the difference between an impersonal space and an interesting one.

Choosing accessories

There can hardly have been a better time than now for buying pretty bathroom accessories, so there's no excuse for not being able to titivate the plainest little space even if – as in rented accommodation – you cannot change equipment, walls or layout. Take towels – they can be worth their weight in gold. Look for the sort of colours that will make an unfortunate shade in equipment or tiles look much more integrated, or buy towels to match or contrast with a predominant colour on walls or floor.

Buy matching porcelain toothmugs and soap dishes, tissue holders and cotton wool jars, cache pots and paper holders. To update a very plain cold space look for those large primary coloured hooks and rails, mugs and holders, or find accessories in pine or brass or clear perspex or plexiglass. These sort of vivid, eye-catching accents can make a dull bathroom seem lively and friendly.

Colourful accents in the bathroom. Yellow, top right, cheers up an all-whie bathroom. Top left: Red and green contrast well with white fittings and pine walls. Bottom right: Wall lights and glass shelves make attractive accessories to the mirror over the traditional style double basin. Bottom left: A fitted towel radiator is almost an objet d'art *in this stunning grey, black and white bathroom.*

BATHROOMS

Heat and light

Warmth is important

One of the most important ingredients for comfort in a bathroom is getting it the right temperature: cosily warm in winter and cool enough in summer. If you can possibly have a heated towel rail you should do so, but beware of one that is run solely off the central heating system. This is fine when the heating is chugging away, but what about when it is not? To make sure of warm dry towels at all times try to get one run off the hot water system itself, or have a supplementary electrically-heated rail, or just an electric rack. If your hot water tank is placed in a cupboard in the bathroom this will also help to keep the room warm as well as making an extra drying place for towels. If you do not have a radiator of some sort, extra warmth can be provided by a wall-mounted fan or an infra red heater mounted above the door or above the mirror.

Avoiding condensation

Condensation which can be such a nuisance in bathrooms, steaming up the mirrors and windows, can usually be avoided to a great extent by steady warmth and adequate ventilation. If you do not want to open a window in winter, you can install an extractor fan on the wall or in the window itself. And the sort of extractor fan that is obligatory in all internal bathrooms will automatically keep a room free from fogging. Mirrors with built-in lights which warm the glass will also eliminate condensation.

The best sort of lighting

If your room is very small, the best solution for general light is a central ceiling fixture, for this, like the kitchen, or utility room, is the one place in the home where you don't particularly want mood lighting.

Lights either side of the mirror or all around as for theatrical dressing rooms are best for make-up and shaving, or just above if only for shaving. You can buy mirors with strips of bulbs all around or at the top, or you can buy separate strips to superimpose yourself.

If you have a large room, perhaps a bath-dressing-room, you can conceal strip lights behind curtains or window treatments of whatever sort, recess spots into the ceiling (if you have a reasonable recess) to pin-point particular objects or plants, or install waterproof downlights and control the whole system with a dimmer switch for glamour. If you have an internal bathroom, you might also consider some of the luminous ceilings available, or try putting light up behind a floating false ceiling – which is also a good idea for any small dark bathroom, with or without windows.

Safety factors

It is absolutely essential that you do not use any electric appliances near water. Radiant electric fires must be suitable for a bathroom, professionally installed high up on a wall and switched on or off by a cord. Lights should preferably be controlled either by switches outside the room or by further cords. Wet hands that come into contact with switches result in tragedy. Never iron in the bathroom and don't dry your hair with an electric hair dryer there or use any other electric appliance.

Above: A neatly recessed radiator underneath the window suits the decor perfectly and provides sufficient heat in this compact bathroom.

Right: Recessed ceiling lights and theatrical bulbs above the dressing-table (reflected in mirror) give excellent overall and make-up/shaving light in this attractive and spacious looking bathroom. Heat is provided by a wall-mounted radiator which also serves to warm the towels.

PAINT FINISHES

INTRODUCTION

Currently, there is a great revival of interest in decorative paint techniques. After a number of years in which large expanses of solid white or pale pastel colours have been the height of fashion, many people have turned to alternative finishes which are less bland and uniform and more colourful.

One of the most attractive features of techniques such as sponging, stippling and colourwashing, is that they introduce subtle gradations of colour into any room setting. Because they are applied in a series of translucent overlays of tinted glaze they avoid the often bland and somewhat harsh look of colour when it is applied in solid, opaque blocks. Moreover, they allow the home decorator to experiment with colour even during the process of application.

For example, if you find that a thinned glaze is not giving you the density of colour that you require, you can add more pigment, or wait until it has dried, before applying a slightly darker tone of the same colour on top. You can even apply a different coloured glaze altogether. Thus, a Sienna brown glaze applied on top of a deep green one will result in a finish in which you can see brown, green and terracotta. The great thing is to experiment as much as possible with different colours.

Another reason why broken colour finishes are so popular now, is that they allow you to introduce a sense of 'movement', and even texture, onto decorated surfaces. For example, dragging and combing involve pulling a brush or comb through wet tinted glaze,

to create a series of parallel stripes or channels in which the contrasting or complementary ground coat shows through. Thus, if applied to the panels of a door, using a combination of reds and browns, the technique will allow you to simulate the grain of a wood such as mahogany. And if you repeat the technique using pastel pinks and greens, you will end up with a pastiche of a woodgrain effect.

This brings us to perhaps the most exciting aspect of decorative techniques such as marbling. *Faux marbre* is an art that goes back to Greek and Roman times, and is a method of replicating/faking the appearance of real marble, just by using paint. To capture all of the qualities of marble in paint is quite remarkable, and to accurately reproduce specific types of marble in such a manner takes years of practice. However, by following the simple guidelines illustrated on page 377 you will be able to create a very presentable example of an attractive marble finish, and one which can be applied to walls, floors, tabletops and even doors.

Finally, all of the broken colour techniques described on the following pages are very easy to follow, and you will soon achieve successful results. Don't be put off if you think a finish like rag-rolling looks like it might be too complicated – it isn't. Half the fun of these techniques is that the end result looks very subtle and sophisticated, whilst achieving it is very easy.

Left: Stencilling can be used to create a range of optical effects. In this elegant living room, a combination of stencil borders has been used to seemingly divide the walls into panels. For a unifying effect, the same design has been used on the rug and coffee table.

PAINT FINISHES

Mixing paints and glazes

When decorating with the broken colour techniques described on pages 372–8, you will need to use a variety of coloured paints and glazes. Indeed, successful results depend on choosing the appropriate glaze for the job in hand, and then mixing it correctly. However, don't be daunted by this. Just follow the simple explanations and guidelines outlined below and you can't go far wrong.

Preparing ground coats

For broken colour finishes to be successful they must be applied on top of a smooth, opaque ground coat. That is, a dense block of plain (often white or pale) colour.

For the best results, use one or two coats of either flat-oil or eggshell finish paint on top of an oil-based undercoat (and primer, if necessary). You will find that the eggshell has more of a sheen than flat-oil, but both are equally effective. All the major paint manufacturers make them in a wide range of colours, and they can be applied straight from the tin, with just a splash of white spirit mixed in for ease of application.

However, if you wish to make up your own colours, you can tint white flat-oil or eggshell with artists' oils. These are available in a wide range of colours from artists' suppliers. You simply mix a little artists' oil with a little mineral or white spirit, in a clean container, until you have a smooth, creamy consistency. then slowly blend this mix with the white flat-oil or eggshell, until you've created the colour you want.

An alternative is to use a latex emulsion paint for the ground coat. Again, apply it straight from the tin, thinned with a little water. However, whilst water-based paints have faster drying times between coats, and do not have to be applied over an undercoat, they can raise the grain if applied to wood, induce rust on bare metal and sometimes partially absorb some of the glazes applied on top, thus spoiling the finish. So, unless you are colour-washing (see page 374) it is preferable to apply an oil-based ground coat.

Mixing glazes

To achieve the subtle, mottled finishes associated with broken colour techniques, you must apply a number of translucent, thinned coloured glazes over the ground coat. Each coat of glaze adds colour to the finish, whilst allowing other colours underneath it to show or 'ghost' through. There are a number of options open to you:

Tinted scumble glaze

Clear scumble glaze is available from artists' suppliers, and when thinned with mineral or white spirit and tinted with artists' oils gives a high quality translucent finish.

1 Put a little artists' oil and white spirit into a small container, and mix to a creamy consistency.
2 Blend in a similar quantity of scumble glaze.
3 Now, slowly stir this mix into the amount of scumble glaze you need for the job, until you have made up the colour you require.
4 This tinted scumble glaze should now be thinned with white spirit, in a ratio of 1 part scumble to approx 2–3 parts white spirit. Basically, the more white spirit you add, the more transparent the glaze becomes.

Thinned oil-based paint glaze

As a slightly cruder alternative to tinted scumble glaze, thinned paint glaze is a flat-oil or eggshell paint thinned with white spirit – again, to the required transparency. Either you can thin the paint with white spirit straight from the tin, or you can mix your own colours using artists' oils (see *Preparing ground coats* above).

1 Put sufficient flat-oil or eggshell paint for the job into a container.
2 In a small container, mix a small quantity of artists' oil with a little white spirit, until you get a creamy consistency.
3 Slowly blend the mix from step 2 into the paint, until you produce the colour you want.

4 Finally, thin the now tinted flat-oil or eggshell with white spirit, in a ratio of 1 part to approx 2–3 parts, until you have a glaze of the required degree of transparency.

Thinned latex/emulsion glazes

Another alternative is to use a thinned water-based glaze. This can give a slightly softer finish than an oil-based glaze, and you can mix your own by adding artists' gouache colours (available from artists' suppliers) to white emulsion. The method of mixing the glaze is the same as for a thinned emulsion glaze (as above), except that, throughout, you substitute water for the white spirit.

However, the disadvantage of an emulsion glaze is that it dries quite quickly, thus giving you too little time to 'work' the glaze to the required finish. This can make techniques such as rag rolling, stippling, dragging and combing almost impossible – especially over a large area. Thus, it is recommended that you use oil-based glazes whenever possible.

Artists' acrylic glazes

Like emulsions glazes, artists' acrylics are thinned with water, and they will dry very quickly indeed. This makes them unsuitable for broken colour applications over a large area (see *Thinned emulsion glazes*, above). However, they can be very useful in a technique such as spattering (see page 376), where you want to build up overlays of colour in as short a time as possible. They come in a wide range of colours and are simply thinned in a ratio of 1 part acrylic to approx 2–3 parts water.

Mixing washes

You will need to use a wash for colourwashing (see page 000). To do this, simply mix up any of the glazes as outlined above (water-based washes are particularly effective for achieving a soft, delicate finish) and further thin the mix in a ratio of 1 part glaze to approx 6–8 parts white spirit/water. The idea is to make the wash very transparent, so that just a hint of the colour is evident when brushed on to the surface. Depth of colour can then be built up with the application of further layers.

Varnishes

Most broken colour techniques require some form of protection from everyday wear and tear, especially in kitchens and bathrooms. So when the glazes have completely dried out, apply a couple of coats of a matt or satin finish clear polyurethane varnish, diluted with just a splash of white spirit for ease of application. Avoid gloss varnishes, as they are very shiny, and reflect too much light off the surface.

Colourwashed walls, marbled shelves and shell design stencilling enliven a large bathroom.

PAINT FINISHES

RAGGING AND ROLLING

Ragging on is a versatile technique that enables you to decorate ceilings and walls in a stylish and quite dramatic manner. You simply use scrunched up pieces of clean rag to dab a coloured glaze, or glazes, over a plain background to produce a mottled finish. Rags made from different materials, such as cotton, hessian or cheesecloth, will produce different effects – so it's best to experiment first on some spare paper before starting in earnest. Also, it is worth nothing that ragging with very strong colours can be rather overpowering over a large area, whereas softer pastel colours are more subtle.

Rag-rolling is a similar technique to ragging, and involves rolling a sausage-shaped rag over a still wet oil-based glaze (don't use emulsions, as they dry too quickly) that has already been applied to the surface with a standard decorator's brush. This has the effect of removing some of the glaze, and creating an elegant marble-type-finish.

Materials:
Oil-based glazes
Mixing bowls
White spirit
Clean rags
Old plate or paint tray
Rubber gloves

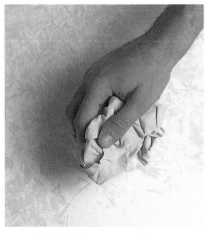

Ragging on:
1 *Pour some thinned glaze (see p.370) onto a plate and dip the bunched-up rag into it. Remove any excess glaze and test the print on spare paper.*

Rag-rolling
1 *Using a standard decorators' brush, apply a thinned eggshell or tinted scumble glaze over a previously painted flat-oil or eggshell ground coat.*

2 *Lightly dab the rag over the previously painted flat-oil or eggshell ground coat – allowing the latter to show through in patches. Continually re-bunch the rag, and when it becomes*

clogged up change it.
3 *When the glaze has dried you can rag over it, at random, using another colour, to achieve a two-tone effect.*

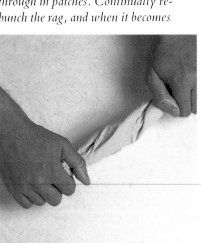

2 *Twist a rag into a sausage shape and roll it up and down and sideways over the still wet glaze. Use the palms of your hands and apply varying pressure on the rag to remove patches of glaze.*

3 *Change your rag regularly, or it will become clogged and simply roll colour back onto the surface.*

SPONGING

Sponging is a very versatile technique which allows you to create a soft speckled finish when decorating walls, ceilings and even furniture. It is an effective way of painting large wardrobes and chests of drawers to make them seem smaller and blend in with the surrounding walls. You have the choice of sponging just one colour over the top of a contrasting ground coat, or building up cloudy layers of complementary colours. But for the most effective results, always use a marine sponge, rather than a synthetic one – the latter will produce too uniform a print.

Materials:
Oil-based glazes
Mixing bowl
White spirit
Marine sponge
Old plate or paint tray

1 Mix up some thinned eggshell or scumble or glaze (see p.370) in the colour of your choice, and pour a little onto the plate or paint tray.

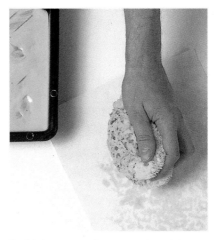

2 Moisten a marine sponge in white spirit, wring it out and dip it into the glaze. Remove any excess on the side of the plate, and test the print a couple of times on spare paper.

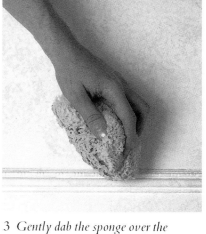

3 Gently dab the sponge over the previously painted, and dry, flat-oil or eggshell ground coat. Don't press too hard, and leave patches of the ground colour showing through.

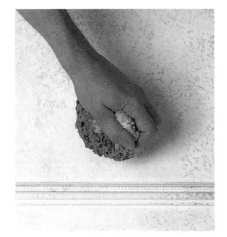

4 Keep changing the side of the sponge that you dab onto the wall, and recharge it with glaze when the print becomes too faint – always removing any excess glaze on spare paper.

5 Whilst the glaze is still wet, or when it has dried, mix up a new batch of glaze in a darker tone or a different colour and sponge over the first coat.

Tips

● Sponge radiators to match the walls

● Check the effect on paper when you recharge the sponge to make sure that you haven't taken up too much paint

● Change your hold on the sponge to vary the print it produces

● Use two or three colours – or shades of one colour – for a subtle shaded effect

PAINT FINISHES

COLOURWASHING

Colourwashing involves building up a number of very thin, almost transparent, coats of glaze over a pale ground coat. It produces a soft, faded look that is particularly appropriate if they are trying to create a rustic or country style. For the most effective results, use water-based matt finish glazes and build up darker tones of the same colour.

Materials:

Latex/emulsion glaze
Water
Large mixing bowl or bucket
Large standard decorators' brush
Polythene sheeting.

1 *Prepare a water-based matt glaze in the colour of your choice (see page 370), and thin it to a wash in a ratio of 1 part glaze to 8 parts water.*

2 *Use a large standard decorators' brush to 'slap' and sweep the wash over the previously painted white or pale latex/ emulsion ground coat. Work in all directions.*

3 *When the first coat has dried, apply 3 or 4 more coats until you have created the depth of colour you want.*

STIPPLING

Stippling is a technique that allows you to create a subtle, elegant and unobtrusive finish over large areas. The method is simple and involves dabbing a stippling brush (an old hair brush or the tip of a standard decorators' brush will do) over the surface to remove tinted wet glaze so that small pinpricks of the contrasting underlying ground coat colours are revealed.

Materials:

Oil-based glazes
White/mineral spirit
Clean rag
Mixing bowls
Standard decorators' brush
Stippling brush/old hair brush

1 *Mix up an oil-based glaze (see p.370) in the colour of your choice and brush it over a small section of a previously painted flat-oil or eggshell ground, using a decorators' brush.*

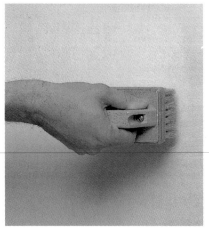

2 *Using a firm, rapid action, dab the stippling brush over the surface to remove tiny pinpricks of wet glaze and reveal the ground coat. Regularly clean brush on white spirit-moistened rag.*

3 *Repeat step 1 and 2 over the entire surface, try to keep a wet edge and blend each section into the next using the stippling action.*

374

COLOURWASHING, DRAGGING AND COMBING

DRAGGING

Dragging is a technique that is derived from woodgraining. It involves pulling a long bristled dragging brush through a wet glaze to reveal stripes of the underlying ground colour. By using natural wood colours you can imitate the grain of woods such as mahogany. And by employing subtle pastel colours over a pale background you can create a very elegant effect.

Materials:

Oil-based glazes
White/mineral spirit
Mixing bowls
A standard decorators' brush
Selection of combs
Clean rag

COMBING

Combing employs a similar method to dragging, and involves pulling the teeth of a comb through wet glaze to reveal stripes of a contrasting ground coat. This tends to produce a very strong pattern that can be overpowering over large areas, but looks very effective on small objects or in door panels.

Materials:

Oil-based glazes
White/mineral spirit
Mixing bowls
A standard decorators' brush
A dragging brush
Clean rag

1 Mix up a thinned eggshell or scumble glaze in the colour of your choice (see p.370), and use a decorators' brush to apply a thin film of it over a previously painted flat-oil or eggshell ground coat.

2 Before the glaze becomes tacky, pull the side of the dragging brush across the surface in a continuous straight line from one edge to the other.

3 Clean the brush on a rag dampened in white spirit at the end of each parallel stroke, and work your way across the entire surface before the glaze dries.

1 Mix up a thinned eggshell or scumble glaze in the colour of your choice (see p.370), and apply a coat of it over a previously painted different coloured flat-oil or eggshell ground.

2 Before the glaze becomes tacky, pull the comb across the surface from one edge to another. At the end of each sweep, clean the comb on a rag dampened in white spirit.

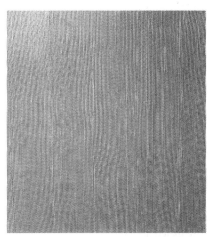

3 Work your way across the surface in a series of parallel sweeps – each time echoing any curves or 'wiggles'.

PAINT FINISHES

SPATTERING

Spattering involves building up droplets or spatters of paint over a contrasting ground coat to produce a speckled, multi-coloured finish. The method opposite describes how to use three coloured glazes, but you can use as few or as many as you want. Artists' acrylics are ideal for this technique, because they dry quickly and thus reduce waiting time between stages. It looks particularly effective on floors and on small objects, such as vases, shelving or occasional table tops, especially if they are spattered with colours taken from the surrounding decor. Because the pattern of spatter depends on the size of the droplets of paint, you will need to practice controlling the technique first on some spare paper.

Materials:
Oil-based glazes or artists' acrylics
White/mineral spirit or water
Mixing bowls
3 angled fitches
Clean rag
Polythene sheeting

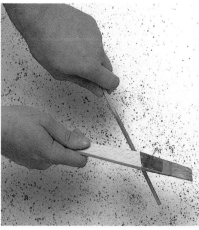

1 *Mix up 3 acrylic or oil-based glazes, in complementary colours of your choice (see p.370). Don't overthin them, or they will run on the surface – a ratio of 1 part glaze to 2 parts white spirit or water is ideal.*

2 *Dip an angled fitch into the first glaze and hold it 8–10 cm (3–4 in) over the previously painted flat-oil or eggshell ground coat. Tap the handle of the fitch with another fitch to spatter droplets over the surface.*

3 *Repeat step 2 using the second colour and another angled fitch. Slowly cover more and more of the ground coat.*

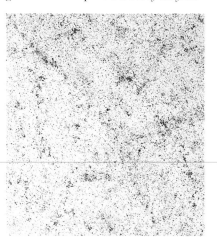

4 *When the second glaze has dried, dip another fitch into the third and darkest glaze. Hold it in position and run your forefinger through the bristles to create a fine spray.*

5 *Seal and protect your work with two coats of polyurethane varnish.*

Tips
● Vary your distance from the fabric to create different-sized spatters

● Carefully blot thick blobs with clean, lint-free rag

● Cover all surrounding surfaces with protective dustcloths before you start – this technique can be very messy!

MARBLING

The paint technique of marbling allows you to simulate the appearance of real marble, which will bring an air of grandeur and style to almost any interior. Copying a specific marble exactly is a job best left to a very experienced professional decorator. However, the method outlined opposite will enable you to create a perfectly acceptable copy of white vein marble – (try to get hold of a piece or a picture of the marble for reference), and by substituting different colours to those specified you could create a dramatic fantasy finish. It is worth bearing in mind that when real marble is used over a large surface area, such as the walls of a room, it is fixed in position in sections – panels. For a more authentic finish you may care to simulate this, by first outlining the panels on the wall using dark grey paint, a fine artists' brush and a ruler, and then marbling each one in turn. However, don't feel bound by this – an unbroken expanse of marbling can look just as effective.

Materials:
Oil-based glazes
White/mineral spirit
Small, medium and large standard
   decorators' brushes
A softening brush
Nos 3 and 6 artists' brushes
Goose feather
Clean rag

1 Using a clean rag, wipe a coat of scumble glaze thinned with a little white spirit over a previously painted white eggshell ground coat.
2 Apply three glazes – each a different

shade of grey (see p.370) – onto the wet scumble, in a series of randomly elongated patches all on the same diagonal. Leave 'channels' of the ground coat uncovered.

3 Pull a dry softening brush over the still wet surface to blend the glazes together. Work in the same diagonal direction as in step 2.

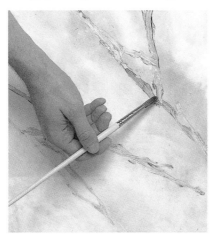

4 Use a translucent mid-grey glaze and a No 6 artists' brush to put on the secondary veins in the darker channels of the ground coat. Immediate blend them with the softening brush.

5 When the secondary veins have dried rub some scumble glaze over them, add a little black to the glaze used in step 4 and apply the primary veins, as in the illustration, using a goose feather.

6 When dry, apply two coats of satin clear polyurethane varnish for protection.

PAINT FINISHES

STENCILLING

The application of coloured paint through a pre-cut shape onto a previously decorated surface, stencilling is a very easy technique to master, and you will find that successful results come almost immediately. With the enormous variety of pre-cut card stencils available today from artists' suppliers and DIY shops, you will be able to embellish many surfaces around the home with all manner of decorative motifs. Indeed, many of the other finishes, such as ragging and sponging, described on pages 372–3 provide ideal backgrounds on which to stencil in a contrasting or complementary pattern and colour.

The dolphin and shell stencils described opposite would look especially good in a bathroom. Just as clown or teddy stencils would be effective in a child's bedroom, and fruit and vegetable motifs appropriate on the doors of kitchen units – just use your imagination.

Materials:
Acrylic paints
Pre-cut stencil card
2 stencil brushes
Low-tack masking tape
Clean rag

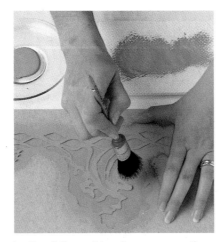

1 *Carefully position the wave stencil on the previously decorated surface. If necessary, hold it in place with low-tack masking tape, so that when it is peeled off it won't remove any paint (or even plaster!). Dip a dry stubby stencil brush into the slightly thinned acrylic paint (see p.370), remove any excess on a piece of spare paper. Dab the paint through the stencil cut-out and onto the surface below, using a light pouncing action. Build up the required depth of colour slowly.*

2 *Carefully peel back the stencil (remove any low-tack masking tape first), making sure you don't smudge the still wet paint.*

3 *When the first stencil has dried position the second and pounce on the paint through the stencil, using a clean stencil brush. Then peel off the tape.*

4 *Position and paint the shell motif. If your stencil has narrow bridges between sections make sure your brush is very dry so that extra paint won't seep under the*

stencil and ruin the look.
5 *When the paint has dried, protect it with 1 or 2 coats of matt or satin polyurethane varnish.*

Painting floors

If floorboards are in bad condition they can be rescued using solid paint which covers a multitude of faults. After painting, the surface will have to be finished off with several coats of polyurethane and given a topping-up coat of polyurethane every year.

You can, of course, paint over vinyl or linoleum, but if you want to stencil, it is probably better to cover the old floor with hardboard or plywood which you have first treated with primer.

Which paint to use?

Although deck or yacht paint is often sold specially for floors, you can use any of the following successfully, depending on what sort of finish and effect you require. It's essential to use an oil-based primer or undercoat first.

Oil-based flat or eggshell paints make a good base for any decorative finish.

Enamel paints give a hard durable finish but are more expensive and have a more solid appearance.

Artists' acrylic, Japan or Signwriters' colours – all obtainable from artists' supply shops – are expensive but good for stencilling.

Oil-based eggshell and gloss paints or epoxy paints are best for any previously tiled surface.

When painting floors the boards must first be given a couple of thin coats of undercoat and left to dry.

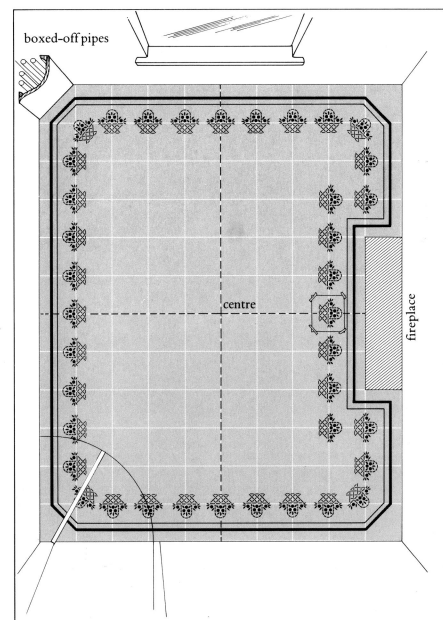

boxed-off pipes

centre

fireplace

Positioning a stencil border

To square off a floor for stencilling you need to take the measurements of the floor first and use them to draw a plan to scale on a sheet of squared paper. The floor drawn here is an average 4 × 3 metre (12 × 10 ft) room with boxed-off pipes in one corner and a fireplace. Measure your stencil block and decide on an appropriate scale. The size of the stencil block used here (see the photograph on page 47 for detail) was 20cm (8in) in diameter. As we wanted a 10cm (4in) space between each stencil we drew up our plan to a scale of 1 square = 30cm (1ft). Find and mark with chalk the centres of the walls and mark off the positions of the stencil pattern blocks, allowing for whatever space you choose between the wall and the stencil border. To take in the boxed-off pipes, we cut off the corner and repeated this device for decorative consistency in each of the other three corners.

If you want to add any stencils in the centre of the floor, you should stretch a piece of heavily chalked string between the centres of both pairs of opposite walls. Where the two lines cross will be the centre of the room. Working from the centre, position any additional stencils at equal distances away from it.

ACKNOWLEDGEMENTS The Complete Book of Home Design – Mary Gilliatt

The publishers would like to thank the following for their kind permission to reproduce the photographs in this book:

Acme Wardrobes 335; Allimilmo Kitchens 115, 131, 152; Alno Kitchens 128, bottom right, 133; Aqua Maison Ltd. 354; B.C. Sanitan 359; Bisque Radiators 363, 365 bottom left; Blasé Design PLC 93, 135, 145 bottom right, 177; Jon Bouchier/EWA 43 right, 47 bottom, 65, 106 bottom right, 178; Michael Boys/Susan Griggs Agency Ltd. 76 top, 175, 204 bottom right, 305, 311, 316 right;

B&Q DIY Supercentres 111; Arthur Brett & Sons Ltd. 172 right; Richard Bryant/Arcaid 72 top left, 143, 206, 207 right; Bulthaup Kitchens 134; Camera Press 43 left, 46 bottom, 49 top left, 51 right, 62 bottom, 72 top right, 72 bottom, 83, 106 top right, 144 left, 157, 181 bottom left, 182 left, 188, 189, left and right, 190, 191 left, top centre and right, 192, 193, 196, 197 left and right, 198, 199, 205, 212 top and bottom, 213, 219 left, 225 top, 227, 229, 231 top right, 241, 249, 250, 253, 255, 256 left, 262 top left, top right, bottom, 263, 265, 266 bottom, 269 right, 273, 274, 277 top and bottom, 289, 290 bottom, 322, 325, 333 bottom right, 339 left and right, 340, 343, 345 top, 365 top right, 365 bottom right, 366; Steve Colby/EWA 50, 128 top left; Coloroll 215, 294; Company Magazine 28 top and bottom; Cover Plus Paints 15 right, 66 left, 236; David Cripps/EWA 66 top right, 308 bottom right; Crosby Kitchens 141 left; Crown Paints Ltd. 33 left, 88 left, 116 top left, 333 top left, 362 bottom; Michael Datoili 38, 321, 329; Designers Guild 68, 323 top right, 33 bottom left, 335; Die Miele Kitchens 100 bottom; Di Lusso Kitchens 139; Dragons of Walton Street 222 top right; Dorma, a member of C.V. Home Furnishings Ltd. 209, 226, 235 left, 296 top, 304, 314; Michael Dunne/EWA 10, 16, 25 top and bottom right, 26, 29 right, 30 left, 34, 49 top right and bottom left, 54, 75, 95, 106 top left, 112, 113 top, 117 left, 119, 127, 153 right, 156, 159 top right, 161 right, 163 right, 180, 181 bottom centre, 278, 293, 298 left, 307 top left, 308 top, 309 left, 320 top, 331 top left, 331 top right, 338 top, 35, left, 352 left; © Peter M. Fine 1983. 159 top left; Fired Earth 42 top left, 144 right; Formica Ltd. 179 top left; The Futon Company 301 left; Hamlet Furniture Ltd. 257; Hammonds Furniture Ltd. 338 bottom; Christine Hanscomb 18, 74, 102, 320 bottom left; Nelson Hargreaves 140; Clie Helm/EWA 41 bottom, 45, 77 bottom, 84, 108 centre left, 113 bottom, 153 left, 237 top right, 247 right, 355; Frank Herholdt 53, 138; Frank Herholdt/EWA 166 bottom, Heuga Kitchens 121 right, 145 top right; John Hill 167; House of Mayfair 51, 225 bottom; Simon Horn Beds 296 bottom right; ICI Paints 214; Interior Selection 60 top, 238; Interlubke 30 right, 64, 66 bottom, 184, 301 right; International Wool Secretariat 239; Junkers 159 bottom right; Ken Kirkwood 62 left; David Lloyd/EWA 42 bottom, 231 centre, 259; Neil Lorimer/EWA 41 left, 81 bottom, 87, 96 left, 104, 123, 130 top, 158 top left, 166 top right, 231 top left, 333 top right; Macpaints Paints 202, 323 bottom; Magnet Plc 129 top, 174, 315, 324 top, 334; Marks and Spencer Plc.

207 left, 264; Marvic Textiles 151; William Mason 105 left; Norman McGrath 216, 217, 221 top left, 228; Chris Mead 287, 326; Meredew Furniture Ltd. 248; Maison Marie Claire 76 bottom 258; Moben Kitchens 122, 124, 128 bottom left; Monkwell Fabrics 52; Mothercare 283; National Magazine Company 58 right; Next Interiors 37 top left, 327; Michael Nicholson/EWA 21 right, 35 bottom, 46 top, 67, 77 top, 82, 85, 89, 100 top right, 117 right, 118 left, 155, 165, 179 bottom left, 179 right, 181 bottom right, 182 right, 203, 296 bottom left, 303 left, 320 bottom right, 350 right; Omega Lighting 37 top right, 309 right; Osborne and Little 15 top, 118 right, 168 right, 181 top left, 295; Osram-GEC 36, 161 left; Spike Powell/EWA 19, 25 bottom left, 59, 126, 181 top left, 218, 245, 251 left; Malcolm Robertson 103, 145 top left, 272; Sanderson 8, 159 bottom left, 168 left, 169, 286, 323 top centre; Jessica Strang 42 top right, 121 bottom left, 136 top right, 141 right, 163 left, 173, 176, 323 top left, 341, 346 bottom centre, 352 right; Tim Street-Porter/EWA 85 right, 145 bottom left, 281; Syndication International 70, 81 top right, 333 top left; Friedhelm Thomas/EWA 86; Transworld Feature Syndicate 21 bottom left, 33 right, 79, 100 top left, 121 top left, 125, 232, 233, 235 right, 256 right, 261, 268, 269 left, 342, 346 left and bottom right; Jerry Tubby/EWA 94, 247 left, 271; Winchmore Furniture Ltd. 106 bottom left, 130 bottom left, 130 bottom right, 136 bottom right; Wrighton Kitchens 136 left, 137, 186, 187; Elizabeth Whiting and Associates 37 bottom, 41 top right, 73 top left and top right, 78, 158 top right, 231 bottom left, 237 top left, 244, 251 right, 292 right, 298 right, 313.

Special photogrpahy
Jon Bouchier 13, 15 bottom left, 32, 44, 62 right, 69 bottom, 98, 101, 107, 132, 142, 148, 160, 162, 288, 290 top, 292 left, 297, 299, 306, 319, 330, 344, 348, 360, 367; Michael Dunne 222 top left, 223, 224, 234, 240, 242 left and right, 243, 252, 266 top, 267, 275, 276; Jessica Strang 29 left, 47 top left, 60 bottom 61, 69 top, 71, 73 bottom, 171, 302, 303 right.

Black and white illustrations by Stuart Perry. Colour illustrations by Ross Wardle/Tudor Art Studios and other black and white illustrations by Greg Jones/Tudor art Studios.

Every effort has been made to trace the copyright holders and we apologise in advance for any unintentional omissions and would be pleased to insert the appropriate acknowledgements in any subsequent edition of this publication.